The Greenpeace Book of

WATER

David & Charles

A DAVID & CHARLES BOOK

Produced by Cameron Books, PO Box 1, Moffat,
Dumfriesshire DG10 9SU, Scotland

ISBN 0 7153 0425 9

A catalogue record for this book is available from the British Library

Translated from the German by Andrew Bird (main text)
and Jill Hollis (captions)
Edited by Jill Hollis
Designed by Ian Cameron
Picture research by Jill Hollis

Filmset by Cameron Books, Moffat
Reproduced by Sfera, Milan, Italy
Paper made by PWA Grafische Papiere, Raubling, Germany
Printed by Artegrafica, Verona, Italy
for David & Charles
Brunel House   Newton Abbot   Devon

The paper used for the contents of this book is chlorine-free
and does not incorporate pulp from eucalyptus plantations, which
throughout the world cause loss of biodiversity, increase soil
erosion and deplete groundwater.

I am grateful to the following for their help: Joan Davis, Armin
Peter, Roland Schertenleib, Martin Strauss and Martin Wegelin
of Swiss Federal Institute for Water Research EAWAG,
Dübendorf, Switzerland; Thomas Kluge of the Institut für sozial-
ökologische Forschung (ISOE), Frankfurt-am-Main; Hans Peter
Duerr; Maika Mason; Harro-H. Müller; Jörg Naumann; Heike
Otremba; Liesbeth Sluiter; Hans Weber; Helmut Winter. Thanks
also to Greenpeace campaigners in Australia, Canada, Germany,
New Zealand, UK and USA. Finally, I wish to thank Astrid, without whose advice and encouragement this book could not have
been written.
                                                        Klaus Lanz

Picture credits
Bryan and Cherry Alexander *front jacket*, p.65, p.102; Dr Alan Beaumont
p.76; Andrew Bird p.13, p.135; Cameron Books (Jill Hollis & Ian
Cameron) p.28 (middle), p.57 (top), p.98; Joachim Chwaszcza p.26
(left), p.44 (bottom), p.50, p.85 (bottom), p.86, p.159; Michael and
Patricia Fogden p.10, p.16 (top), p.19 (top), p.70, p.77, p.78 (top and
bottom), p.79, p.111; Ecoscene (Richard Glover) p.11, (Wayne Lawler)
p.15, (Michael Cuthbert) p.53, (Andrew Brown) p.59, (Jim Winkley)
p.63, (Chinch Gryniewicz) p.91, p.103, p.112, p.117, p.147; Mary Evans
p.45, p.46, p.47, p.48 (bottom), p.55 (bottom), p.62; © Gesellschaft für
ökologische Forschung/Ossi Baumeister p.107; Grand Council of the
Crees of Quebec (Luis Eguren) p.140, p.142, (Barry Tessman) p.141;
Greenpeace Communications (Hoffman) p.40 (bottom), p.128
(bottom), (Edwards) p.66, (Visser) p.67, p.74, 120, (Cortesi) p.97,
(Morgan) p.110, (Hodson) p.125, (Greig) p.127, (Nimtsch) p.128 (top),
(Munday) p.151 (bottom); Greenpeace Germany (Nimtsch) p.4, p.12,
p.16 (bottom), p.36, p.40 (top), p.52 (top), p.71, p.75 (top), p.94, p.113,
(Lutz) p.30, (Langrock/Zenit) p.35 (top), p.123, (Venneman) p.73,
(Kuidin) p.96, p.123, Sarah Hollis p.131; Holt Studios International
p.72; Images of Africa p.21, p.23, p.55 (top), p.56, p.58, p.83 (left and
right), p.104, p.157; © Institut für Strömungswissenschaften p.18 (top);
Katz Pictures p.133; Klaus Lanz p.19 (bottom), p.64, p.138, p.146; Look
(Florian Werner) pp.2-3 (*endpapers*), p.18 (bottom); Medimage
(Anthony King) p.108; Bipinchandra J. Mistry p.42, p.43; Harro-H.
Müller p.60, p.85 (top); National Institute of Public Health and
Environmental Protection (RIVM) and Institute for Inland Water
Management and Waste Water Treatment (RIZA), Bilthoven, The
Netherlands; Panos Pictures (Jean-Léo Dugast) p.20, p.68, (Jeremy
Hartley) p.87 (top), (John Clarke) p.89 (top), (Jimmy Holmes) p.93,
(Jon Levy) p.99 (bottom), (S.B. Nace) p.105, p.115, (D.K. Hulcher)
p.116, (Liba Taylor) p.130, (David Reed) p.156; Poseidon (Michael
Nicholson) p.25 (top), p.48 (top), (P.Terry) p.25 (bottom); Nick Rain
p.80, p.81; Rex Features p.61; Monika Rößiger p.24 (top), p.87
(bottom); Michel Roggo p.69; Select/J.B. Pictures (Ed Kashi) p.33
(bottom), p.41, p.99 (top); Roderick Simpson (Architect) p.148, p.149;
Liesbeth Sluiter p.152, p.153, p.154; Still Pictures (Edward Parker) p.22,
(Hjalte Tin) p.28 (top), (Bryan and Cherry Alexander) p.28 (bottom),
(Chris Caldicott) p.28 (right), (Jorgen Schytte) p.29 (right), (Mark
Edwards) p.34, p.38, p.49, p.92, p.101, p.126, p.139, p.143, p.144 (top
and bottom), p.145 (top and bottom), (Paul Harrison) p.52 (bottom),
(Nigel Dickinson) p.57 (bottom), (Heldur Metocny) p.84, (Andy
Crump) p.137; Swiss Federal Institute for Water Research EAWAG
(Michael Schurter) p.151 (top), (Martin Wegelin) p.29 (left); Mike
Tyler p.14; Vera Miljø, Norway p.54 (right); Hans Weber p.89 (bottom);
Johanna Wesnigk p.9, p.24 (bottom), p.35 (bottom), p.54 (left), p.82;
Windrush p.5, p.106; David Woodfall p.17, p.31, p.33 (top), p.37, p.75
(bottom), p.95 (left, right and bottom), p.118, p.121, p.122, p.124; Dr
Paul Yule p.26 (right).

Cameron Books would like to thank Tim Birch, Pat Costner,
Chris Harris, Sandra Marquardt, Stephanie Mills, Jörg Naumann,
Bonnie Rice, François Tanguay and especially Astrid Hotopp, all
of Greenpeace, for the help they have given in the production of
the book.

CONTENTS

Foreword

For thousands of years, the fact that water had to be valued and looked after was sufficiently obvious to human society that every civilisation, every small community, organised ways of preserving the purity and abundance of supplies. Water's magical, life-giving properties provoked awe and respect, giving it a natural, important place in all the world's major religions. Alien though this spiritual appreciation of water may now seem to someone in the industrialised world, we are by no means immune to its inexplicable, mysterious attractions. Taking a shower, even just splashing one's face with water, refreshes in a way that nothing else can imitate, and anyone who has watched the utter absorption of children playing in water can be in no doubt as to the delight it can bring. Towns and villages built along the banks of rivers or lakes have a special quality that soothes the spirit and calms the nerves. Nobody needs an excuse to stand or sit gazing at a lake or watching a river flow by.

In general, though, modern lifestyles in what we think of as the developed world exclude the kind of direct contact with water in the environment (and therefore an understanding of its place in nature) that formed such an important part of human life until relatively recently. Supplies are cheap and constant, and all that most people are aware of is the stream of water as it passes between tap and drain. It arrives along invisible mains and disappears into equally invisible sewers. Any shortages are immediately tackled by the unquestioning exploitation of new sources; wherever water poses a threat, it is dammed up or confined between dykes. All too often water is seen as a natural asset put at the exclusive disposal of humanity – just one more consumer item with large customers even entitled to discounts. Industry lines river and lake shores using vast quantities of water, among other things, as a cleaning and rinsing medium, a cooling agent and a generator of electricity. Modern agriculture has a seemingly insatiable thirst for it. Streams, rivers, lakes, even groundwater are bombarded with a deadly cocktail of industrial and domestic waste and pesticide-laden, nutrient-rich agricultural run-off.

Only three per cent of the world's water is fresh rather than salty, and 99 per cent of this either lies deep underground or exists as glaciers or icecaps. This small proportion of available freshwater would nevertheless be ample to satisfy the needs of the human population on the planet in a sustainable way, if only it were shared more equitably, and current levels of waste as well as damage to water and wetlands were tackled.

In the global ecosystem, a much broader context than that of mere humanity, water performs a whole host of crucial, life-giving tasks – about which we know little and often seem to care less. If the current abuse of the world's water continues, it is not just the rest of the natural world that will suffer, but people too.

Early morning on the River Li, near Guilin in southern China.

CHAPTER ONE

WATER AND THE PLANET

The Global Water Cycle

Some of the greatest expeditions of the 19th century into the heart of the African continent, undertaken by explorers like David Livingstone (1813-73), John Speke (1827-64) and Sir Henry Morton Stanley (1841-1904), were prompted by a desire to find the answer to an enduring mystery concerning the waters of the River Nile: why did they rise and fall with such regularity when there seemed to have been no rain anywhere nearby? The answer, they believed, must lie at the river's source, and that was what they set out to find.

The idea of a river having a single source remains beguiling, even today, but rivers do not of course originate in one spot. Countless tiny rivulets and streams of rainwater feed into the main watercourse above the ground and more seeps into it underground through the soil. Even if a single spring can be identified as the source, it will already be carrying rainwater from a wide catchment.

As Speke rightly surmised, most of the Nile's water comes from Lake Victoria in Uganda. The largest river feeding into Lake Victoria is the Kagera, which rises in the Ruwenzori mountains to the west. In

the dry season, when there is little water flowing down from the mountains, the middle section of the Kagera's length, which passes through completely level swampland, comes to a virtual standstill. At this point it is fed mainly by the many trickles running out of the sponge-like land, and with no gradient to help the water on its way, the Kagera's current may even reverse. Seeing this must have been the last straw for the baffled explorers, and they had to return home still no wiser as to the source of the Nile. Had they but known it as they gave up the search, some of them were actually standing on the

Opposite. Rainforest wreathed in clouds in the Penas Blancas Valley, Costa Rica. At any one time, 12,000 cubic kilometers of water are airborne as clouds and atmospheric moisture, equivalent to a third of all the water deposited each year by rivers into the world's oceans.

Sunset over Melbourne, Australia. Clouds are crucially important in the regulation of temperature and climate at the earth's surface. Where there are no clouds and little atmospheric moisture over land, the sun is relentless, and there is devastating heat during the day, followed by bitter cold at night.

answer. The Ancient Greek historian Herodotus (c.484-c.425 BC) perhaps best encapsulated the idea of rivers being fed by rainwater: the Nile, he wrote, has its source in the clouds.

How the water cycle works is now clear: water evaporates from the oceans, the land and vegetation to form clouds. These are driven by wind across the continents where they discharge their rain, feeding the rivers, which then carry the water back to the sea to complete the cycle. It might seem that this powerful natural process is entirely independent of human activity, that it is indestructible and permanent, and that we can therefore place total reliance on it unfailingly to replenish and purify the planet's water supplies. In subscribing to this reassuring idea, humanity is in danger of making an assumption as monumentally wrong as that made by the Nile explorers, but this time with far more serious consequences.

The crucial aspect of the water cycle which is so often overlooked is the importance of the rate at which water travels around it. This is largely determined by the presence of vegetation: the denser and lusher it is, the more rain is retained by it, the moister the soil, the milder the climate and the more constant the flow of the rivers. This interaction of vegetation and

water finds expression in a number of ancient religions in which the god of rain is identical to the god of the forests. People learned from experience that it was only by respecting water – looking after even the humblest little stream – and by caring for the soil, that forests would survive and sustain themselves in the long term. They were entirely aware that destroying trees meant risking the loss of rain.

The sheer scale of the global water cycle and the mistaken belief in its indestructibility threaten to blind us to the fact that the human race is undermining, or a least compromising, its integrity. If the cycle is to continue to provide the world with generous supplies of fresh, clean water, we have to recognise and maintain what supports it: rich diversity in vegetation, healthy soil, naturally flowing rivers and streams and undisturbed wetlands. The global water cycle is not a hydraulic pumping and drainage mechanism, it is a living and vulnerable organism.

Climate

However chaotic or fickle the weather may seem in any particular place on any particular day, over a period of years it is remarkably reliable: the average annual precipitation in any given region is surprisingly constant, as are the levels of atmospheric moisture and temperature at any specific season. In North America and northern Europe, for example, we still expect winters to be cold and summers to be warm.

Clouds are the visual evidence of moisture moving around in the atmosphere. As water traps warmth from the sun's rays, clouds perform the important function of evening out distribution of the sun's energy on earth. Temperature differences on the planet would be much more marked were it not for the moist air masses which are blown from the tropics to more temperate zones.

The water in the atmosphere — most of which exists not as clouds, but as invisible water vapour — also helps to retain the sun's warmth on earth. Nowadays, 'the greenhouse effect' often signifies to people the climatic havoc wrought by human activity. In fact, the natural greenhouse effect performs a crucial role in maintaining the planet's climate. In conjunction with other gases, in particular carbon dioxide and methane, water vapour traps the energy from the sun's rays in much the same way as do the panes of glass in a greenhouse. Water vapour accounts for 65 per cent of this effect. The lower the atmospheric humidity, the faster the air and the land will cool off once the sun has set.

As water vapour effectively acts as an insulator, it can also protect against too much heat. When the sun warms the air, it also has to warm the water vapour. The more moist the atmosphere is, the longer it takes to warm up and to cool down again later. The greater the distance from the oceans – as the providers of moisture – the drier and also the tougher the climate becomes. In one of the coldest inhabited places on earth, the town of Oymyakon in Siberia, temperatures drop to -70°C in winter, but they can climb as high as 35°C during the brief summer season.

Water thus plays a critical role as a global distributor of solar energy: Siberian rivers, for example, carry a hundred times more solar energy into the Arctic Ocean than it receives directly from the sun. The Gulf Stream, to which Europe owes its relatively mild climate despite its northern latitude,

Wherever there are mountains, water is slowly but surely wearing them down. If there is no stabilising layer of vegetation, as here at Landmannalaugar in Iceland, erosion happens all the more rapidly.

Were it not for the rivers in the Siberian taiga, the climate there would be very different. The Ob, the Lena and the Yenisei bring with them the sun's heat from where they rise, further south; without them Siberia would be as uninhabitable as the Antarctic, even in summer.

heats up the atmosphere over the Atlantic at a rate equivalent to burning 200 billion tonnes of coal an hour. Large areas of the planet would be uninhabitable were it not for water's ability to redistribute heat.

But this system, which has held itself in balance for millions of years, seems now to be getting badly shaken up as a direct result of the impact on the atmosphere of human activity: the evidence is the intensification of the greenhouse effect. An increase of just one degree in the mean temperature of the earth's atmosphere will cause a dramatic change in the amount and distribution of rainfall all over the world. Massive climatic changes, such as those already becoming apparent on the peripheries of deserts, would then threaten the entire globe, endangering not only natural vegetation, but also farmed crops and thus the human food chain.

Water and the Landscape

The origins of water are as obscure as the creation of the planet itself. Rocks dating from the beginning of geological time show clear traces of contact with water; there is in fact no evidence of it ever having been absent from the earth. Had there not been a constant succession of mountain chains being raised up by movement in the earth's crust – a process that continues today – the action of rain would long since have left the planet with little more than inconspicuous ranges of hills. If we could flick at lightning speed through the history of the earth, we would see many mountains come and go, rising up only to be eroded by the rain. Even the oldest ranges known to us today, such as the Appalachians in North America, are relatively recent arrivals in the context of the

age of the earth, and the Himalayas actually postdate the dinosaurs.

Were it not for the brevity of human existence, we might be more aware of the role played by rain in the formation of the landscapes around us. Rainwater can dissolve stone, it can crack massive rock formations and carry them in pieces far down into the valleys. As the sand, gravel and rocks carried by streams and rivers grind along the river bed, they gradually carve out a deeper channel for the water. At the foot of the mountains, where rivers are able to spread out and their waters become calmer, they relinquish part of their load. Over the millenia, sediments accumulate to form the basis of fertile river plains. As the water moves towards the mouth of the river, it deposits finer and finer material, which gradually extends the delta into the sea. This process can take thousands of years or, as in the case of some larger rivers, it may be observable in the space of a single human lifetime.

Although water has left its mark on every landscape on earth, the way it behaves when it flows is still only poorly understood. It remains impossible to describe or predict precisely how water will move. Laboratory experiments have shown that, left to itself, water rarely (if ever)

flows in a straight line, even when it is sent along a straight, artificial channel. As it rushes down a gradient, it will twist and turn, whirl and sway, until it finally spills over its banks.

Even a river that appears at first sight to be just flowing quietly along is actually behaving in a highly complex manner. It may form standing waves, or spiral backwards along its banks or simply sway almost imperceptibly from bank to bank. The exact amount of energy released when the level of a river carrying a specific volume of water drops by, say, one metre, can be calculated. But the use to which the water puts this energy – how it reshapes its bed, its banks and its surroundings – is as impenetrable as human nature. Rivers lead their own lives, and each has its own character. When the waters of two rivers converge, for example, they may flow for several kilometres, one alongside the other, without mixing.

All of this precludes any reliable judgements about a river's precise movements or the effects it may have. Any watercourse will constantly reshape its bed, frustrating attempts to map it exactly. As the Greek philosopher Heraclitus (?535-?475 BC) famously declared, 'You never step into the same river twice.'

Plant life

Water is by far the largest single constituent of living organisms. It is the very basis of life, playing an essential part in all living processes. Life on earth began in water and has always been reliant on it. Indeed, plants and animals had evolved to a relatively advanced level before they emerged on dry land. Hundreds of millions of years earlier, water had already created plains with moist soils rich in nutrients and mild climates favourable to the development of life, but for aeons, this promising environment lay desolate and void.

The first plants to grow on land were still dependent on an uninterrupted supply of water and could survive only on regularly flooded river banks and in swampy lowlands. Higher plants, which now predominate on land, have developed the capacity to absorb water from the soil through roots that grow downwards and are sensitive to moisture. Over the millenia, different species have adapted their root systems to suit specific water conditions; you can usually tell from the plants growing in any particular place how much water is available there.

The demonstrable fact that water is carried upwards from the roots to the tops of

the tallest trees, defying gravity, baffled scientists for centuries. The fact is that the energy for this elaborate upward flow is provided by evaporation: the faster the water evaporates through the minute pores on the undersides of leaves, the stomata, the greater the suction generated at the plant's roots. Biologists have been able to observe dry spots appearing in the soil at the tips of the tiny root hairs when a plant is exposed to a dry atmosphere. If the suction becomes too great, however, the system may collapse, causing the plant to wilt and die. In response to environmental conditions, higher plants can regulate the amount of moisture lost by opening or closing the stomata. Deciduous trees have adapted to their seasonal exposure to freezing conditions by shedding their leaves in autumn, avoiding loss of moisture to the air when they are unable to take up water from the frozen ground.

Decaying leaves and the dead remains of plants contribute to the structure of the soil, introducing organic material – humus – that helps in the retention of moisture and nutrients. Heavy showers are absorbed by the humus-rich soils of forest so that even during dry periods there is water available. Without this organic content, the water would drain away much faster. Plants growing on the forest floor benefit from the shade cast by the leaves of the trees above, which helps to keep the soil cool and moist, even on hot days. Thus, plants not only create favourable microclimates, but have a moderating effect on the climate of entire regions. The older an ecosystem is, the more stable and bio-diverse it will be, protecting soil from damage and helping to support a slow water cycle.

The Limitations of Science

The interrelationship of water, soil and vegetation is intricate and highly complex and has thus far resisted all attempts to describe or identify it precisely, let alone

to reproduce it in artificial models. Such variables as temperature, moisture and concentration of nutrients are regulated in nature by buffering systems which interact to maintain a balance, guarding against excessive change. For example, a lake can absorb quite a lot of acidity before it actually becomes acid itself, but once its limit has been reached and its buffering capacity exhausted, the lake will abruptly become acidic making it toxic to its flora and fauna. How stable ecosystems are, how much change they can cope with, is as difficult to predict as the weather.

Ecological science relies more on careful observation of recurring natural patterns of action, than on knowledge deriving from laboratory research. A fisherman who has put out to sea all his life uses the clouds, the wind and the colour of the sky to predict the weather he will have to face, often more accurately than meteorologists using scientific data. Sometimes a trained eye can detect changes in an ecosystem too subtle to be measured by scientifical instruments. An experienced and patient observer is often the most likely to be rewarded with insights into the secrets of nature.

Lying in the path of the north east trade winds in Panama is a belt of luxuriant rainforest. The dense canopy is highly efficient at trapping and storing rainwater, enabling the spider monkeys (Ateles geoffroyi) in the picture opposite to enjoy a drink from a water-filled balsa flower.

Water is present at all stages of growth and decay. Leaves shed in autumn by deciduous trees gradually turn to humus. Earth formed of organic matter makes an ideal storage place for water and nutrients – the basis of new life.

Like countless others in northern Europe, this lake fringed with pines, alders and birch in the Wigierska National Park in Poland is a relic of the last Ice Age, carved out by glaciers over 10,000 years ago.

The Secret Life of Lakes

Anyone who thinks that lakes are just hollows in a landscape filled with water is very much mistaken. Lakes have a life of their own, and humanity's understanding of some of the mysterious things that go on in them is still very incomplete.

It is only recently, for example, that scientists have been able to explain a process in which lakes take deep 'breaths', revitalising themselves each year in a great upheaval that literally turns over their waters. During the warmer months, there is a stable division between the the upper layers that are warmed by the sun and the cold water in the depths; the sudden difference in temperature between these layers can be quite dramatic. No exchange of water, nutrients or algae takes place between the deep water and that nearer the surface. When the air temperature begins to fall in the autumn, the surface water cools down, and a spectacular event takes place. The cooler, denser water sinks, mixing with the lower layers right down to the bottom of the lake. This sudden, powerful circulation causes the whole lake to heave, as if taking a deep breath.

Even if there is no wind, the surface will seem strangely choppy and change colour.

The lake's plant life is restricted to the few metres of water close enough to the surface to be reached by the sun's rays. For a long time it was thought that beneath the warm surface layer, the depths of the lake formed a calm, almost immobile, body of water. But recent research has shown that here, too, there are strong currents. Some of this unexpected dynamism is caused by the arrival of water from rivers and streams which is generally colder than the topmost layer of the lake and so sinks, mixing with other water and causing it to move. Studies of Lake Lucerne in Switzerland have shown that in some of its deeper reaches, long believed to be virtually static, the waters are exchanged laterally from one part of the lake to another.

Exact measurement has also been able to reveal another phenomenon that is still only partially understood: in almost all lakes, oscillations, known as seiches, sometimes occur, during which the lake's entire contents swish around like milk in a bowl. This motion is so slow, however, that it is not visible to the naked eye. Some seiches are evidently caused by strong winds, and

lakes have been known to go on swaying for days after the wind has dropped. The slowest single oscillation so far detected in studies on Lake Michigan and Lake Zurich took around 100 hours. Physicists suspect that this movement may be related to the rotation of the earth.

Seiches can be detected only by precise measurement, but the rise and fall of the water level of Lake Wakatipu on New Zealand's South Island – a good five centimetres overall every ten to fifteen minutes – is quite visible. So far, no one has found a satisfactory explanation for this phenomenon, though Maori legend has it that a giant who had been burnt as a punishment for his misdeeds stepped into the lake to ease his pain; changes in the water level of Lake Wakatipu are caused by the giant's breathing.

Much of what goes on in lakes happens so slowly that it is scarcely perceptible: in sharp contrast to rivers, it may take decades, or even centuries, for the water of large lakes to be replaced. Similarly, while rivers are constantly refreshed with oxygen which mixes with the water as it flows, still water takes in oxygen only very slowly. Although scientific understanding of lakes has advanced enormously in recent years, they have yet to yield up all of their secrets.

More than just H₂0

Anyone with a smattering of scientific knowledge who is asked what water is, will answer H_2O – the chemical formula describing molecules made up of two atoms of hydrogen and one of oxygen. An exhaustive scientific description of a water sample will measure the substances dissolved in it – its salt and gas content – and its temperature. If two samples share the same chemical make-up, they are regarded as identical. But this kind of description does not even begin to explore the true nature of water.

The variety and transmutability of water are proverbial. It is the only naturally occurring substance that freely changes between what geologists and chemists call the three states of aggregation – solid, liquid and gas – under conditions found at the earth's surface. The shapes it takes are

infinite: no two snowflakes falling from the sky are identical; at least ten different crystallisation patterns of ice have been discovered to date. In extremely cold conditions, in Siberia, for example, water that is forced up out of the depths freezes instantly on contact with the bitterly cold air, to form a kind of glacier. The legendary ground ice of Ulachan-Taryn, known as aufeis, is created in this way, expanding in winter to a thickness of four metres and covering 180 square kilometres.

Even in its liquid state, water can take a variety of forms. Photographs of laboratory experiments reveal that when, for example, a series of water droplets hit the surface of a sample of water from a mountain stream, quite different flow patterns are created from those made by an identical series of droplets falling into a sample of tap water. Even if the chemical make-up and temperature of two water samples are identical, their respective origins may be reflected in different flow patterns.

As a result of studies of this kind, some researchers now believe that water in its liquid state can retain and even pass on certain properties regardless of its chemical make-up. Further experiments, again with two samples from a mountain spring and tap water, have involved diluting these with distilled (chemical-free) water

Photographs taken in the course of a test developed by a German research institute showing the different currents created when distilled water was dropped into water samples taken from an ancient spring (left) and city tap water (right). The spring water shows far more complex and defined flow patterns than the treated river water.

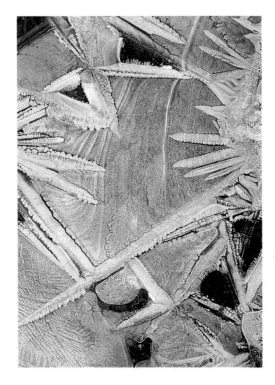

The Inuits – inhabitants of the Arctic – have over a hundred words to describe ice and snow; the variations in patterns made by ice are infinite.

(in a ratio of $1:10^{50}$) until they have effectively no chemical content and then introducing a very fine suspension (or colloid) of gold chloride into both. Although chemically identical, the samples still coloured the colloid differently, appearing to retain some 'memory' of their different histories. Quite how this memory works is unknown. It may have to do with the internal structure of the liquid, which is in a sense midway between ice crystals with their geometrical patterns and amorphous vapour with no discernible pattern. It may possibly contain clusters of water molecules whose relative (at present undetectable) arrangements carry 'information'.

It is likely, too, that the curative effect of mineral springs cannot be put down exclusively to the presence of dissolved salts. Numerous springs which have been shown to have a therapeutic effect do not, according to conventional science, contain

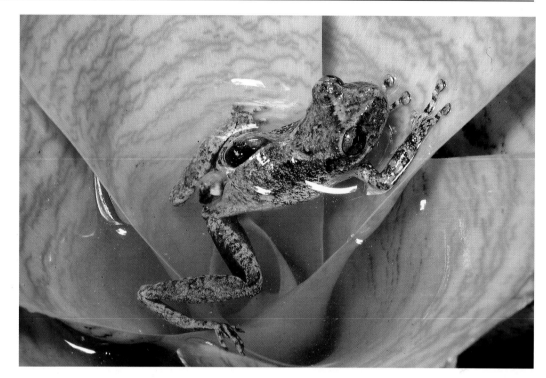

Above. Entrusting a future generation to a tiny but secure reservoir of water, a pygmy marsupial frog (Flectonotus pygmaeus) releases tadpoles from its pouch into a bromeliad growing in Venezuelan cloud forest.

Detail of the Mangorewa river near Rotorua, North Island, New Zealand, showing one of the limitless patterns created by flowing water.

enough minerals to be of any consequence. It seems that water which has spent thousands of years maturing deep below the earth's surface acquires special properties which cannot themselves be measured, even though their curative effects are quite clear.

All that can be said for sure is that water in its liquid state is a great deal more complex than our hitherto rather simplistic view of it might suggest. Many scientists continue to believe, however, that what cannot be measured does not exist.

Water – showing us the way

The sheer complexity of natural systems makes it extremely difficult to predict exactly what impact humanity is having on the environment. What is certain is that the greater the intervention, the more significant the risk that serious damage will be done. But trying to take account of uncertainties of this kind is not a popular way of thinking. It is much easier to rely on scientific theory to justify human actions and allay anxieties about any negative consequences they might have on the environment. But this blinkered way of making decisions ignores the fact that scientific predictions are not always accurate, and fails to take account of the close

mutual dependence of the natural systems that ultimately govern our own beneficial relationship with the natural world.

People who have for generations lived in close contact with nature are only too well aware that it makes sense to work with rather than against its forces. Their very survival depends on the need to limit their exploitation of nature's gifts. Many of the techniques used by so-called 'primitive peoples' are highly sophisticated and based on experience and wisdom gathered over hundreds, even thousands, of years. What they invariably have in common is a deep respect for nature. In general it is taken as read that ecosystems should be disturbed as little as possible by farming; that only modest numbers of animals should be hunted or fished so as to safeguard long-term populations. Natural processes are made use of but not undermined – wild fruits are harvested but the parent plant is not damaged.

It goes without saying that this attitude stands in sharp contrast to the modern industrialised view of nature, which is almost always that of user or exploiter. Technologies have for a long time been developed quite independently of natural processes and based instead on the limited knowledge provided by scientific research.

Much of human society now acts as

though it were no longer part of nature. It is as if we are pushing away the natural world, entrenching ourselves in artificial environments, denying any dependence on dangerous, unpredictable, threatening nature. Springs have been replaced by taps, rainfall by irrigation pumps. We swim in sterile, tiled swimming pools full of chlorinated water rather than diving into clear lakes or steadily flowing rivers. Soap and detergent are considered more important than the purity of water.

The belief in a huge and everlasting water cycle which cannot be thrown out of balance allows modern industrial society to dodge any responsibility for the amount of water it extracts from nature and the use to which this is put. But the assumption that the source will never run dry is a dangerous illusion: in overexploiting water resources, increasing the velocity of the cycle and slowly eroding its foundations,

we are in the process of taking the bread – and water – out of our own mouths. As people become more insulated from the natural world, though, the dangers of such arrogance become harder to appreciate.

We have to decide whether to be guided in our water use by the ways in which water naturally behaves, or to continue in what will inevitably prove to be a vain attempt to organise it along exclusively human-centred lines. One look at how water is behaving is enough to show whether or not people are treating it properly: is it clean or is it dirty, is it threatening to wreak havoc or controlling its own flow, is it in constant supply or running short?

If humanity continues to waste and abuse this gift of nature, the future looks bleak. But if water is once again treated with intelligence and sensitivity, it will continue to sustain us indefinitely.

Woman collecting water vegetables on a canal in the Mekong Delta, Vietnam.

Opposite. Samburu warrior drinking from a pool in the sand in a dried-up river bed near Tum, Nyiru range, northern Kenya.

CHAPTER TWO

DRINKING WATER

For humanity, as for most life on earth, regular supplies of water make the difference between life and death. Each of the billions of cells in the human body contains a minute amount of salty water which scientists believe is remarkably similar to the water in the primeval oceans that covered the planet millions of years ago. On average, 70 per cent of the human body consists of water; the figure is a little higher for babies and a little lower for old people.

Even the slightest drop in the body's water content will affect the metabolism. If the water deficit in the body reaches 0.5 per cent of normal water content, we feel thirsty. At 5 per cent, light fever will ensue, and at 8 per cent, the glands no longer produce saliva and the skin begins to turn blue. A person whose water level is 10 per cent below normal can no longer walk; once the figure has reached 12 per cent death is not far off.

Bare medical statistics of this kind give no indication of the horrible suffering caused by dehydration. One of the most powerful descriptions of what it is like to come close to death from thirst was given by the French pilot and author, Antoine de Saint-Exupéry, who crash-landed in the Sahara in 1935 and, together with his co-pilot, was lost in the desert for days without water: 'The west wind is blowing, which can dry out a man in nineteen hours. My gullet is still open, but it is hard and painful. I can already perceive a soft rattling noise. Soon the cough I have been told about and which I have long been waiting for will start. My tongue gets in my way. But the worst thing is that I can see bright spots. When these turn into flames, I will collapse.' This gradual blurring of the senses ultimately triggers hallucinations,

fear and aggression, as well as muscle cramps and an unbearable burning sensation in the skin. The vocal chords dry out, making it impossible to speak.

The two French pilots were lucky and were saved in the nick of time by an Arabian shepherd who found them wandering through the desert sands. 'A miracle, a miracle! He approaches us like a deity walking across the ocean! He has looked into our faces, has placed his hands on our shoulders and we have listened to him and lain down. Here there is no such thing as race, no such thing as language, no such thing as political parties. A poor nomadic shepherd has laid angelic hands on our shoulders. We have waited for his return, pressing our faces into the sand. And now we are drinking, lying on our stomachs, our heads in the pool like cattle.'

Each day, the body needs around 1.5 litres of water so that, through the production of urine and faeces, it can get rid of undigestible waste, the by-products of metabolic activity and the salts consumed in food. A further 0.4 litres per day are carried to the membranes of the lung to keep them moist, then released as we breathe out. Anyone living in a cold climate will have noticed the small cloud of fog (or condensation) produced on a crisp winter's day on breathing out. Whenever the air is dry, either at high altitudes or in cold weather, the moisture loss is particularly high. A significant amount – 0.6 litres per day – passes out through the skin, again to keep it moist and supple. But the largest quantity of water is used to regulate body temperature: surplus body warmth produced by strenuous physical activity is brought into balance through the evaporation of moisture, which is why people perspire. A person working in the sun for eight hours at a temperature of 18°C can lose four litres of liquid in perspiration, and, at 30°C, as much as eight litres. The body uses the same mechanism to bring down a high temperature caused by illness.

Whenever people travel into areas where there is no water, they have to take with them sufficient supplies of liquid. Being obliged to carry two to five litres of drinking water per person for every day of travel places severe restrictions on the distances

that can be covered. The Bedouins of the Arabian desert have developed water conservation to a fine art. Their caravans can travel for days without having to find fresh water supplies and can thus cover hundreds of kilometres – even in the infamous Rub' al Khali (Empty Quarter) in southern Arabia that would be impossible to cross without such measures. Here, Bedouin caravans travel only at night. Moisture loss is reduced to a minimum by adopting a slow and measured pace, and by hardly

speaking. Loose, billowing clothing makes it easier for air to circulate around the body and thus to avoid perspiration as far as possible. The day is devoted to rest, in the shadow of rocks, well out of the heat of the sun.

Astronauts face similar restrictions: every extra litre of water they take into space means an additional kilogram to be catapulted out of the earth's gravitational field. The American space station, Skylab, for instance, had 3,000 litres of water, or three

Opposite. A farmer of the Dogon tribe draws water near Bandiagara, South Mali (West Africa). In regions with clearly defined dry and rainy seasons, groundwater is the only reliable year-round source. Engine-driven pumps have made water extraction easier, but in many places supplies have been rapidly exhausted as a result.

Turkana girl watering cattle at a waterhole near Lorugumu in northern Kenya (East Africa). In arid areas like this, cattle, goats, pigs and sheep are prized possessions, not least for the nutritious milk they produce, even when grazed on the scantest vegetation.

tonnes, on board when it went into orbit in 1973 – enough, with substantial recycling, to supply the crew for about 100 days. More extended travel in space is impossible because of the scale of water reserves that would be needed.

Ancient Water Supplies

In many ancient societies the phenomenon of pure, clear spring water issuing from the soil seemed nothing short of miraculous. Springs and rivers, as well as rain, were regarded as gifts from the gods and worshipped like deities.

Although some of the earliest settlements were set up on the banks of rivers, spring water was generally preferred for drinking because of its purity and cool temperature. Wherever the water did not come to the surface of its own accord, holes were dug in the ground to find it. As water

holes became deeper, they had to be lined to guard against collapse. Well-building had begun. Brick-lined wells have been found even in the most ancient settlements so far discovered: a round well, carefully lined with brick and several metres deep, was found completely intact in the Indus city of Mohenjo-Daro, now in Pakistan, which is over 4,000 years old.

In many areas, there was only a limited supply of well water, and fair distribution had to be regulated by law. Highly complex regulations controlling the use and protection of wells and springs were enshrined in Hebrew and Arabic law, in particular. A clear hierarchy was stipulated: drinking water for people (followed by domestic animals) had absolute priority; what remained could be used for washing; only then was it permitted to be used for watering fields, flower beds and trees. Many of these traditions survive in the Middle East

today. Nomads' desert wells are designated for the exclusive use of passing caravans. No thirsty man may be refused a drink of water, but once a water hole is occupied, any new arrivals have to move on. When the first caravan leaves the well, the water becomes public property again. In ancient legal systems, private ownership of water was as unknown as private ownership of land: water was indivisible, a gift from God. Interference of any kind with the water, whether polluting it, diverting its course for individual use or causing damage to wells, was strictly forbidden.

Wherever groundwater was in short supply, or salty – as in brackish coastal districts, rain was the only source of drinking water. For islands with no spring water, storing rain was an essential prerequisite to human habitation. Island peoples all over the world – in the Mediterranean, in the Pacific and off Northern European shorelines – developed sophisticated methods of storage using cisterns. These were usually hewn out of the rocks or excavated. They often consisted of two basins: after collecting in the first basin, where dust and other particles could settle, the water ran into a covered basin for storage as drinking water.

As the populations of towns and cities expanded, the growing demand for water could no longer be satisfied by supplies from wells and cisterns alone, and it was not long before more elaborate schemes were developed for supplying water to conurbations from other areas. The phenomenon of designing water supply to meet demand, rather than tailoring consumption – and therefore population size – to locally available water had begun. In Asia Minor (now the Middle East), monumental tunnels and aqueducts have been discovered that are almost 3,000 years old.

Hermitage on the Sinai peninsula. The improbable sight of trees in this parched place indicates skilful collection of the sparse rain and protection of the water from evaporation.

Butt to catch rainwater from gutter on private house in Oneroa on Mangaia in the Cook Islands, South Pacific.

Some of these are still in use. The oldest known construction of this kind served the town of Tushpa, today known as Van, in Anatolia, as early as 790 BC. Tushpa, the capital of the Kingdom of Urartu, was situated on the shores of Lake Van, whose waters are undrinkable and of no use for irrigation because of an unusually high natural concentration of sodium carbonate. On the orders of King Menua (805-785 BC), and at a vast expense, a 56-kilometre canal was built across steep and unsafe terrain to carry water to the town from springs in the Engil-Chaji valley. This canal still forms part of Van's water supply infrastructure today.

It is worth noting, however, that uncontrollable growth in urban populations resulting in importation of water is not an inevitable progression, as the example of Ladakh in northern India shows, where for centuries the sizes of communities have been deliberately limited so that the populations could be supported by existing water resources.

The Romans have often been credited with inventing the long-distance water main. But when Rome's first large-scale aqueduct, the Aqua Appia, was completed in 317 BC, the Tushpa supply network (and for that matter others in Asia Minor) was already over 300 years old. The scale of the Roman edifices, however, far surpassed anything that had gone before them: the Aqua Marcia was some 91 kilometres in length, and ten kilometres of it passed along magnificent arched aqueducts. Rome had an enormous population – in the second century AD it became the first city in history to reach the million mark, and by then the quality of its water resources was degrading rapidly. Such quantities of filth were carried into the Tiber by the city's sewers that its waters were utterly unfit for human consumption. Roman aqueducts are rightly considered to be masterpieces of architecture and engineering, but they are also monuments to the phenomenon of urban populations outstripping the local natural resources essential to their survival.

Not all the twelve aqueducts built to serve Ancient Rome supplied water suitable for drinking. One supply line, the Aqua Alsietina, carried undrinkable, murky

Above. The Pont du Gard in the south of France – an aqueduct constructed by the Romans as part of a scheme to bring pure water from the mountains to Nemausus (present-day Nîmes) in spite of the fact that the city is rich in springs – testament not just to engineering skill but to an early impulse to import supplies from other regions.

Below. The Roman water mains at Ephesus (now in Turkey) which were used not just to transport drinking water, but also to service a splendid nympheum, *a huge, ornamental wall in the centre of the city over which water constantly flowed – a kind of early water sculpture.*

water from Lake Martignano mainly for washing streets and watering gardens. Occasionally, Alsietina water was deployed for a *naumachia*, when an amphitheatre would be flooded for dramatic stagings of historical sea battles.

Despite the elaborate infrastructure needed to deliver it, drinking water was available free at every public fountain. All but the very rich had to carry it home in jugs and other vessels. Any excess water (*aqua caduca*) not required at the fountains was piped or channelled to wealthy households for a fee (*vectigal*). The amount supplied and the fee charged depended solely on the size of the feedpipe – there were no taps to turn off the water, and so

In Ancient Greece and in the Roman Empire, almost all settlements, including small farms, were equipped with capacious cisterns to collect rainwater. The practice was no less widespread in the Arab world. The picture on the left shows the rainwater collection cisterns at the fort of Zafar Dhi Bin in North Yemen, dating from c.1200. In the 20th century, mains water is for the first time becoming preeminent, and an immensely valuable source of water – rain – is increasingly ignored.

Qanats are an ancient and ingenious method of tapping groundwater thought to

have originated in what is now western Iran in about 700 BC. They provide both drinking water and the means to irrigate crops in otherwise dry areas and are usually found in places where rainwater collects not in rivers but in layers of gravel at the base of mountains. Qanats or tunnels are dug horizontally into the water-carrying gravel; vertical shafts from the ground above provide both air and access to remove excavated material. The spring at the top end of the qanat can be over 60 metres beneath the mountain's surface. Many of the oases in northern Africa and central Asia owe

their very existence to 2000-year-old qanat systems, which, without the use of any kind of pump, provide a constant flow of cool, potable water. Drinking water networks and irrigation canals alike can be fed by water flowing out of the opening in the mountainside. Until 1930, Tehran, capital of Iran, depended exclusively on qanat water for its supplies.

The picture on the right shows the interior of a falaj, another name for a qanat, in Central Oman.

it flowed day and night from the springs to the aqueducts, to the public fountains and baths and finally into the villas of the wealthiest citizens, whose sinks, fountains and private baths were supplied with thousands of litres of fresh water 24 hours a day. Statistics revealing the immensely high per-capita consumption of the Romans are therefore of little more than curiosity value. Most of the water was not used at all and simply flowed straight out of the city again. Modern experience of the use of public standpipes suggests that the daily household consumption in Ancient Rome is unlikely to have exceeded 50 litres per person because of the hard work involved in fetching and carrying it. Families who could afford slaves to collect their water may have used up to 1,000 litres a day.

During the later centuries of the Roman empire, water was made private property for the first time in the history of humanity (a privilege that has continued to the present day in some countries, among them Italy and Spain). Only rivers, springs feeding aqueducts and rainwater collected in cisterns or mountain lakes remained public property; all other springs and water became part of the property of the relevant landowner.

By far the greater part of the world's population has always lived in rural areas, far away from towns or cities. In spite of rapid urban growth, this is still the case today. Most settlements were established where there were good, productive springs, so water shortages were probably rare. Little faith was placed in rainwater, or in springs which tended to run dry. If at all possible, people used springs which flowed reliably all year round, or set about gaining access to groundwater by digging wells or constructing other systems such as the qanats common in North Africa and large parts of Central Asia. Knowledge about where the best water could be found – how to recognise it, test it, and discover its properties – was passed down from one generation to the next. At least in the countryside, every family was ultimately responsible for its own drinking water. Springs, streams and wells have traditionally been carefully looked after in all cultures.

It is only in the second half of the 20th century that the human race has had the temerity to assume that it can improve on the free supplies of water that for centuries have been garnered directly from nature. On most Italian islands, the ancient cisterns that have been a reliable source of water for the island populations and their crops and animals since time immemorial are now being neglected and falling into disrepair. Instead, the inhabitants are coming to rely on the daily arrival of shiploads of water from the mainland, which are then pumped into the islands' central network. In places where careful use of the little water available used to be a natural part of everyday life, people are now able to enjoy the luxury of apparently inexhaustible surplus.

This expensive, thoughtless and short-sighted abandoning of naturally available water epitomises humanity's changing attitudes to water. In modern industrial society, what was once welcomed as a gift from the gods is now taken utterly for granted. In our unquestioning belief in the limitless progress of science and technology, we have been happy to abandon the tedious task of arranging and looking after our own water. Just as we see health as a matter for doctors, and justice as the preserve of the lawcourts, we have handed over the responsibility for the basis of life – water – to politicians and water engineers.

Today's Water Supplies

The majority of people who pick up this book are likely to live in households with both a source of running water and drains connected to sewers. These conveniences are nothing special in the industrialised world, but seen in a global context, they are an exceptional luxury. According to World Health Organization (WHO) statistics, less than 20 per cent of the world's population enjoys these facilities. Around two-thirds of all people fetch their drinking water just as their ancestors did a thousand years ago, balancing it on their heads in clay jugs (or often, nowadays, tin cans or plastic buckets) or loading it onto mules. In rich countries, water is available to almost everyone in unlimited quantities at any time of day. In developing countries,

up to a third of the daily calorie intake of women and children is used up solely in obtaining water.

It is not easy for people who are used to the convenience of taps and running water to judge how difficult it is to live without them, and the usual assumption is that providing these facilities unfailingly raises living standards. Large numbers of water projects funded with development aid, however, have not been accepted by the people for whom they were intended, even though they have brought water much closer. Women evidently still often prefer to fetch water from streams which seemed to well-intentioned aid workers unreasonably far away. In Africa, especially, ancient water laws regulating the use and distribution of water still apply, and any modern development project must take account of them. It is almost invariably the women of a community who are responsible for obtaining water, and plans implemented without involving them are unlikely to meet with much success, however well-meaning they may be.

For decades, water policy for or in many developing countries has been formed over the heads of those who will be affected. As recently as the 1980s, which were declared the Water Decade by the United Nations, little importance was attached to the idea of involving the local population in plans to construct supply systems for drinking water. The UN's stated objective was the provision of sufficient clean water and adequate sanitary facilities for everyone in the world by the year 1990. WHO analysts, who hold poor hygiene responsible for as many illnesses as are caused by impure drinking water, were intelligent enough to set the target volume at well above the subsistence minimum of five litres a day. All water supply projects were therefore to be designed to provide a daily volume of 40 to 50 litres per person – in other words, a family of six would be carrying home the equivalent of 300 kilogrammes of water per day, and so the WHO target was to provide a water supply point no further than 200 metres from any house.

In the course of the Water Decade, developing nations invested some $70 billion in water supply systems and sanitary facilities; $30 billion more were contributed

For millions of people (though mainly women and children), the first task of the day is fetching water: from a public standpipe near Lake Baikal, Siberia (top left), from a communal water tap and wash house on the island of São Tiago, Cabo Verde (centre), as a block of glacial ice in Greenland (bottom) and from a village well near Jodhpur, Rajasthan, India (top right).

by foreign aid agencies. By 1990, the situation had improved, but the target of providing clean drinking water for all was still almost as remote as it had been in 1980: in towns and cities in developing countries, 240 million people (18 per cent of the population) were still without 'reliable water supplies', and the same applied to a further billion (37 per cent) in rural areas. From the point of view of the industrialised world it had seemed quite logical to use itself as a model and build water mains leading to every house. But even a rough estimate shows that the necessary construction work involved – for dams, wells, waterworks, and Western-style supply and sewer systems – would far exceed the entire national wealth of most developing countries. Even more basic strategies, such as piping water from a stream to a public standpipe, are too expensive for people in very many regions. The only water systems which make sense in these places are those that are installed in full consultation with the local population and can be maintained by them: boreholes with manual pumps, shallow wells and tanks for collecting rainwater.

Of the $3 billion a year contributed by the rich world towards water systems in developing countries between 1981 and 1990, only four per cent was targeted at projects with technology appropriate to specific locations and needs. Many technical facilities broke down within a few months of installation and could not be repaired by locals. In addition, the development agencies setting up drinking water programmes almost always overlooked the fact that water has to drain away after use.

As drainage systems were rarely included in the budget, pools and puddles of stagnant water began to accumulate near supply pipes providing ideal breeding grounds for malaria-carrying mosquitoes.

Slowly, the realisation is dawning that Western water and sanitation technology cannot be applied indiscriminately to any climatic, ecological or social context. They probably cannot be paid for, either: UNICEF, the United Nations Children's Fund, estimated in 1990 that it would cost at least $357 billion to supply drinking water for all to a point within 200 metres of each household and hygienic sanitation by the year 2000. $247 billion of that sum would be swallowed up by creating urban infrastructures based on Western models. According to UNICEF, a simple but comprehensive solution for the entire world could be provided for only a third of this sum, around $110 billion.

Inexpensive and robust systems of the kind proposed by UNICEF consist largely of locally available materials. Pumpless gravitational systems conducting water out of streams, through pipes and to public standpipes are easy to build and maintain, and are also highly durable. One of the greatest successes of the UN's Water Decade may well have been the introduction of the standardised India Mark II handpump: there are now people in practically every Indian village who know how to fix this sound, cheap device. Low-tech solutions are far more successful in poor countries than expensive Western high-techology; it can only be hoped that water planners and engineers elsewhere will follow this impressive example.

Water for the Rich

Some water engineers are now beginning to ask whether the technological strategies of Western water management, which have hitherto gone unchallenged, really present such perfect solutions, even for industrial countries. Larger and larger amounts of high-quality drinking water are turned straight into waste water, and the costs for collecting and treating it are soaring ever higher: this pattern of procurement and disposal not only puts too much strain on natural water systems, but also threatens to become unaffordable. Experience in developing countries shows that equally good results can be achieved with considerably less technological sophistication. Making use of rainwater, and separating different types of waste water, so that some of it can be recycled, are tested methods which, in a number of regions, have made a reliable supply of water possible in the first place.

Modern industrialised societies are now having to face up to the unexpected and unwelcome discovery that their water supplies are limited. It may still be possible to make water available whenever and wherever necessary, but only at great expense. And ultimately money will not be able to guarantee supplies of water on the current scale. As pollution continues to make more and more sources unusable, increased demand can be catered for only by drawing on the steadily shrinking supplies of clean water left to us.

Although water suppliers have long since opted to concentrate on sources in rural areas, they have still not escaped the blight of pollution. Hundreds of sources,

Sand and gravel filters are far superior to chemical disinfection for making water safe to drink. The water passes through a coarse filter of gravel or similar material, like the brick fragments used here in the Sudan, and then through a sandpit that filters out disease-carrying organisms and substances. An installation of this kind can provide 5,000 to 10,000 litres of clean water per day.

Far right. The India Mark II handpump, developed by UNICEF. Reliable and robust, it is made from standard components and easily maintained.

in areas far from conurbations, have been closed because of contamination, and even remote reservoirs tucked among low mountains are not safe. The principal sources of water pollution in the countryside are agricultural fertilisers and pesticides which have been used in increasing quantities mainly since the 1960s. Intensive livestock farming has also proved disastrous, because the enormous volume of slurry (liquid manure) spread on the land contaminates the groundwater. Where there are centres of meat, egg and milk production – such as the Po valley in Italy, Lower Saxony in northern Germany and large tracts of land in the Netherlands and Britain – the groundwater has long since ceased to be of any use for drinking because of high nitrate levels, and these areas are now just as dependent as industrial areas on water brought in from other supply regions.

Poisoning the Well

Today the few pristine water resources that are left are coming under more and more pressure; ultimately such a pitch of overuse is reached, that streams run dry and the groundwater level begins to drop. Inflated demands made on the water supply result in massive changes to the natural environment. A recent survey in England and Wales by the National Rivers Authority documented 43 cases of severe damage to streams and rivers as a result of water extraction. At least 16 cases have been caused exclusively by the water industry. Initially, there is little to distinguish the ecological consequences of such changes from those of a summer with little rain, but slowly the water regime is affected, moisture-loving plants disappear, frogs and toads are unable to survive, and

woods dry out. In many places, local residents are protesting against this theft of water and the slow, insidious destruction of the countryside around them. In the north of Spain, there is opposition to plans to divert much of the water from the Ebro River into the industrial areas of Bilbao and Tarragona; ultimately a significant proportion of the river's water will not even discharge, as it always has, into the Mediterranean, but into the Atlantic. A number of successful campaigns have been organised in Germany, like the one in the Vogelsberg mountains, to the east of Frankfurt-am-Main, which mobilised opposition to plans for extracting still more groundwater for the banking metropolis.

In the Mediterranean region, a crisis is rapidly coming to a head because of huge and competing demands on the limited water resources by agriculture and industry.

Yellow water lilies (Nuphar lutea) *in Snowdonia, North Wales. Wherever too much water is extracted from nature, causing the groundwater level to sink, large numbers of plant species die out.*

Opposite. Slurry spread on a snowy day in the Schwäbische Alb region of southern Germany. In many intensively farmed areas, the earth's power to act as the guardian of groundwater has long been undermined by overdoses of slurry, sewage sludge, fertilisers and pesticides.

Groundwater supplies along the entire coastline and on many islands have been decimated and on many islands sea water is now penetrating the substrata from which the groundwater has been pumped. Once groundwater becomes salty, it is irretrievably lost as a drinking water resource.

Shortages in the supply of drinking water would be far more apparent if waterworks were not able to resort to deep-lying groundwater. For many areas of Switzerland, Denmark, Germany and France, pumping groundwater from deep underground is now the only way of getting

clean water. The port of Hamburg is by no means exceptional in pumping its fresh water up from depths of more than 400 metres. Harmful substances used in industrial processes and agriculture have already made most rivers and shallow groundwater (groundwater near the surface) unfit for drinking, but the poisons have not yet penetrated as far as the earth's deeper substrata. When water is mined from these sources deep below the earth's surface, it is done at some risk: the suction generated underground by powerful pumps causes water from the surface to be drawn rapidly

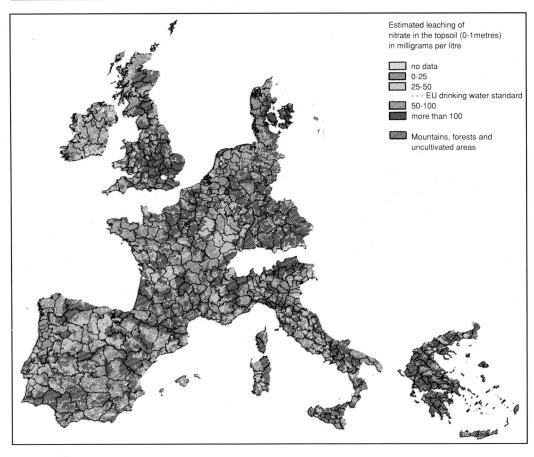

Estimated leaching of
nitrate in the topsoil (0-1metres)
in milligrams per litre

no data
0-25
25-50
--- EU drinking water standard
50-100
more than 100

Mountains, forests and
uncultivated areas

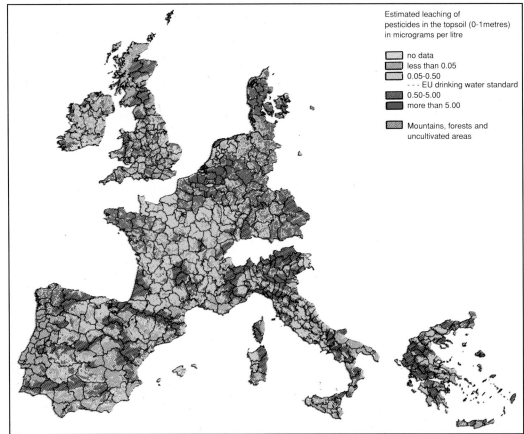

Estimated leaching of
pesticides in the topsoil (0-1metres)
in micrograms per litre

no data
less than 0.05
0.05-0.50
--- EU drinking water standard
0.50-5.00
more than 5.00

Mountains, forests and
uncultivated areas

Pesticides are used to wage chemical warfare on plants, insects and fungi considered undesirable by farmers. In the European Union alone, 300,000 tonnes of pesticides are used every year. In the absence of any comprehensive survey, nobody knows precisely how much of these highly active biological substances leaches into the rivers and groundwater.

This map is based on a computer model created by the Dutch Environmental Protection Agency to show levels of pesticide concentration in shallow groundwater based on soil permeability, levels of rainfall and the leachability of certain agricultural chemicals. These findings (backed up by random tests) indicate that the groundwater of 65 per cent of the arable land in the European Union (and any drinking water taken from it) breaks the limit of contamination permitted by the EU Drinking Water Standard.

The American Environmental Protection Agency has identified 98 different pesticides in the groundwater of 40 states from which the drinking water of more than 10 million American citizens is taken. Virtually nothing is known about damage to ground and drinking water in developing countries. Tests carried out on irrigation canals in intensively farmed land show high pesticide concentrations, but soil contamination is probably still far lower than it is in Europe or the United States. As the water-soluble herbicides (weedkillers) that are responsible for most of the infractions of drinking water standards in the developed world are expensive, they are still relatively rarely used in non-industrialised countries.

The second map indicates nitrate pollution of shallow groundwater, which typically reflects the distribution of intensive agriculture, including specialised cultivation such as market gardening, vineyards and tree nurseries.

The dark-red and orange areas on the map, signifying acute, health-threatening concentrations of nitrates, often coincide with intensive meat, egg and milk production, where vast quantities of slurry are spread on the land. The only solution to this is an entirely different approach to raising animals. If the number of beasts is limited by the feed crops or pasture that can be grown locally, the relatively small amount of resulting manure can be safely recycled in the cultivation of more fodder.

Nitrates cannot economically be removed from water, making the shallow groundwater beneath 25 per cent of agricultural land in the European Union virtually unusable for drinking.

Along many coastlines, fresh groundwater constantly emerging from the land effectively holds the seawater at bay, thus protecting against salinisation. If, as here on the Coto Doñana in Spain, the surrounding settlements and irrigation agriculture take too much groundwater, the flow reverses: the precious layers of fresh water lying deep underground are invaded by sea water, and rendered useless to all plant and animal life (including humans).

down to the underground reservoirs, carrying with it any poisonous substances it may contain, and thus polluting the source. Sometimes the process disturbs still deeper layers of enclosed salt water – the remnants of prehistoric oceans – causing it to mix with the highly-prized fresh water which then becomes unusable. Pristine water from deep sources such as these is sometimes as much as 10,000 years old, and is replenished only very slowly. And yet huge quantities of it are being sacrificed to modern society's unquenchable thirst, sometimes exhausting the source within the space of only a few years.

Shallow groundwater is replenished far faster than resources deep underground and provides good drinking water. A good rule of thumb is to exploit only those aquifers that will be replenished over at most the life span of one generation. No-one has the right to plunder ancient deep-lying aquifers which have taken many thousands of years to form.

If we are to rely exclusively on shallow groundwater for supplies, however, it must be protected from non-biodegradable chemicals. Before the industrial age, the waste discarded by humanity presented little problem, because bacteria in the soil could break down both it and any accompanying microbes to produce substances that could play their part in natural processes. It is thanks to this simple but effective mechanism that our well and spring water remained pure and fresh until the early part of this century. But many of the chemicals that are now used are highly persistent and cannot be broken down by the soil. The only way to prevent

lasting damage to the groundwater from all the pesticides, detergents, solvents and oils which are unaffected by the soil's detoxification system is to replace them with biodegradable alternatives.

In a vain – and damaging – attempt to replenish pristine groundwater in areas where even the water companies admit that it is overexploited, these companies are attempting to copy nature by putting the soil to work. Huge seepage fields are set up into which waste water or river water is forced. The idea is to clean the water and artificially replenish the groundwater, a process known as artificial groundwater recharge. But these schemes take no account of the fact that we are no longer dealing with the biodegradable natural substances of the pre-industrial age. Although the water is treated before it enters the fields, the removal of all toxic substances and salts is impossible. Wherever the seepage technique is employed, and no matter how sophisticated is the technology for purifying the waste or river water, a cocktail of thousands of unknown substances passes through the soil and gradually accumulates in the groundwater.

Artificial groundwater recharge, long-distance pipelines, extraction of ancient groundwater, when it comes to it, none of these technologies (which are supposed to secure future drinking water supplies) are tackling the underlying problems. By using high technology and grossly interventionist strategies of this kind, politicians and water companies create the illusion of never-ending water supplies, while pollution and overexploitation alike continue unchecked. In the long term, pursuing a

Doha desalination plant, Kuwait. There is no technical obstacle to desalinating sea water, but it uses a great deal of energy and so cannot be used for large-scale purposes such as irrigation. Small-scale solar-powered installations have been in use since the 1960s – many ocean-going vessels and some of the Aegean Islands, for example, use small evaporators to produce their own fresh water. But a centralised desalination plant would need to gather solar energy from a huge area in order to have access to sufficient power to function. It is only in the oil-rich Gulf states that desalination for general domestic purposes is affordable.

Acid Rain

Crystal-clear water is not necessarily pure water. Hundreds of lakes in the northern hemisphere, notably in Sweden, Norway, the United Kingdom and North America, which appear to contain pristine, fresh water are in fact as sterile as a chlorinated indoor swimming pool – tragic victims of acid rain. In summer, a healthy lake often has somewhat cloudy water, an effect caused by the presence of tiny algae that thrive in the top, sunlit layers of the water and form the beginning of the food chain.

As lakes become more acid – the end result of constant, large-scale atmospheric emissions of sulphur dioxide and nitrogen oxides in car exhausts, and from industrial processes and coal, oil and gas-fired power stations – their fish, amphibian and invertebrate populations gradually die; finally even the tiny algae can no longer survive, leaving nothing but toxic reservoirs.

The fact that not all lakes exposed to acid precipitation have suffered this fate is because some have benefited more than others from the neutralising effect of the soil through which the rain passes before it drains into them. In most regions, the mineral content of the soil includes calcium carbonate and magnesium carbonate which are able to neutralise acid. They are, however, washed away in the process; eventually the soil's buffering capacity will be used up, leading inevitably to long-term acidification. Once the soil is too acid and its mineral content is depleted, it will no longer be able to support the life that used to thrive in and on it, and the ecosystem's ability to break down harmful substances will be affected, which ultimately damages its capacity to maintain the purity of groundwater.

It is usually only when the first trees start to die off that people begin to realise the scale of destruction. Woods on hillsides where there is particularly high precipitation are often worst hit. Even in dry weather, trees catch and collect acid dust particles and tiny droplets of water carried on the wind. Once the soil's neutralising potential has been exhausted, the acid will penetrate further into the valleys – a development familiar to many water companies whose upland reservoirs are becoming increasingly acid. Alkaline substances have to be added to the water to correct the balance so that copper and lead pipes are not corroded by it. But this is not the end of the problem, for acid in the soil will trigger the release of any aluminium

it contains, contaminating drinking water reservoirs and making it necessary to put the water through an elaborate and expensive detoxifying process.

Ongoing research in Norway has demonstrated just how persistent the effects of acid rain can be. A transparent cover was placed over an area of soil that had become acidified years before. Rainfall was allowed to collect on the cover, then neutralised and finally distributed over the soil. After five years, the soil

Lake Övre Bergsjön, near Göteborg, Sweden – a last-ditch attempt to save an acidified lake by dumping lime into it. Every year Sweden spends lavishly on liming, with only limited success in reversing the effects of acid rain.

showed little improvement. Its original acidity had been retained and its fertility was still markedly reduced. Even direct applications to the soil of lime and other alkaline substances had little effect in aiding the soil's recovery.

policy of continually broaching new water sources in order to avoid polluted ones, will inevitably lead to more and more acute shortages in drinking water supplies and catastrophic ecological consequences.

Water suppliers have long been aware that their moves to exploit previously untouched water reserves would inevitably fail. But instead of launching an outcry against polluters, who were (and still are) wrecking the natural resource on which we all depend, they have quietly moved away from their original philosophy of putting only pure, natural water into their pipelines with as little treatment as possible. When naturally clean water began to run out, the age of treated drinking water dawned. Artificial production of drinking water from polluted resources became the rule rather than the exception: today, more than half the citizens of the industrialised Organization for Economic Cooperation and Development (OECD) nations are supplied with treated drinking water, and the figure is as high as 70 per cent in the United States.

No matter how carefully water is purified by technical means, it is never as pure as unpolluted natural water. Even the most advanced purification methods are not a hundred per cent effective. And we have only limited knowledge of the effects of chemical residues, which in the case of drinking water may also include residues of substances used in the purification process. Toxicologists warn that merely a few molecules of some substances may be enough to trigger allergies and cause illnesses. There is no substitute for naturally clean, unpolluted drinking water.

Profiting from the Water Crisis

Resourceful entrepreneurs realised as far back as the 1970s that worsening water pollution was likely to be a source of lucrative business in the future. They recognised that environmental organisations had raised awareness about issues such as clean water, and had awakened consumers' anxieties as to whether drinking water might be polluted, making them a great deal more willing to pay for good water. Indeed, who would not be prepared to pay a little more for clean drinking water?

Outfall into the River Ohre, a tributary of the Elbe, from a chemical factory in the Czech Republic, photographed in June 1994. In the long term, even the richest nations will be unable to afford to abandon the rivers as sources of drinking water and will have instead to stop mindlessly polluting them.

The environmental technology market was launched. In addition to tackling the problems surrounding the preparation of drinking water, engineering and technology companies addressed themselves to the processing of sewage and refuse – another opportunity presented to them by the green movement. An entirely new branch of high-tech industry was born. Today, there is a huge market for technology designed to process our increasingly poor quality raw water to produce drinking water that still conforms to official standards. Products or techniques that use rainwater or reduce water consumption are few and far between in this industry. All you can buy is damage limitation.

The environmental industry has mushroomed over the past ten years, and this growth has been reflected in the price of water. It is not just the treatment plants that have to pay for themselves, but every new long-distance pipeline, every subsurface pump and every reservoir. Waterworks'

Mineral Water

It is bottled and costs the consumer around 1,000 times the price of tap water. It is regarded as pure, authentic and health-giving. Yet mineral water sources and wells are not immune to the poisons of our modern, chemical civilisation. Valuable sources have had to be shut down because of impurities in the water.

Poor-quality tap water produces a rise in turnover for the mineral water industry. In 1991, around 34 billion litres were sold worldwide; the European market has doubled over the past ten years. But people have to be able to afford it: 97 per cent of all mineral water is sold in Europe and the United States, though the level of consumption varies widely from country to country. On average Britons drink a mere eight litres a year, where Germans consume 90 litres, the French 100 litres and the Italians 116 litres.

Mineral water is a product with a future, say market researchers. Multinational food companies have already secured the best sources: the Swiss company, Nestlé, for example, owns Perrier, Contrex and Vittel in France, Fürst Bismarck Quelle and Neuselters Mineralquelle in Germany and has a one-fifth share in San Pellegrino water from Italy. In the United States, Nestlé is the market leader with brands such as Arrowhead, Poland Spring and Ice Mountain. The company controls around 20 per cent of the mineral water market worldwide. Expansion is a certainty: bottled water is now being vigorously marketed in the economic boom region of the Far East.

Mineral water vendor in Beijing, China.

running costs are also on the increase: whereas their costs used to be limited to pumping water and pipe maintenance, today they also have to cover the energy and chemical costs associated with treatment. The prognosis for water prices is that they will continue to rise steadily until they reach the pain threshold. But where does the pain threshold lie? Unlike more competitive markets, there is only one supplier of water: each regional water supplier holds a monopoly.

Nowadays, in many countries, the water monopoly has ceased to be an operation run by the state or local authority, but is increasingly in private hands. Based on the French model – where over 70 per cent of the country's water supply has been controlled by private companies for some time – waterworks in England and Wales have recently been sold off to private companies in the face of vigorous popular protest. For the first time, water suppliers are there primarily to make a profit; the price of water has gone up, while its quality has in many cases worsened. Local communities can no longer participate in decisions about long-term development, such as whether future shortages should be dealt with by saving water or by building another reservoir. In Scotland, strong public pressure managed to prevent privatisation, and plans to sell the country's water were abandoned in 1993, a decision not unconnected with the unsatisfactory

experience of England and Wales. In February 1994, Strathclyde Regional Council, itself opposed to water privatisation, organised a referendum on the water issue. The turnout was colossal. Out of those who voted, 97 per cent were against privatisation. In Spain, a quarter of the population is already being supplied by private water companies, and similar steps are being considered in Belgium and Portugal. Even in Germany, where supplying water has traditionally been one of local government's fundamental responsibilities, many towns and communities are finding themselves unable to cope with increasing pollution, particularly in the face of financial cuts and are turning to private groups to shed the pollution: Rostock and Frankfurt an der Oder in former East Germany have both delegated control of their waterworks to private companies in recent years.

The booming water market – treatment, civil engineering, water sales – has led to the formation of substantial multinational water companies, the largest of which are the French giants, Générale des Eaux and Lyonnaise-des-Eaux-Dumez with a joint turnover of FF 49 billion ($9.5 billion) in the water sector alone. Like most companies in the water business, they have mixed interests and also own large construction companies and engineering consultancies. This means that they are not limited to supplying water, but also plan and construct their own pipe networks, treatment

plants and dams. Drinking water is not the only commodity they deal in – they also run sewage plants and set up refuse incinerators and landfills; their operations cover the entire 'environmental' field. They also carry out port, motorway and underground transport systems construction.

These multinationals enjoy the prospect of assured, almost unlimited growth, especially in the area of drinking water. The industry predicts that the world market for construction projects related to water will continue to grow by 30 per cent a year for some time. The European Commission expects an increase in environmental investments from 250 billion ECUs in 1993 to over 325 billion ECUs by the turn of the century. Consumers have so far been willing to pay, persuaded that these improvements are necessary to protect both health and the natural environment. In fact, almost all of these measures are simply attempts to repair existing damage. In most cases, precautionary and preventative strategies would be of greater benefit to the environment as well as a lot cheaper.

At present, a number of governments are lavishing care and attention on the environmental industry, recognising it as an important field of economic growth, and banking on the willingness of environmentally conscious citizens to pay up. The water industry benefits directly from pollution of water resources; today's poisons are a guarantee of future business. The

Filtration unit for the final stage in drinking water treatment at the waterworks in Dresden, Germany.

Opposite. Water dripping slowly but surely through luxuriant mosses and rich earth emerges purified and fresh. This process beats any water filter currently on the market.

more polluted the resources become, the more purification technology will have to be installed, and the higher the prices that can be demanded from consumers. It sounds absurd, but there is very little money to be made in merely distributing clean water from protected sources. Every increase in chemical pollutants will improve turnover, as new purification plants or long-distance pipelines will be needed. And turnover is what brings profit, in the water industry as in any other.

This depressing analysis is vindicated by observation of the water multinationals' own buying policies. The poorer the quality and the lower the availability of water, the tougher the competition will be to acquire waterworks that are being privatised. Générale des Eaux and Lyonnaise-des-Eaux-Dumez have not only bought their way into private English and Spanish water companies; they also run the supplies in Sydney (Australia), where water is relatively scarce, and – together with Aguas de Barcelona from Spain and Anglian Water from England – will in future be supplying the eleven million inhabitants of Buenos Aires with drinking water. These leading companies are also active in the former Eastern Bloc: Lyonnaise, for instance, is involved in supplying drinking water to Vilnius, the capital of Lithuania, and is building a sewage works for Warsaw. The complicated infrastructure involved means that in the developing world only large cities in growth regions such as Indonesia, Brazil and Venezuela are of interest to the multinationals.

Meanwhile, in the companies' home markets, water prices continue to rise merrily. Consumers are charged not only for the water they have used, but for the effects of years of failure on the part of the state to protect water resources. Harmful chemicals from industry, agriculture, transport and energy production are being removed from drinking water at the consumer's expense, while those who have caused the damage get away scot-free. In some cases, they even receive preferential treatment. In Germany, industrial companies drawing amounts of over 50,000 cubic metres a year from waterworks are charged an average 26 per cent less than domestic consumers.

Caracas, Venezuela. European water companies are falling over themselves to land water management contracts in the mega cities of South America, attracted by the prospect of massively remunerative plans to construct dams, long-distance water mains and treatment plants. More sustainable strategies like local usage of rainwater or recycling greywater are of no interest to these multinationals because they would produce much less profit.

1991 Domestic Water Prices per Cubic Metre

Australia	$1.69
Belgium	$0.85
Canada	$0.43
Finland	$1.02
France	$1.06
Germany	$1.40
Ireland	$0.56
Italy	$1.36
Netherlands	$0.88
Norway	$0.34
Sweden	$0.84
United Kingdom	$0.93
United States	$0.53

These prices are national averages; in some regions, the price per cubic metre has already risen above $3, to which have to be added the booming costs associated with maintaining sewers and sewage works. But resistance is growing, particularly in those rural areas which now have both to import their water from other regions, and to pay to pump their sewage to distant treatment plants. Before consumers have been able to organise themselves to demand reparations from the polluters, the water industry itself has become active, namely by campaigning for a drop in drinking water standards – which is certainly one way of lowering purification costs. The most striking example of this development to date is that EUREAU, the European Association of Waterworks, is allowing itself to be coerced by the chemical industry into campaigning for the abolition of the basic principle of pesticide-free drinking water. Their reassuring contention is that there is no scientific evidence to demonstrate that this is necessary.

Behind the scenes of European Union bureaucracy in Brussels, a tough battle is being waged over drinking water standards. Industrial spokesmen and farming bosses are lobbying hard for legal permission to pollute the groundwater. Their intention is for Europe to be divided up into protected and pollutable areas: only in protected areas would activities likely to damage water supplies be stopped, while groundwater lying beneath the rest of the surface area could be quite legally sacrificed to almost unlimited pollution. In most countries, current legislation makes water polluters liable for the damage they cause

– a major risk from the point of view of industrial and agricultural concerns. In spite of the obvious wrong-headedness of the zoning strategy – groundwater cannot be persuaded to stay within any boundaries drawn by man – Eureau persists in supporting it.

Curtailing Demand

It is sometimes said that cheap water naturally encourages wastefulness, that it is only when you have to pay a high price that you value something. This may be true now, but when water was still seen as a precious and limited resource, people were economical with it as a matter of course. If one accepts that water is now seen as a commodity, one way of forcing consumption down might well be to put up the price. Ultimately everyone's entitlement to this gift from nature must be calculated in the light of how much nature can afford to give without sustaining damage. For domestic consumers, whose supply should always have priority over that of industry or agribusiness, a statutory quantity (per person) could be provided at a price in line with the cost of delivery – a logical concomitant of the responsibility assumed by the state for organising the supply of water. Anything over and above this basic amount could be made more expensive to discourage waste. In order to avoid poor families having to bear the brunt of the real (and high) cost of their water supply, some countries are levying part of the cost as a universal tax. Industrial allocations of water supply could be traded, with the price going up or down according to demand within a limited water budget.

Water Priorities

In most regions, there should never be a problem in supplying domestic consumers. Shortages arise only because of the immoderate demands made by industry and agriculture, and because of the loss of previously good resources through pollution. Water consumption in the industrial nations has increased five-fold since World War II, and so far the water industry has met all demand, however excessive. Ever greater supplies of water have been seen

as a sine qua non of economic growth, and governments and water boards have enthusiastically sought access to new resources.

For decades, water planning has been entirely demand-led. As most politicians have regarded water as an inexhaustible resource, there have been no moves to restrict its exploitation. It should come as no surprise that there is a limit to how much water can be extracted from a region (whether it is a river catchment or an administrative area) without severely upsetting the balance of nature. This upper limit, however, has long been exceeded in most conurbations, many of which now regularly import water from neighbouring regions – always a sign of overexploitation. Demands made on these back-up supply regions are now also often excessive and causing grave environmental damage.

Far-sighted water planners today refer to 'supply planning', meaning that every region should cope within the 'budget' of its own water resources. For many cities and centres of industry, that means managing with a great deal less fresh water than they have hitherto enjoyed. This does not mean that either the economy or living standards will have to take a step backwards. First and foremost, in many places, large water resources – both rivers and groundwater – which have had been abandoned because of pollution, could be cleaned up and put to work. Rain, too, could once again become an important additional source, for example, for washing and for watering gardens. Secondly, there is still ample scope – no matter which country one looks at – for making savings in industrial use and agricultural irrigation as well as in domestic consumption. Recycling water means not only multiplying its use, but also reducing the amount extracted from nature.

There is no doubt that the establishment of legally enforceable regional water sustainability – obliging each region to cover its demand solely with its own water – would represent a significant and very valuable corrective to current water policy. Daily decisions made in water management would then take on a different character: instead of further water extraction being sanctioned, current levels of

Above. Such is the degradation of much of the natural water around us, that it is easy to forget how an undamaged environment should look – as here in a forest clearing in northern Germany.

Left. The dried-up river bed of the Darent in Kent – the result of overexploition by the local water authority, Thames Water, in 1992.

exploitation for industry, irrigation and public supplies, and pollution should be cut back. All rivers, lakes and groundwater should be protected and polluted water cleaned up.

Pollution and overexploitation are directly responsible for persistent rises in the price of drinking water supplies, a development that benefits no-one except the water and environmental industries. Prevention of pollution and sustainable use, on the other hand, will guarantee a long-term supply of good-quality drinking water, as well as keeping prices under control. The importance of the concept of regional sustainability can easily be seen by glancing at what is happening in poorer countries. Crisis management – involving long-distance importation of water, exploitation of deep groundwater and high-tech drinking water treatment – is already becoming difficult for the wealthy nations of Europe and North America to afford and is prohibitively expensive for the less well-off. Clean drinking water must not become a luxury.

CHAPTER THREE

WHAT PRICE CLEANLINESS?

The Sanctity of Water

Water is indispensable for cleaning. People use it to wash not just themselves, but clothes, household crockery, windows, floors, toilets – in short, everything that is inhabited or used by humans is cleaned or rinsed down with the aid of water. Once used, it turns into a transport medium for all manner of dirt and rubbish. Outdoors, streets and squares are doused with water which then flows through subterranean drains carrying its cargo of dust, filth, dog dirt, spittle, chewing gum, fragments of rubber tyres and shoes, in other words, all the flotsam and jetsam of urban life.

In many earlier civilisations, using rivers to dispose of rubbish would have been regarded as straightforwardly sacrilegious. As water was assumed to have the power to heal, to revitalise and even to effect transformation, it was accorded great respect.

Images of paradise in cultures and religions across the globe are replete with references to water. The Koran describes 'gardens, quickened with streams' as a

Moslems wash before praying in the fountain of a mosque in the old city of Damascus, Syria.

synonym for paradise, and a Buddhist text says: 'All sorts of river flow in this country . . . All of the rivers are refreshing. They run with water fragrant with all manner of sweet scents . . . and their murmur is full of sweet music.' The most famous psalm in the Bible proclaims: 'The Lord is my shepherd . . . He maketh me to lie down in green pastures: he leadeth me beside the still waters.'

Pure springs and swiftly flowing rivers were the most likely to have purifying powers attributed to them and to be considered sacred. In some belief systems, water has been employed to drive out of the body the evil spirits and demons judged to be responsible for illness, and the practice of bathing in certain rivers in order to be absolved of wrongdoings and receiving forgiveness is not confined to Christianity.

Ritual washing and bathing are important components of some of the world's oldest religions. Often it is difficult to draw a clear line between spiritual purification and washing to keep clean. Indeed, some religious washing rituals read just like instructions for personal hygiene, and it is fairly safe to assume that at least some of the rituals were based on an awareness that contact with rubbish, animal corpses or faeces carried with it the risk of disease and fatal illness. Whatever the origin of water's central role in religion, its importance as an agent or symbol of spiritual cleansing and transformation is beyond doubt.

In orthodox Jewish life, strict observance of ritual washing remains of paramount importance. If a person becomes unclean (*tame*), for example, by touching a corpse, he or she can become entirely clean or pure (*tahore*) again only by total submersion in so-called 'natural water'. Religious

Opposite. Coloured water plays a crucial role during the spring festival of Holi observed by Hindus.

Some cultures still retain a strong respect for water and gratitude for the blessings bestowed by rivers. Pious Hindus make sure that they bathe in the holy water of the River Ganges at least once in their lives.

prayers from everyday life. A more extensive cleansing ritual, in which not even the tiniest patch of the body may remain dry, can be performed only in an Islamic bath (*hamam*). Again, it is of great importance that running water is used, and a continuous flow of water is maintained in and out of the *hamam*.

The Christian ritual of baptism originally took the form of a bath in the river – John the Baptist demonstrated his transformation, his turning to God, by submerging himself in the River Jordan. Today, even though in many churches this has been reduced to a sign of the cross made on the forehead with water by the priest, baptism remains the ceremony marking entry into a Christian community. In Indian religious life, there are countless rites involving water, usually focusing on sacred rivers. In Hindu rituals of detachment, observed when someone dies, all members of the family are required to take a bath every other day after the death – if possible, in a river or in the temple pool. The idea is that these baths release the spirit of the dead person from the world of the living and restore the inner calm of the bereaved. The first intensive phase of mourning is concluded with a final bath on the eleventh day – water has aided spiritual transformation. People in despair and those seeking enlightenment make pilgrimages to the waters of the sacred river, the Narmada. Even being in the vicinity of the holy river is said to bring consolation and relief.

Washing – Changing Habits

As far as we know, the Ancient Greeks were the first to take baths to clean the body rather than for purely religious reasons. Homer's description of Odysseus taking a bath in the *Odyssey*, written in the 8th century BC, almost certainly reflects the practice in his own day. The dividing lines between religious rite, hygienic act and enjoyment of water for water's sake were probably as unclear in Hellenic society as elsewhere.

For the early Romans, who seem to have been more prosaic, washing with water was purely a means of promoting hygiene. They despised the aesthetically minded

households still wash all new crockery in 'natural water' before using it for the first time. 'Natural water' used to be taken straight from springs or wells. Increasing urbanisation has forced believers to turn to rainwater, collected according to strict rules in a pool known as a *mikwe*. The rainwater must pass into the *mikwe* as directly as possible, without being pumped or carried there in other vessels. Modern *mikwes* bear little resemblance to their ancient counterparts, but the principle of immersion and

tahora (ritual purification) has remained unchanged for almost 4,000 years.

In Islam, too, water has always played a central role. Before every visit to the mosque, every prayer and every reading from the Koran, Moslems must perform a ritual cleansing. For this, flowing water is essential, and so most mosques have their own water source. Believers have to wash hands and forearms, feet, face and certain parts of the head. It is as if ritual cleansing symbolically separates the five daily

Greeks as weaklings and made fun of their hedonistic bathing habits. Baths were banished to small chambers with almost no natural light (*lacatrina*), where hands and feet were washed daily. Once a week, the early Roman citizen submitted him- or herself to what in the cramped conditions must have been a pretty joyless experience – a full bath.

All this changed radically around 50 BC with the introduction of the hypocaust, an underfloor space and water heating system. The population, who were used to having to wash in cold water, took to the new heated baths with great enthusiasm. Water temperatures of 35° to 36°C and room temperatures of up to 30° soon made the new baths popular meeting places. Both public and private baths became centres of cultural life. In 33 BC, the Roman general Agrippa (63-12 BC) counted as many as 170 baths in Rome. At the height of the Roman Empire, some 350 years later, urban Romans were able to choose between 856 public baths.

In Rome, there was no shortage of water – whether cold or hot, standing or flowing. Soap, as we know it, did not exist. People either used a primitive kind of soap, *sapo*, made from animal fat and potash, or scrubbed their skin with rough towels or pumice stone and clay. After this

Built for eternity: the 3,000-year-old triangular temple (a construction known as a nuragh) at the pozzo sacro *(sacred well) of Santa Christina in Sardinia.*

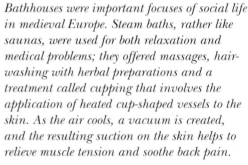

Bathhouses were important focuses of social life in medieval Europe. Steam baths, rather like saunas, were used for both relaxation and medical problems; they offered massages, hair-washing with herbal preparations and a treatment called cupping that involves the application of heated cup-shaped vessels to the skin. As the air cools, a vacuum is created, and the resulting suction on the skin helps to relieve muscle tension and soothe back pain.

Opposite page. For the French aristocracy of the 17th century, washing with water was avoided at all costs; instead a tedious process of dry rubbing with towels was adopted, followed by various cosmetic procedures including powdering.

astringent treatment, the skin was anointed with oil.

The destruction and neglect of the monumental Roman baths at the fall of the Roman Empire brought an end to the culture of bathing for the general population. In the 7th and 8th centuries, there was a revival of the art of bathing in the Eastern Roman capital of Byzantium (now Istanbul). Eventually, the Byzantine Empire, too, came to an end, but the emerging Islamic nations, attracted by the Roman traditions of washing and bathing, incorporated them into Islamic washing rituals. When the Arabs conquered and occupied the Iberian peninsula in the second decade of the eighth century, they brought with them Moorish customs which led to the construction of hundreds of beautifully designed public baths. Around 1000 AD, there were allegedly some 900 in the southern Spanish city of Cordoba alone. When the Christian crusaders from further north drove the Moors out of Spain, they returned home with the idea of warm baths,

and so the taste for them spread across Europe.

For much of the middle ages, taking a weekly bath was a luxury confined to the nobility. It was not until the 13th century that public baths began to be established in the larger European cities; they had little in common with their Roman antecedents. There were no pipes supplying fresh water, no large bathing pools, and certainly no marble halls. Water was heated in large cauldrons, and a mixture of herbal essences was poured over hot bricks to produce thick clouds of aromatic steam. Washing and cleaning the body, which had once been the purpose of public baths, had given way to the pleasure and relaxation of steam baths.

Much scholarly debate has centred on whether or not medieval bathhouses promoted sexual impropriety. Certainly they were popular meeting places, and it is true that men and women bathed and sweated it out side by side in many establishments. The Church was in no doubt,

however, and bathhouses were roundly condemned as dens of iniquity and lechery. Gradually, public baths became associated with criminality and fell into disrepute. By the early 15th century, every public bathhouse in London and the surrounding district had been closed, largely as a result of being associated with criminal behaviour (disturbances of the peace, theft, even manslaughter). As the century progressed, large numbers of bathhouses were shut down across Europe. But it was the medical profession that ultimately sealed the fate of bathing. Syphilis became prevalent in Europe from around 1495, and doctors began to attribute the spread of the disease to physical contact in public bathhouses. As if that were not enough, medical opinion suddenly decided that infection with the plague – which had been around in Europe for more than 200 years – was likely to result from bathing. As pestilent clouds of air could penetrate the skin, it was stated, anything which raised the body's temperature had to be avoided, including, of course, any form of warm bath. bathhouses in 15th-century France were banned as a direct result of these abstruse medical theories.

By 1610, such views were so widely accepted that the French nobility regarded taking a bath as a potentially lethal act. Henri IV once sent a messenger to summon his minister, de Sully, only to find him taking a bath. There was no question of de Sully appearing before his monarch either that day or the day after. According to the royal doctor, Du Laurens, the dangerous after-effects of a bath were likely to last for several days.

From this time on, the well-to-do refused to use water for washing. Instead, people relied on simply rubbing the dirt off and powdering and perfuming themselves. A 17th-century French source warns: 'Washing with water damages the eyes, causes tooth-ache and catarrh, makes your face pale and more sensitive to cold in winter and heat in summer.' At most, water was used for washing hands or rinsing out the mouth.

Although rubbing down and powdering is far removed from today's concept of hygiene, it would be wrong to regard the age of 'dry cleaning' as unclean. The avoidance

A drop of London drinking water and its imagined inhabitants in an 1850 edition of Punch *magazine. The reputation of river water for drinking was already decidedly tarnished, and the construction of main sewers simply exacerbated the situation.*

Opposite page. Illustration from La Science Illustrée *(1892) showing precautions being taken against cholera in Hamburg by the provision of pure spring water in tankers. The cholera epidemics that afflicted European towns and cities in the 19th century were soon attributed to the polluted drinking water being taken from rivers. In 1892, Robert Koch proved that the pathogens responsible for the disease were getting into the water via the faeces of infected people. But the obvious conclusion from this – that faeces should be kept well away from rivers – was never drawn.*

of water did not mean that people stopped looking after their bodies. What now mattered was to appear clean, so care and attention were concentrated mainly on the parts of the body and clothing that were visible in public. A decent appearance was regarded as a sign of respectability, orderliness and reliability. The word *propre* (clean) came into use in the French court to describe character or behaviour, much like one of the senses of 'proper' in modern English.

Developments in physical cleanliness followed an entirely different course for the rural population. According to documentary evidence dating from the 13th century onwards, farming families and farmhands took sauna-like steam baths in simple bath-houses or huts. These baths were infrequent and irregular, because of the expense of firewood, but they were not the only way of keeping clean. Peasants generally kept washing and cooking water separate, washed their hands before pre-

paring a meal and knew from experience or from folk wisdom that only boiled water should be used for cleaning wounds.

Even in the 17th century, when the upper classes' aversion to water was at its height, ordinary people blithely continued to use water to remove dirt. Craftsmen like dyers, butchers and tanners, soap-boilers and washers, who spent all day working at the river's edge rinsing away such by-products of their work as blood, oak tan, dyes and fat, would certainly not have rejected a bucket of water in the evening to wash themselves. Perhaps another function of the powdering and perfuming habits of the rich was to distinguish them from the masses, making the use of water as clear a social indicator as coaldust on the faces of miners has been this century.

In the Islamic empire, which for centuries stretched as far as Pakistan, India and Uzbekistan, high standards of hygiene were observed as part of a religious

code, and public bathhouses could be found in every town. Medieval Islam never subscribed to European theories about the dangers of water.

In Japan, too, a centuries-old tradition of bathing survived the Middle Ages intact, much to the astonishment of travellers like Heinrich Schliemann, who noted in 1865: 'Everyone, no matter how poor, goes at least once a day to one of the public bathhouses that can be found in every town.' A Japanese family got into the hot water (minimum temperature 43° C) in strict hierarchical order – first the father, then the eldest son, then the wife and other children – but before they could do so, they had to give themselves a thorough all-over wash. This ensured that the water in the bath was still relatively clean and pleasant for the children, who were the last to enter it. People go about bathing in much the same way in modern Japan, except that in public baths men and women are now segregated.

Sanitation in European Cities

18th-century European cities were suffocatingly filthy. The problem was at its most acute in what were then the world's two largest cities: London and Paris. Despite the passing of countless laws designed to keep the streets clean, the people could apparently not be induced to do so. By the end of the 18th century, the upper classes began to become concerned about the unhygienic conditions in which most people lived, for it was beginning to be recognised that the masses were going to be crucial to economic success – 'the basis of the power of nations', as an 18th-century French commentary put it. It was important that the potential workforce be kept healthy – no easy task in the large towns and cities, where the streets overflowed with faeces, rotting left-overs and animal corpses. There was still a general belief in the idea of miasmas – bad or stale air thought to cause illness. The stench of rotting meat,

for example, was supposed to be lethal.

As the 18th century drew to a close, the age of public hygiene dawned; it was to culminate in our present-day ministries of health. In spite of the upper classes' enduring water phobia, municipal authorities saw water as the key to solving the cities' hygiene problems and banishing urban stench. Parisian city planners dreamed of streams of running water washing the paved streets clean of stinking liquids. Sparkling fountains in market squares would wash away ordure without a trace; foul and rotting matter would be whisked out of sight along drains to disappear into the River Seine. All that was missing was the water, but to bring such quantities into the city, a vast network of mains would have to be constructed – and that was a costly proposition. In the early 19th century, the municipal authorities in Paris finally erected a series of water towers. These were designed with huge gates that opened, releasing water to sluice down

the streets of the city, much like the action of flushing an enormous toilet.

In the first half of the 19th century, water mains similar to those constructed by the Romans some 2,000 years earlier were built in Paris. Around the same time, inhabitants of London and of American cities began to enjoy the benefits of tap water for the first time. There were, however, still no directly piped supplies to apartments in the more modest quarters of Paris. Poor people continued to haul their water home from wells or from public standpipes; dirty water was simply poured into the street. There was a certain amount of new provision for personal hygiene, however: public baths were opened by the River Seine, where the poor could pay a small fee to wash themselves in luke-warm water. In 1819, when the city had a population of 700,000, a total of 600,000 baths were taken in these places, meaning that many people never even saw the inside of a public bath.

As more and more water was pumped into the towns and cities along the new mains, the amount of waste water which had to be disposed of grew concomitantly. Old drains and open sewers were already overloaded with rainwater; streets were increasingly surfaced with cobble-stones, which prevented the rain from seeping into the ground as it had always done before. In the course of the 19th century, subterranean sewer systems – some of them of gigantic proportions – were constructed in all major European cities (the main collecting sewers in Vienna and London, which are now well over 100 years old, are almost the size of underground train tunnels). Any water arriving in the city, whether through water mains or in the form of rain or snow, now ended up a few hours later in the nearest river, carrying with it any dust, dirt or rubbish it picked up on the way.

What 19th-century European town planners did not understand was that in building the sewers they were about to compromise their most important source of drinking water – the rivers. Water, once regarded as a purifying and revitalising force, had been reduced to the role of rubbish carrier. The lack of regard for rivers signalled a tacit rejection of the wisdom accumulated over generations that had allowed people to make use of water without significant harm being done either to it or ultimately to themselves.

The Fatal Error

The fatal error in disposing of waste water was not long in the making. In spite of urgent warnings from a number of eminent scientists, all the major cities in Europe and North America began connecting their cesspools and latrines to central sewers in the late 19th and early 20th centuries. This meant that faecal matter was being flushed straight into the rivers. Medieval cities in Europe had had latrines on river banks, but their impact was infinitesimal compared to the mass of faeces – and with it harmful bacteria – now being dumped in European and American rivers. It was not long before the rivers themselves were little better than stinking sewers, providing ideal conditions for the spread of epidemics.

Communal latrines at Dougga, Tunisia, built by the Romans, which would have been washed through with a constant flow of water.

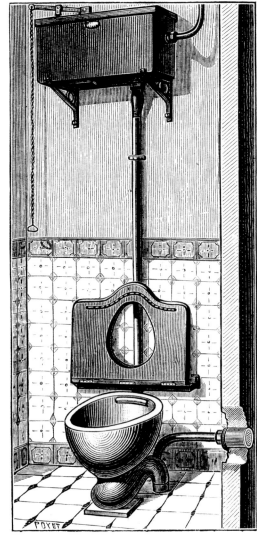

Opposite page. For centuries open sewers (often doubling as property boundaries) have carried away both rainwater and domestic waste water in urban areas, though until relatively recently, faeces (or night soil) were collected separately. Here, in a town in northern Italy, untreated water (including sewage) is discharged directly into the river.

As far as dealing with human waste is concerned, the predominant technology nowadays is scarcely more advanced than what could be obtained in Victorian times, as this illustration from an 1886 edition of the journal La Nature *shows.*

Hundreds of thousands of people died of cholera in the 19th century – victims of drinking water taken from rivers contaminated with faecal matter. The sad irony was that this disaster was sparked off by administrators determined to rid the towns and cities of all faeces because of the risk of infection.

Using water to flush away faeces vastly complicates the management of water resources and leads to unnecessary pollution of huge amounts of water. Human excrement presents a potential risk because even the faeces of otherwise healthy people may contain bacteria that can spark off epidemics such as cholera or typhoid. Our ancestors seem to have been entirely aware of the dangers: rivers in many religions were sacred; any pollution with excrement or rubbish was regarded as sacrilege and strictly forbidden. The Greek historian Herodotus (c.484-c.425 BC) was moved to write of the Persians: 'They neither urinate into rivers nor spit into them, and they do not wash their hands in them. They do not tolerate anyone else doing so either, and have a very special respect for rivers.' Archaeologists have been able to demonstrate that toilets with water-flush systems did exist in earlier times – for example, in Babylon, in ancient Athens, and in the 4,000-year-old town of Mohenjo-Daro on the Indus River. What they have also discovered is that in almost all cases the waste water was channelled into a soak-away, often with a primary sedimentation basin, rather than being allowed to flow directly into a river. After this initial stage of purification, the water seeped back into the groundwater, with no risk of anyone coming into contact with the raw excrement that had been flushed away.

The Romans were the first people to fall victim to the idea that the way to deal with all waste water was simply to conduct it into the nearest river. Several huge sewage tunnels drained from Rome into the river Tiber, the largest of which was the Cloaca Maxima, that still exists today. This sewage system took up excess water from fountains and Roman baths, together with kitchen waste and faecal matter from the houses of the wealthy and from public toilets. This practice was partly responsible for the state of the Tiber, which was evidently appalling, even in those days.

It should have been possible to learn from the Romans. The fact that town councillors and administrators have since the 19th century persistently opted for the system of sanitation that is the most expensive, most wasteful of water and most likely to pass on infectious diseases can probably be put down to psychological rather than scientific reasons. Instead of separately collecting and purifying 'greywater' – the moderately polluted waste water from bath or kitchen use – and 'black water' or excreta, everything goes down one pipe just as it did in the 19th century. It costs huge amounts of money to equip sewage treatment plants to deal with water contaminated with human waste, because elaborate processes have to be used to remove nutrients like nitrates and phosphates, which come almost exclusively from urine and faeces (providing phosphate-free detergents are used). If these processes could be avoided, treating water would produce a cleaner result as well as being cheaper. In addition, the risk of diseases being transmitted through waste water would be avoided. As it is, some pathogens are able to elude modern sewage treatments or even to multiply once they find their way into the rivers. Since many towns rely on river water, they are compelled to disinfect and filter their supply at great cost before it can be used as drinking water.

Counting the Cost

Europe and America are evidently still willing to support the vast costs of this illogical and ineffective system for disposing of human excreta. Water supply and sanitation consume a full two per cent of the gross national product of many rich industrial countries. The building industry is the main beneficiary: the total spend in Europe on new sewerage systems and treatment plants was over $19 billion in 1990, and is expected to have grown to an annual $24 billion by 1995. The driving force behind all this construction is the European *Directive on Urban Waste Water Treatment (91/271/EEC)*, which was drawn up in 1991. This prescribes that all communities in the European Union with over 2,000 inhabitants must have a central sewer and sewage works by 31st December 2005. The colossal investments needed will be financed by a combination of sewerage rates paid by users and substantial one-off payments by those forced to connect to the system. The expenditure is always justified with claims of protection for the environment. But the fact is that sewage plants consume immense amounts of energy and chemicals and ultimately produce millions of tonnes of sewage sludge which have to be dried and stored in special dumps at further cost, while still contributing to the ongoing pollution of rivers. The obvious alternative – separate collection and treatment of excrement and greywater in on-site or small-scale community systems – does not seem even to have occurred to the sanitary authorities.

The flush toilet has become a symbol of progress and development all over the world. Despite the visibly catastrophic consequences for the health of the environment, Western hydraulic engineers continue with impunity to plan central sewage systems for all major towns in

The inhabitants of the famous high buildings of Sana'a in the semi-desert of southern Arabia (now Yemen) have traditionally kept faeces and urine strictly separate. Excrement from every floor falls into a collection tank, from which it is taken every day to be dried in the hot desert sun for use, ultimately, as fuel. Urine and the small jugful of water that is used in Islamic countries instead of toilet paper are allowed to flow down the outside walls of the buildings. As the air is extremely dry, the water evaporates immediately, and there are no unpleasant smells. There are now plans to replace this virtually water-free system, which has been in use for hundreds of years, with western flushing toilets courtesy of finance from a German development bank, KfW (Kreditanstalt für Wiederaufbau). Where the water – as much as 50 litres per resident per day – is to come from is not at all clear, but the Germans are thoroughly convinced that their plan is a good one. Development aid workers associated with the project did not even bother to take a look at the existing system.

The practice of keeping urine and faeces separate – which makes good sense as it is generally only faeces that harbour harmful bacteria – is by no means confined to Yemen. In Vietnam, for example, human urine (which contains a high concentration of nitrogen and in healthy people is normally free of pathogenic bacteria) is collected separately and used on the fields as a fertiliser.

Even the most sophisticated treatment plants, like this one in Hamburg, Germany, cannot solve the fundamental problems caused by the adoption of centralised sewage systems. The best they can offer is a small amount of damage limitation in circumstances where the real solution is to keep bath and kitchen waste water separate from toilet and industrial wastes.

Opposite page. Guests at the An Tigh Mhor Timeshare near Loch Achray, Scotland, probably have little idea that the idyllic pond in the grounds is not just a pretty part of the scenery, but also purifies the castle's waste water.

Africa, Asia and Latin America, as if there could be no such thing as progress without flushing toilets. The enormous expense of installing sewage works and the unavoidable running costs involved (not just in operating a treatment plant, but also in treating polluted river water to make it drinkable) will be enough to cause most projects to founder. It is perhaps worth remembering that even the richest communities in the industrialised world would not be able to afford to build new sewage systems of this kind from scratch.

Viable Alternatives

The principle of mixing greywater and faecal matter creates many more problems than it solves and is a pernicious model to foist on developing countries. Yet most of the funds earmarked for sanitation projects are still used for the construction of western-style water-borne waste systems. However, the World Bank, the largest provider of loans for development projects, is beginning to have second thoughts and is starting to look for alternatives. The key to the installation of effective, hygienic sanitation in poor countries is the use of advanced, low-cost technologies that can be built and maintained by local labour from locally available materials. Greywater from kitchens and bathrooms should as far as possible be treated on site, using low-tech sustainable methods, such as greywater gardens. One example is small reed beds, in which the plants break down and absorb the pollutants that would foul river water – a method that will work as long as the water contains only biodegradable matter. Even when waste water is contaminated

Slums in Jakarta, Indonesia, where makeshift latrines empty into open canals. There are no easy formulae for water management in large conurbations. In monsoon regions, for example, sudden, heavy rainfall renders western sewage systems useless. Only a careful analysis of social, ecological and economic conditions is likely to lead to an appropriate choice.

with excreta (from neighbouring buildings equipped with flush toilets, for example), on-site biological treatment can be feasible. In India and China, fish ponds, which thus have a dual function, are used for this purpose: aquatic plants and algae consume the nutritional elements of the waste and are in turn eaten by fish, which ultimately provide protein for people. Techniques such as these are currently being rediscovered by sewage engineers in the developed world as an inexpensive alternative to our own, more costly, but less effective solutions. For densely populated, high-rise development areas in vast urban agglomerations, trials are being undertaken with vacuum toilets like those used on aircraft. These are fitted with a vacuum pump, and require less than half a litre of water per flush; excreta are deposited either into the sewage system

or – preferably – collected in tanks installed in the basements of buildings, or under the street, where they are allowed to settle, eventually turning to compost which can be used either as fertiliser on agricultural land or broken down anaerobically to produce bio-gas for fuel.

Of course, water-free toilets vastly reduce water consumption. At least one third of water used each day in the North for domestic purposes, usually over 50 litres per person, literally goes down the toilet. Every region and city requires its own tailor-made water policy, not just for the distribution and supply of water, but incorporating appropriate management of excreta and greywater. Are the region's resources generous enough to provide the luxury of conventional water-flushing toilets? Is the river into which the city's sewage flows used for obtaining drinking

water or for irrigating farmland further downstream? And, finally, as far as faeces are concerned – a touchy subject in all cultures – the treatment of water and excreta must take people's beliefs and religions into account. The Maoris of New Zealand are not alone in believing that a river is ruined if waste water (no matter how sophisticated the treatment it has undergone) has been poured into it; they then regard its waters as useless for fishing or bathing, let alone for use as drinking water. People who doubt the seriousness of habitual and religious requirements should ask themselves how they would feel if it were stipulated that, as from tomorrow, they had to wipe their backsides with a hand and a little water. It would be equally difficult to enforce a toilet paper culture in Arab countries or in Asia, where it is customary to rinse yourself with water.

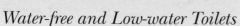

Water-free and Low-water Toilets

There are many good reasons for using very little or even no water to carry away excreta. It saves enormous quantities of water, and, in places where sewage flows directly into open ditches and rivers, the spread of faecal pathogens and the concomitant risk of disease are avoided. Huge sums of money can be saved when there is no need for expensive sewerage systems and sewage treatment plants to collect and process excreta-laden waste water, and the cost of bringing river water to drinking standard is greatly reduced. Moreover, the natural environment no longer has to suffer the devastating consequences of conventional sewage treatment, among them eutrophication resulting from nutrients originating in excreta, chemical pollution where waste water is disinfected, and the long-term problems of sewage sludge disposal.

Many people may be surprised to discover that they are already familar with low-flush toilets – the vacuum toilets fitted in aircraft use a mere half litre of water, as opposed to the massively wasteful nine or ten litres disposed of by the average flush toilet. The argument for keeping faeces and urine strictly separate from greywater is so compelling that even in countries where flush toilets are the norm, systems that either compost excrement or turn it into biogas to be used as fuel are beginning to be installed. Over the last twenty to thirty years, spurred by environmental concerns and by the pressing need for affordable

hygienic sanitation in poor countries, great efforts have been made to develop effective, technologically advanced biological toilets that are user-friendly and ecologically sound.

In Europe and North America, various models of biological or composting toilets are already in use. In some areas of Sweden, where buildings are constructed on solid rock, digging sewers or installing septic tanks is impossible. Most hikers' and climbers' cabins in remote mountain areas have always relied on compost systems in an attempt to prevent the pollution of rivers and lakes. Increasingly, people are opting to install biological toilets when they build new properties or renovate old ones, particularly in rural areas where the cost of installing a new water-based sewage system is often very high.

Of course, at least two-thirds of humanity will never have the chance even to consider western-style water-flush toilets, simply because of the huge costs involved in laying on piped water and installing sewerage systems, not to mention the generous supplies of water that are needed.

Which system is right for which place or culture depends primarily on conventions of anal cleansing. In parts of Asia, for example, small quantities of water are used (poured from a jug), while in Africa, a dry wipe with paper or similar material is the usual method.

Where water is used, the pour-flush toilet is now the most widely adopted low-cost solution: this has a small U-shaped bowl, and, like conventional flush toilets, a small amount of water lying in the bend of the waste pipe provides a seal between the toilet and the storage chamber

Two composting toilets – a simple, home-made one (left) on a Pacific island and the other (right) designed for the sensibilities of the North American and European markets, where customers are more used to flush toilets.

beneath. Excreta and cleansing water collect in the chamber which is pumped out periodically. If pumping is not feasible, the chamber is filled in with soil, a new one is dug a few metres away, and the toilet is reinstalled.

Where a dry system is acceptable, a water-free toilet with an aperture leading to a vented chamber that guards against bad smells is now usually the best option. The waste gradually accumulates in the chamber and turns to compost. In one year, one person generates only about 50 litres of compost. In some countries, among them Vietnam, biological toilets have two pits that are filled in alternate years to ensure thorough composting.

One of the greatest stumbling blocks to getting biological toilets accepted where people are used to flush toilets is lack of familiarity, but it can only be a matter of time before it is generally recognised that, far from being smelly and disgusting, they can be cheap, efficient and hygienic. Even more importantly, people might at least begin to consider the value of human waste, the use to which it can be put if treated properly, rather than always regarding it as an embarrassment to be disposed of at all costs.

Greywater – A Crucial Concept

Keeping greywater and excreta separate is crucial to the protection of the natural environment from damage done by problems originating in domestic use. Greywater from kitchens and bathrooms can be treated with little effort and reused before being reintroduced into the local water regime, as long as it contains only biodegradable substances (such as soap as opposed to most modern detergents). In this way far less water is extracted from nature, avoiding importation from other regions.

Unfortunately, the mixture of water to be found in municipal sewers today is not at all susceptible to easy recycling. Needless to say, domestic households are by no means the only, or even the main, contributors of non-biodegradable chemicals to sewers. A host of trades and small businesses ranging from dry-cleaners to photographic laboratories and dentists' surgeries work with chemicals that are difficult or impossible to remove from sewage. Far more seriously, it is common practice all over the world for industry to get rid of its usually toxic waste via municipal sewers, frequently accounting for a large proportion of the persistent chemicals and heavy metals in the treated waste water and sewage sludge emerging from sewage works. Emissions from non-domestic sources should never be allowed to flow into standard municipal drains.

It was in the 1950s that the water going down domestic drains began to pose a serious environmental problem. Ecologically damaging detergents began to be

Soap advertisement dating from 1926, less than twenty years before detergents deriving from the petro-chemical industry appeared in households for the first time, marking a new, dangerous threat to the health of rivers.

The Fourteen Falls on Athi River near Thika, Kenya, showing clear signs of pollution. Cleaning agents now known to be highly damaging to the environment and so prohibited in some rich countries often continue to be sold in developing countries, frequently by the very manufacturers forced to discontinue sales at home.

sold on a wide scale – as a by-product of the burgeoning petro-chemical industry. The new detergents (in which the active ingredients were branched alkane sulphonic acids) were cheap and quickly replaced older, biodegradable products based on natural oils and fats. It was not until 30 years later that their huge drawback became fully apparent: the bacteria in rivers and soil were unable to digest them or break them down, and their residues were building up in soil and river sediment.

As far back as the 1960s, scientists were already warning that phosphates could lead to excessive fertilisation of our waters and eutrophication (when algae is just about the only form of life that thrives and biological diversity is dramatically cut), but there are still very few countries which have converted to phosphate-free detergents. Even phosphate substitutes,

such as NTA and EDTA, have come into disrepute because they can cause heavy metals that have accumulated in river sediment to be released and introduced into the food chain – a highly subtle, but equally serious ecological change.

A further component of modern detergents, polycarboxylates, have also caused controversy among experts. They are unaffected by sewage treatment and so pass unchanged from waste water into the sewage sludge, which is frequently spread on cultivated land as fertiliser. Polycarboxylates do not break down at all and have the potential to change the nature of the soil: research has shown that they absorb plant nutrients such as magnesium and calcium, and could thus impoverish the soil. In Germany alone, around 21,000 tonnes of polycarboxylates are used every year in cleaning agents and detergents,

and are then quietly and irresponsibly allowed to pass into the environment with no adequate investigation of the effects they might have on it.

Most of the washing-up liquids and washing powders, detergents, soaps and shampoos currently in use contain substances that cannot be filtered out of waste water even given the most advanced purification technology. Some of these give rise to a second generation of persistent chemicals when they are used. As over a third of the solid material in domestic waste water consists of detergents, it is essential that measures are taken to ensure that all domestic cleaning aids are biodegradable. Only then can natural biological processes turn greywater back into pure water.

Running a household that avoids the use of harmful chemicals is no longer

Municipal washhouse at Assomada, São Tiago Island, Cabo Verde.

Opposite page. Washing spread out to dry on the banks of the Upper Nile in Uganda next to the thundering waters of the Bujagli Falls.

People from the nomadic Penan tribe washing in a river near Belaga in Sarawak, Malaysia.

utopian. Dirty clothes and dishes, as well as floors, tiles, windows and furniture can be cleaned perfectly efficiently using natural substances, such as soap and vinegar. Manufacturers of modern cleaning products, including those containing chlorine, push the idea of cleanliness to a point where they are effectively promising a sterilising effect. Quite apart from the fact that research has shown that some pathogens survive even the most aggressive chemical cleaners, these products do indeed eliminate a whole range of bacteria, including those that are harmless to people but essential for purifying used water. Anything living in water must be killed off, it seems, even if it could be of use to us, not to mention the natural environment.

It is now clearer than ever that the passion for washing whiter, using phosphates, phosphate substitutes, polycarboxylates, has fatal, albeit delayed, consequences. What is needed is comprehensive investigation and regulation of the production and use of cleaning materials with direct regard to environmental safety. Fully biodegradable alternatives that leave no residue already exist for most conventional substances. In spite of this, millions of tonnes of detergents, bleaching agents and conditioners are sold and used every year; no-one knows what the ecological consequences will turn out to be once these products have been 'tested' on the environment.

What Is Clean?

Improvements in western-style standards of living also mean a rise in the annual tonnage of shampoos, soaps, deodorants and shower gels washed away into sewers from bathrooms. People are rarely aware of the ecological responsibility involved in using a particular product. Can it be properly dealt with in sewage treatment plants? Is it poisonous to fish? Does it encourage the excessive growth of algae? Questions of this kind remain largely unanswered because manufacturers are intent on keeping their formulae secret; in contrast to the food industry, they are under no obligation to disclose the contents of their products.

The wisdom of subjecting our bodies to continual chemical attack is also worth

Rendille elder washing by a desert well near the village of Korr, west of Marsabit, northern Kenya, after raising water for his animals.

thinking about. Many people expose both their skin and their hair to an aggressive cocktail of chemicals and detergents as often as twice a day. Dermatologists believe that this exaggerated use of soaps and shampoos is responsible for a rapid increase in skin complaints, both fungal infections and allergies. Rather than taking baths and showers because they are dirty, many people seem to take baths and showers for fear of smelling – or perhaps just out of habit. Rarely do they realise that by undergoing this voluntary deodorisation, they are subjecting themselves to a mechanism which has more social than hygienic significance. Since the end of the 19th century, total absence of body odour has gradually become the essential prerequisite of social acceptability. Since then, cleanliness has been equated not just with hygiene and health, but also with respectability.

There is just as little proof that an odourless body is a medical necessity as there is scientific conviction that living environments must be utterly disinfected and dust-free. According to the French sociologist, Georges Vigarello, 'Cleanliness essentially has its roots in inner, personal compulsions which are difficult to explain, primarily because they seem so self-evident to us.' Standards of cleanliness that seem to us like second nature date from only just over a hundred years ago,

when there was enormous social pressure to conform to new hygienic standards of cleanliness. Nowadays, this still finds its expression in the boom in the 'personal hygiene' market, which includes endless deodorising products. The meaning of 'clean' has changed radically, even over the last few decades. A key to self confidence seems to be persuading oneself that one is clean, and that may well be more difficult than convincing other people.

Today, in the Western world, up to half of our entire domestic consumption of water goes down bathroom drains – and that does not include water used for flushing the toilet. The ambitions of the sanitary industry go even further. Today's trend is towards even higher water consumption – an individual en-suite bathroom for every bedroom, power showers that pump water at high velocity. Sophisticated consumers are lured with the promise of sensuous water treats. The humble bathroom is now to become a fitness and leisure experience, with plants and lumps of rock tastefully setting the scene. At the very moment when more and more rivers, streams and wetlands are being deprived of their water by ever-increasing urban demand, with all the destruction that this implies, people are still kidding themselves (or being kidded) that there is an inexhaustible supply of this natural element at hand for whatever aquatic fantasy that attracts them. It is not unusual for someone who enjoys taking baths or showers to use as much as 500 litres of water per day. The fact that water is part of nature rather than a consumer item, and that extracting it in large quantities is likely to harm the environment, is conveniently ignored. The provenance of the water that pours from our elegant taps and showers is something we choose not to reflect upon.

One might even argue that, without anyone noticing, the mundane task of keeping

It was only when overexploitation of California's Mono Lake had drained it to a level fourteen metres lower than normal, exposing the extraordinary calcite deposits laid down over much of the lake's bed, that the authorities put a stop to the huge demands made on it by Los Angeles.

clean has in the late 20th century become inflated almost to the level of an ideology, demanding the use of batteries of soaps, lotions, oils, expensive apparatus, and, inevitably, ever-greater quantities of water.

Of course, the majority of the world's population does not have to think about weaning itself off excess use of water and mindless use of pollutants in washing: shortages of both water and money mean that water management based on Western models mainly does not exist; where it does it is almost invariably doomed to failure. To cover drinking, cooking, doing the dishes and the laundry, cleaning the home and personal washing, the World Health Organization reckons that a person needs an absolute minimum of 20 litres of water per day; 50 is considered an adequate supply.

Gradually the developed world is bound to have to start accepting the natural ecological limits to its exploitative behaviour. This will have its effect not just on the politics of the 21st century but on our whole attitude to what is important or appropriate in our own lives. 25 years from now, a life-style that recognises the needs of the natural environment as well as human desires, will be regarded as modern and socially acceptable. This does not mean reverting to such peculiarities as powdering instead of washing, but it does mean changing wasteful, polluting habits. This should be no more difficult than it was for people to adjust to the idea of daily washing a hundred years ago.

CHAPTER FOUR

HEALING WATERS

It is hard to say precisely when humanity discovered the curative properties of water. As far back as the New Stone Age, over 4,000 years ago, people seem to have been drawn to certain springs, which were regarded as sacred, washing themselves in the waters in the belief that wounds would be healed and pain eased. Sickness was often regarded as a sign of divine wrath; archaeological finds near springs of coins and sacrificial objects suggest that washing and bathing in curative waters probably had a dual function, serving as a rite for placating the gods as well as a means of healing the body. High up in the Sudety Mountains near Jelenia Góra in southern Poland is the 'Good Well', which, like many other healing springs, has been much venerated. For thousands of years, people have made the long climb up to it, even though there are plenty of other springs much closer to their villages.

Ancient or folk knowledge of the healing properties of springs is based on careful observation and experience, and the wisdom is passed down from one generation to the next. By contrast, the modern scientific approach towards them is to try to unlock the secrets of their healing powers through chemical analysis. Many medicinal springs do indeed differ considerably from others in their chemical content, which often includes elements such as magnesium, iron, sulphur, iodine and especially calcium. Like any groundwater or spring, medicinal springs began as rain, snow or dew before seeping into the ground. The longer the path followed by the water and the more soluble the layers and strata it has passed through, the more mineral salts will be dissolved in it, ranging from a few milligrams per litre to a concentration many times that of sea water. The famous medicinal springs of Karlovy Vary in the Czech Republic, for instance, bring to the surface 10,000 tonnes of Glauber salts (sodium sulphate) and 12.5 tonnes of fluorspar (calcium fluoride) each year.

If you wanted to know exactly how the water bubbling out of a particular spring had got there, you would need an X-ray view of the subterranean world through which it had passed. This, of course, is impossible, but in the course of drilling through the substrate and taking random samples of rock, scientists have been able to take advantage of the resulting peepholes to observe something of what is going on deep underground. Droplets of rainwater or melting snow seep into shallow groundwater (lying close to the earth's surface) which flows fairly directly, following the gradient, into the nearest river. Some of the water is trapped beneath impermeable

Left. Water being drawn from an especially valued spring on the island of São Miguel in the Azores.

The Széchenyi Fürdö bath in Budapest, where thermal baths are an important focus for the city's social life.

layers of rock; if these strata lie at an angle, the water will be forced downwards, sometimes travelling so deep that it will take thousands of years to re-emerge at the earth's surface. Arriving at a cleft in the rock or any other point offering access to the surface, the water will be forced upwards by the pressure of the mass behind it and burst out of the ground.

Only rarely is it possible to gauge how long a given sample of water has spent on its underground journey before it resurfaces in a spring. Recently, however, the age of several medicinal springs in Switzerland has been estimated. Traces of the natural radioactive isotope, Argon-39, indicate that the water issuing from most Swiss medicinal springs must have spent

some 10,000 years under the earth's surface. It had probably seeped into the ground as rainwater or melting snow in the last Ice Age when Europe was still partially covered by glaciers. Analysis of the hydrogen isotope, tritium, in it suggests that this medicinal water originally percolated down into the earth at temperatures around freezing point.

The water of each spring has its own history, and the mixture of minerals it contains is as unique as a human fingerprint. Some water is so ancient that it is almost impossible to imagine its origins. Long, long ago in the planet's history, when oceans and salt lakes evaporated, large amounts of water remained sealed in the remaining sediment. This water, thought to be some 250 million years old, is saturated with salts, and now feeds brine springs such as those at Battaglia Terme near Padova in Italy, and at Gmunden in the Salzkammergut in Austria.

Water and Medicine

The development of medicine is inextricably bound up with the healing powers of water. Hippocrates, who was born on the Greek island of Kos in around 460 BC and is generally considered to be the founder of medical science, prescribed sweating and bathing cures as a normal part of treatment. Over several decades, he observed the effects of the island's spring waters on his patients, building up valuable medical knowledge. Hippocrates espoused a holistic approach to medicine, considering all parts of the human body in relation to one another, as well as to the body as a whole, and to the environment. He regarded illness as springing from disturbances in the relationship between the body and the soul, and prescribed treatments designed to strengthen the patient's vitality. Bathing in the springs of Kos was an essential part of the therapy.

In medieval Europe, medicinal bathing was common, especially among the poor, who were unable to afford medical treatment and bathed to rid themselves of illness. The practice came to an end when medical opinion began to attribute the spread of the plague and syphilis to the use of public bathing places – whether they

were communal baths or healing springs. Medieval doctors were in any case mainly opposed to therapeutic bathing on theoretical grounds. A Swiss physician and chemist, Philippus Aureolus Theophrastus Bombastus von Hohenheim, better known as Paracelsus (1493-1541), dissociated himself from the holistic classical medicine practised by the Greeks and Romans, subscribing instead to the theory that all illnesses could be traced back to deficiencies in specific substances. He pioneered an approach that attempted to remedy particular complaints by administering specific chemical substances, anticipating the pharmacology of today. According to Paracelsus, it was impossible for a bath in curative water to have

After public baths had fallen into disrepute in the 16th and 17th centuries, many spas began to promote the drinking of their mineral waters instead, and some became fashionable places for the gentility to meet and promenade, as this 1904 illustration of people taking the waters at the Mühlbrunnen in Karlsbad (now Karlovy Vary in the Czech Republic) shows.

Opposite page. Where groundwater is in contact with the internal heat of the earth in zones of seismic activity, the most spectacular geological sights are created: mud pools, geysers and even monumental terraces like these at Mammoth Hot Springs in Yellowstone National Park, the oldest and largest national park in the United States.

therapeutic effects. Generations of doctors have followed him in this belief.

Modern western medical theory draws its conclusions almost exclusively from detailed research into the physiology and biochemistry of the human body; as a result it refuses to acknowledge that balneotherapy has any curative powers, unless this can be proved scientifically. There have been attempts, for example, to put down the effects of sulphur or brine baths to some kind of chemical exchange through the skin, but even the most elaborate studies have failed to show any such thing.

In an attempt to achieve scientific recognition for balneotherapy, balneologists have for decades been observing and recording the physiological effects of water on the human body. Blood circulation is stimulated by hydrostatic pressure, and the buoyancy of the body, together with water resistance, helps to improve articulation impaired by accidents or surgical operations. Most companies dealing with health insurance, however, refuse to recognise curative bathing, complaining that it has no scientific basis.

Sadly, it seems that in medical terms balneotherapy has reached its historical nadir. The curative effects of thermal and

mineral springs, like those of homeopathy, are rejected by many as mere superstition. As a result, knowledge gained through experience over generations is likely to be lost, at least in the Western world.

Early this century, the waters of the Good Well in the Sudety Mountains were subjected to detailed analysis, which revealed that as far as measurable properties were concerned, they were not significantly different from those of other springs in the area. Finding no unusual concentrations of minerals, the scientists rejected all claims for the spring's curative powers. The local people, however, were quite unperturbed and continued to use the Good Well as they always had. After 1945, Polish scientists carried out a further study. By this time radioactivity – entirely unknown when the first analysis was conducted – had been discovered, and low levels of natural radioactivity were found to be present in the water, a characteristic the Good Well has in common with a number of other healing springs.

Many springs whose curative properties have been valued for hundreds, even thousands of years, have been abruptly downgraded by chemical analysis to the status of normal, non-mineral springs.

Few have been lucky enough to be rehabilitated by more recent scientific discoveries. The source of the Seine, for instance, venerated for its curative water for over 2,000 years, is today officially regarded as having no special value because of its low mineral content. However, increasing numbers of scientists now regard merely listing the chemical components of a water sample as an incomplete description, suspecting that such characteristics as the internal structure of water – as yet only poorly understood – may well have something to do with its curative powers.

Thermal Springs

Hot water rises to the earth's surface at numerous points across the globe, spectacularly in the geysers of Iceland, mysteriously in the incessantly steaming cauldrons of America's Yellowstone National Park. For aeons, thousands of thermal springs have been bringing water up to the earth's surface. The colossal heat at the earth's core becomes gradually more evident as the earth's crust is penetrated: on average, for every 30 metres of depth, the temperature rises by one degree centigrade. In some places, where the crust is especially thin, notably near fault lines and volcanoes, warm or even boiling water emerges through cracks or fissures.

Archaeologists have discovered evidence of early civilisations making use of thermal springs, among them, the Chimú and the Inca in South America. The warm water was prized both for relaxation, and to heal wounds and cure sickness. Sulphur springs are particularly beneficial for treating skin infections and wounds, those bubbling with carbon dioxide are invigorating, and bathing in springs containing iodides or bromides is calming for the nerves.

Bathing in thermal waters has never been just a treatment for the sick. Anyone who has ever entered a thermal bath in a state of exhaustion on a cold winter's day knows that it serves not only to warm the freezing body, but also to calm and soothe the spirit. Thermal baths have been valued since time immemorial – more than once, springs that have been buried in landslides have been dug free, with all the effort that that entails. In Japan, a country rich in

thermal springs because of its volcanic origins, hot springs are known as *kami no yu*, or divine baths. Here the daily bath has for centuries been valued as promoting physical and spiritual well-being.

In Europe, visitors to Budapest can still find plentiful evidence of the history of occidental hot bath culture. A book on the city written in 1968 contained an eloquent description of the experience of using a thermal bath: 'The greatest pleasure of all is submerging oneself in this tender, transparent element; rocking gently in it, feeling the soft slap of the waves as they merge and sway, listening to the rush of the steaming water as it pours down, feeling for warmer streams beneath its surface with your hands and feet, and, lying carelessly stretched out, listening in the silence to your heartbeat as you float motionless through time.' A total of 123 thermal springs with temperatures of up to 78°C surface here on the shores of the Danube – nowhere else in Europe do they occur in such profusion. The Celts were probably the first to make use of the hot springs, and in around AD 150, the Romans founded their settlement of Aquincum here; the ruins of their public baths can still be visited today. More than a thousand years later, the Hungarian King Sigismund (1361-1437) established a bathhouse at a spring which is still in use today – the Rácz Fürdö. Budapest's reputation as the European capital of thermal bathing rests largely on its days under Turkish rule (1541-1686). It was Turkish pashas who built the Király and Rudas spas, also still in operation

today, and introduced highly sophisticated bathing and healing methods. Steam baths, mud packs, moving from cold to hot water and the inhalation of salt spray as a cure for bronchial catarrh are some of the therapeutic ideas introduced to Europe from the Orient at that time. Since early this century, visitors and patients from all over the world have come to stay in luxuriously appointed surroundings, but Budapest has nevertheless remained true to the most important aspects of its Turkish tradition: its spas are still first and foremost places where the city's residents go to wind down and enjoy themselves.

Wherever a region is blessed with hot springs, use has been made of their curative powers. In New Zealand, Maori traditions, passed down by word of mouth for generations, attribute special properties to individual springs. In Kaikohe, local Maori meet at the village of Ngawha Springs to talk, meditate and cure any ailments at Nga Waiariki, or 'Chiefly Waters'. The pool they choose to swim in will depend on their mood or need: there is the quietly bubbling greenish Rata (also called The Doctor) where countless illnesses are said to have been cured, the somewhat cooler Waikato where old people get together for a chat, or the hot and dark water of Korohuhu a Maikuku, in which a Maori called Maikuku is said to have sought relief from pain after first giving birth some 500 years ago.

But even these centuries-old, much-loved springs, regarded by the Maori as their birthright and enjoyed by thousands of

Luxurious surroundings are not a prerequisite for successful water cures. Thousands of visitors come to Ngawha Springs on New Zealand's North Island to benefit from their healing and therapeutic effects.

Right. Bathers in the Blue Lagoon, a swimming pool in the outflow of a geothermal power station in Iceland. This spectacle, of industrial and leisure interests both being satisfied, is a rare one. Many geo-thermal fields exploited for power generation cause valued hot springs either to turn cold or to run dry.

visitors every year are not immune from the greedy interest of energy planners. It is only the stubborn resistance of the local Maori people that has so far managed to prevent the government from tapping the

underground sources of steam for electricity generation, which would inevitably turn the hot springs cold.

Arguments about water tend to centre on scientific and ecological issues, focusing on the availability of drinking water for people and the health of the natural environment. It is often forgotten that our careless treatment of water is denying us spiritual as well as physical benefits – nothing makes this clearer than the disdain shown by modern industrialised society for curative springs. Neglect may not yet have destroyed them, but we are in danger of forgetting how valuable they can be.

CHAPTER FIVE

FRESHWATER HARVEST

In 1870, servants in the Saxon city of Dresden, on the River Elbe, requested that they should not be given salmon to eat more than five times a week. In Scotland, similarly, salmon was regarded as a poor man's dish. Rivers which are now little more than industrial drains, such as the Elbe, the Rhine, the Thames or the Mersey, were full of fish only about a hundred years ago. Thousands of fishermen made a living from putting out salmon nets or setting eel traps in Europe's rivers. Today, however,

Fishermen working the polluted waters opposite ENCE's pulp and paper plant in the Ria de Pontevedra, the estuary of the Rio Lerez, north-western Spain. Where fishing and industrial interests collide, sooner or later the fishermen have to retreat.

the straightening and damming up of large rivers has destroyed the habitat of many species of fish, which have disappeared altogether from our rivers. The few that have stubbornly remained have fallen victim to industrial pollution: in Germany, selling fish caught in the Rhine or the Elbe is now illegal for that reason.

Healthy rivers are among the most productive ecosystems on the globe. Natural fluctuations in water level and gradually sloping banks provide ideal living conditions for countless riverside and aquatic

The Great Lakes

The Great Lakes – Lakes Superior, Huron, Erie, Ontario and Michigan – together contain more than a fifth of the freshwater on the earth's surface and form one of the most important systems of inland waterways in the world. They support an extremely productive and diverse ecosystem, but have also acted as a magnet for industry.

It has been clear, at least since the 1970s, that nature and industry as it currently functions are, to say the least, incompatible. The quality of the water in the lakes has suffered grievously from industrial waste-water and sewage outfalls. In at least 43 places the lakes have been officially declared so polluted as to be unsafe for either bathing or fishing. Even where fishing is not yet prohibited, there is cause for grave concern. More and more birds whose diet is dependent on fish are being found to have gross abnormalities, and it is possible that the neurological problems manifesting themselves in some children who live near the lakes can be put down to their mothers' regular consumption of lake fish.

Opinions as to what action should be taken to brook the damage being done to the Great Lakes are a focus of great controversy. There is no shortage of data on the effects of pollution – more research has been done on the Great Lakes than on any other freshwater system on earth, making it likely that decisions made here will be taken as international precedents for future environmental policy.

Industry shrinks at the thought that what becomes law here could tomorrow be set as a worldwide standard for production.

The International Joint Commission for the Great Lakes (IJC), which was set up jointly by the American and Canadian governments in 1909, is advocating a completely new approach. Confronted by increasing environmental pollution and health problems in the region, they have decided that it is no longer sufficient to ban the use of individual chemicals with a particular reputation for toxicity. They wish to stop the entry into the lake of any substance that does not biodegrade by at least 50 per cent in at most eight weeks. Experience has shown that waste-water treatment alone cannot achieve this, so the Commission is recommending a total ban on the use of substances such as lead, mercury and chlorinated compounds in any stage of production or manufacture.

But the IJC is toothless. It has no power to make laws – this has to be done by the legislatures in Washington and Ottawa, which are besieged constantly by powerful lobbyists for industry, in particular chemical concerns, determined to preserve the status quo, which effectively block any ecologically enlightened strategy.

Outflow from Elken Metals polluting Lake Erie, Cleveland, Ohio.

plants and micro-organisms that provide food for fish. The sheer richness and diversity of life in freshwater, especially in tropical rivers, is breathtaking. Over 1,000 different species of fish have been identified in the Amazon and its tributaries alone, and almost as many in the catchment of the River Zaire in Africa. Much the same can be said of tropical lakes – well over 200 species of fish live in Lake Tanganyika in East Africa. Low-lying areas that flood regularly, such as deltas and flood plains, provide rich pickings for many species. The fertile silt that is deposited on them from time to time promotes the growth of lush vegetation and a feast of nutrients for fish, crustaceans and countless invertebrates. The shallow water provides excellent conditions for spawning grounds and nurseries for the young of many species.

For millions of people, fish is and has always been the most important source of protein. Today, in Asia alone, one billion people – a fifth of the world's population –

live in the deltas of the ten largest rivers. In Bangladesh, five million earn their living by fishing. A fundamental tenet of traditional fishing involves the protection of even the most productive fishing grounds from over-exploitation. In many societies, fishing has been regulated by strict laws for hundreds of years, with the size and number of fish and shellfish that can be caught being stipulated by the community. Fishermen keep a keen watch on their fishing grounds and stop at the first sign of fish stocks declining – often noticing a change too subtle to be picked up by anyone without their generations of experience.

Traditional Fish Farming

Methods of raising particularly valued fish have evolved over the centuries. Some Maori families in New Zealand, for example, have detailed knowledge of how to increase river eel populations. Traditional methods of harvesting tend to work hand

Fishing with a square net in the Mekong Delta, Vietnam. In the densely populated delta areas of Asian rivers, fishing plays a vital, life-supporting role. If the delicate ecological balance of these rivers is disturbed, hunger is an almost inevitable outcome.

in hand with ecological laws that avoid disturbing the natural balance of a habitat.

The earliest exponents of this principle were almost certainly the Chinese. Fish-farming in ponds has been carried out in China for over 3,000 years. The Chinese ensure that there are at least four different types of fish in a pond: one plant eater, two plankton eaters (one for animal and one for plant plankton) and one bottom-feeding fish that will eat virtually anything. The ponds are fertilised with animal or human excrement and rotting plant matter from, say, vegetable trimmings or food left-overs; this encourages the growth of algae and, via the food chain, various other forms of life which in turn nourish the fish.

The principles of Chinese polyculture spread right across south-east Asia. As rice paddies can double as ponds, fish is an important source of protein for many farmers and their families. The variety of systems is as wide as the climatic differences between regions: in northern China, for instance, where it is too cold to keep mud carp, common carp or bream are used instead; arid regions, where there is little vegetation, dispense with plant-eating fish altogether. The pond system is designed to enable virtually all plant or animal and human waste matter to be fully utilised by the fish. As a result, the ponds also act as purification plants: by the time the water drains out of them, it contains very few nutrients. A well-maintained fish pond imitates natural ecological processes rather than opposing them.

Aquaculture – Industrial Fish Farming

Global fish consumption has increased enormously since World War II. Traditional coastal fishing has been largely replaced by deep-sea fishing using sophisticated equipment. Echo-sounders, radar and satellites track shoals of fish in even the most

Brown trout (Salmo trutta fario) *on one of the few spawning grounds left in Europe in a tributary of the Aare River in Switzerland. Practically all freshwater trout are now raised in breeding stations, then reintroduced into rivers to grow into targets for sport fishermen.*

remote parts of the ocean, and modern factory ships comb the seas with huge trawl-nets. Five times more fish, molluscs and crustaceans were taken from the world's oceans in 1990 than in 1948, a rise from 20 to 100 million tonnes. These enormous catches cannot be sustained in the long term. In 1990, the United Nations Food and Agriculture Organization classified the stocks of almost all edible fish in the world's oceans as 'depleted, fully-exploited or over-exploited'. Since 1989, there has been a drop in the number of fish caught – it appears that within the space of a mere 50 years humanity has succeeded in emptying seas that had seemed perennially abundant.

Until the 1970s, freshwater fish farming was the poor cousin of the booming ocean fisheries, but latterly, much attention has been paid to developing more efficient ways of producing fish. With the model to hand of intensive animal rearing, in which large numbers of chickens, pigs or cattle are squeezed together in extremely confined spaces for maximum return, it was not long before fish farming became an industry. This new factory-farming of fish – or aquaculture – has little in common with the ecologically sensitive, sustainable fish farming of the past. As many fish as possible of a single species are kept in cages, basins or ponds – aquaculturists express the number of fish as kilogrammes per cubic metre of water. The fish are fed not with waste products, but with high-quality protein – soya, chicken meal and

even fish meal – just as in industrial livestock farming. Water carrying the excreta of fish passes into the lakes or rivers where farms are located and has an effect as disastrous as that of effluent from piggeries. An eight-hectare salmon farm will cause as much pollution as the untreated sewage from a town of 10,000 inhabitants.

Not surprisingly, in such crowded conditions, the fish also get sick. Attempts are made to control infections by injecting or feeding them with antibiotics. In Norway, in 1987, 50 tonnes of antibiotics were used in salmon farming – more than the total used by the country's human population over the same period. The crowding also encourages parasite infestations. Farmed salmon, for example, can quickly become infested with sea lice, a problem unknown in natural environments. Inevitably aquaculturists then resort to insecticides which are poured directly into the water in large quantities. Ciba-Geigy, the multinational pharmaceutical and chemical company, expressly recommends that Nuvan, one of its insecticides, should not be used in salmon farms. This has not stopped it becoming the market leader for dealing with sea lice.

Genetic engineering is another well-established element in aquaculture's repertoire. On 14th May 1993, Fidel Ramos, President of the Philippines, presented to his country's fish farmers the product of a collaboration between Norwegian and Philippine scientists: a new variety of tilapia (an important freshwater food fish in the region). Billed super tilapia, it grows 60 per cent faster than normal. Genetic engineers working in salmon farms have been experimenting for years with human growth hormones to make the salmon grow faster and thereby to increase yields.

Aquaculturists like to claim that their business makes a major contribution to feeding the world's population. In fact, the fish farms that have grown up in the past 20 years are geared exclusively to producing luxury fish for Japan, Europe and the United States. Shrimps, salmon and lobster are grown all over south-east Asia, in Chile and in El Salvador, even in Zaire. Aquaculture involves far too much costly equipment and supplies to make it a viable alternative food source for poor countries, quite apart from its disastrous ecological

consequences. Cultivating fish spawn requires complicated technology, and fish feed, antibiotics and insecticides have to be purchased, all of which adds to the cost of the fish. Only investors with a great deal of capital are able to survive in this business – many of the shrimp and salmon farms on Chilean fjords, for instance, belong to Scottish and Norwegian companies.

Expense is, however, not the only reason why industrially farmed fish can never become a basic foodstuff. There are two essential prerequisites for aquaculture that are in short supply all over the world: water and land. One hectare of land devoted to agriculture produces a far higher nutritional yield than the same area dedicated to fish farming, so aquaculture has been able to establish itself only on apparently useless land. Situated on brackish coasts and in marshy deltas, 'wasteland' of this sort, suitable neither for agriculture nor for industry or settlement, has been purchased on a large scale by international fisheries consortia, even though, in some cases the land is traditional commonland belonging to the local community. As a result, unique and unspoilt natural habitats are destroyed and the locals lose their right to earn a bit extra by collecting the naturally occurring shellfish and crustaceans.

All over the world, a variety of plans for development are now competing for the opportunity to destroy these so-called useless areas situated between sea and land, which are exceedingly rich in wildlife. Many species of birds, often migrating long distances, breed in these unique habitats. In Thailand and India, over 80 per cent of mangrove swamps have already been destroyed, as have over 70 per cent of those in Bangladesh, Somalia, Pakistan, Kenya and Ghana. Fish farming represents yet another threat to these endangered ecosystems. In Greece, bass and bream farming increased ten fold between 1989 and 1992. Drainage pipes, green with algae, that discharge from gigantic concrete fish tanks into the Gulf of Amvrakikos in Greece are accelerating the process of eutrophication in the calm waters of the Gulf.

It is imperative that coastal marshflats and deltas – the spawning grounds and habitats for huge numbers of fish species – are rigorously protected. Further destruction of these areas would place even more pressure on the already severely depleted fish populations of our over-exploited oceans.

Overfishing

Over half of the fish caught across the world is consumed in the rich nations of the northern hemisphere. Out of a total annual catch of almost 100 million tonnes in commercial ocean fisheries, one third is turned into fish meal. At least a further 20 million tonnes of (mainly dead) sea creatures are rejected and thrown back overboard by the floating fish factories. While such vast quantities of fish are simply thrown away or processed as animal feed, it seems nonsensical that there should be any attempt to boost fish production.

Nonetheless, international development banks such as the World Bank and the Asian Development Bank are still making massive investments in aquaculture. Where traditional river fishing is in danger of dying out because of the construction of dams or industrial plants (also funded with development aid), aquaculture is presented as appropriate compensation for lost food supplies. The spiral of environmental damage which starts with the internationally subsidised destruction of traditional fishing in rivers such as the Mekong, Amazon and Zaire, thus spins irrevocably on.

Fish farming could only make a genuine contribution to feeding the world's hungry if it were possible to establish and maintain it without causing any environmental damage and without using any additional land or valuable water resources. The principles of traditional Chinese polyculture indicate the path that must be taken if fish farming is to become an ecologically sound, integrated part of land use. In Calcutta, for example, the city's household sewage flows into an artificial wet area some 5,000 hectares in size where Indian carp, Chinese carp and tilapia are kept in polyculture. Four thousand families make a living from fish farming here, and further downstream the water is used for a second time to irrigate 6,500 hectares of farmland. Calcutta benefits from this system in two ways: sewage and organic waste are disposed of cheaply and effectively, and large amounts of valuable foodstuffs are produced at the same time.

Mangroves are one of the very few plant species that are equally tolerant of fresh or salt water, making them an invaluable form of vegetation along coasts where the climate allows them to thrive as here at San Blas on the Pacific coast of Mexico. Many marine species make use of the relative safety of the waters around mangroves to breed and raise their young.

Opposite page. A last, tiny, unspoilt corner of Teufelsmoor – or the Devil's Moor – an area of wetland near Tessin in north-east Germany, most of which had already been destroyed by peat extraction by the time this picture was taken in 1993.

CHAPTER SIX

WATER IN A STRAITJACKET

Draining the Land

Ditches running alongside roads and paths are such a common sight that we rarely stop to wonder why they are there. Yet they are evidence of one of the most significant human interventions in the landscape: the comprehensive manipulation of the water regime to force water to drain away from where it might inconvenience people: on transport routes, in settlements, on farmland.

Undamaged ecosystems can store huge amounts of rainfall in their soil and vegetation, which absorb water like a sponge, then later gradually release it. Large parts of the earth's surface consist mainly of water: swamps and marshes, lakes and ponds, flood plains and river valleys. Siberia is as marked by water as are the rainforests of the tropics.

The importance of moors and marshes for the ecology as a whole does not usually become apparent until the effects of their destruction begin to be felt. Left intact, they slow down the rate at which rainwater drains away, guaranteeing a flow of fresh water into streams and lakes, even in dry periods. They are also highly efficient at absorbing excess nutrients washed out of fields and meadows (from fertilisers and dung). According to Swedish estimates, a wetland of only two square kilometres will every year prevent up to 2,000 tonnes of nitrogen from entering rivers or streams. This protects them from over-nutrification

Specialised dyke-clearing machine operating in the fen country in eastern England. Where once wetlands supported rich ecosystems, vast prairified fields for arable farming have been created by determined drainage – an artificially created landscape that requires constant maintenance.

which would lead to the rapid growth of certain algae, a much reduced oxygen content and hence greatly impoverished wildlife – a process known as eutrophication. Moisture held in wetlands is also crucial in regulating local climate. When wetlands are drained, a cycle of dehydration is set in motion. Decreased soil humidity leads to higher soil temperatures, so condensation is reduced and less atmospheric moisture (dew) is deposited on the land; in addition, clouds are less likely to form over the now warmer ground, ultimately leading to less and less rainfall.

History has shown that it is not unusual for human beings to squeeze the water out of a landscape without having any real use for the land. Scarcely any victory over nature has been more enthusiastically received than the reclamation of swamps. In the 18th century, ponds, marshy fields and even small puddles were thought lethally dangerous, as illnesses and epidemics were believed to originate in the miasmas they emitted. Such malign places had to be dried out. The history of hydraulic engineering in the western world is pervaded by a vague, abstract fear of swampy land, an antipathy to ground too wet to stand on. Even modern schemes aimed at draining wet areas sometimes have a touch of the irrational about them.

In Europe and North America, the delicately balanced natural processes that store and transport water have been under relentless attack over the last 50 years. Thousands of kilometres of pipes have been laid to facilitate the drainage of wetlands on both sides of the Atlantic so as to ensure that rainwater runs off as quickly as possible, making soggy land tenable for tractors and for building.

Since 1900, at least half of the world's wetlands have been destroyed in the name of agriculture, the expansion of urban areas and, most recently, the creation of tourist developments. 60 per cent of wetlands in Asia have disappeared. Even in Africa, where relatively little land has been exploited for intensive agriculture, one third of the continent's wetlands have already been drained.

Engineered Catastrophe

No-one who has witnessed the sheer power of a river bursting its banks and inundating streets and houses would blame anyone for trying to protect themselves against the effects of flooding. Indeed, for thousands of years, immense effort has been put into attempts to contain large rivers by building embankments and reinforcing riverbanks.

Each time a river loses some of its floodplain behind embankments or dykes, the water has no choice but to flow faster and more violently – it is confined to a much smaller space, making floods occur more

Pumping out for Mining

When miners dig into the earth in search of metal ore or coal, what they mainly come across is water. This has always been seen as an obstacle. 'Anyone involved in mining', wrote the medieval German scholar, Paulus Niavis, 'avoids water above all else and curses springs and sources above all else when searching for ores.' The task of keeping mining shafts dry when they could be hundreds of metres deep was difficult and arduous and was judged worthwhile only because the minerals being mined were so valuable.

The development of powerful pumps in the 20th century has made many more mining enterprises possible. In German lignite (or brown coal) mining, which is carried out in open pits up to 500 metres deep, the groundwater is taken down to a level below that of a coal seam, so that the excavating machinery and conveyor belts can be kept dry. In the space of a few years, the rainfall of centuries is unceremoniously pumped out. The damage is phenomenal: the groundwater level drops dramatically over entire regions, leaving wetlands and streams dried out as far as 100 kilometres from the mines.

The brown coal workings near Cologne, Germany. In June 1989 Greenpeace activists scaled the colossal excavating machinery and fixed a banner to it in protest at the destruction caused by this industry of one of the largest groundwater reservoirs in Europe.

suddenly and more menacingly. Higher and higher dykes are supposed to protect residential or industrial areas from rivers, but in many places the strategy has been taken too far. Had all the levees along the Mississippi held up during the summer of 1993, the cities along the river's lower reaches would have been swamped on a scale never seen before. Dykes and embankments may prevent local flooding, but they merely exacerbate the overall problem because the sheer force or volume of the water will eventually either break through or overflow flood defences further downstream.

As navigable rivers are effectively turned into racetracks for shipping, both the speed of flow and the risk of flooding rise dramatically. Bends and sandbanks, viewed as inconveniences and obstacles, are removed.

Much of the Rhine, for example, has been reconstructed to form a perfectly straight channel, with barrages artificially guaranteeing a minimum depth. Once-majestic rivers like the Volga have been reduced to a series of shallow reservoirs or, like the Mississippi, are tightly corsetted to make them shorter and deeper.

The combination of draining land and manipulating rivers inevitably has serious knock-on effects: rainwater is no longer stored in the soil, but immediately diverted into drains, ditches, streams and rivers, creating the potential for flash floods. The price of the attempt to master water can be gauged most clearly in Europe where the general belief is that water is perfectly under control. In towns and cities, rainwater falls on concrete or asphalt and is spirited away to the nearest river through

the sewers, while in the country it is carried off along ditches or drainage pipes.

For some time now, experts have realised that rainfall can no longer carry all the blame for increasingly serious flood damage. Water authorities have acknowledged that rivers have become unmanageable partly as a result of their own construction work. Along the Rhine and the Mississippi, feverish attempts are now being made to find areas into which rivers can safely be channelled through controlled breaches when the water rises past a certain point. But no farmer is likely to agree to his fields being submerged, and no local authorities are prepared to sacrifice land that could accommodate future development.

In spite of the experiences of Europe and North America, huge flood control projects are currently being proposed for

developing countries. In Bangladesh, the World Bank aims to provide a permanent antidote to the floods that inundate large parts of the country on a regular basis by constructing dykes along both banks of the country's two great rivers, the Jamuna and the Brahmaputra. This Flood Action Plan, which would cost over $10 billion and take more than 20 years to complete, is, however, facing strong opposition from concerned Bangladeshi and international experts alike. Abnormal or unpredictable floods, like those that caused extensive damage and loss of life and made international headlines in the late 1980s, which are known as *bonna*, are rare. The normal monsoon floods, the *borsha*, which regularly leave a third of the country under water, are regarded as beneficial by the Bangladeshi, who have organised their lives around the annual arrival of water on their fields that brings with it fertile silt and washes away the dreaded salt which would otherwise render their land barren (see Chapter 7). The planned embankments would cause drastic changes to the water regime and the ecology of the rivers and their floodplains. Many Bangladeshi fear that, if the scheme goes ahead, their country will become 'a land without water', that they will be deprived of the

benefits of the *borsha* without receiving any real protection from the devastation of the *bonna*.

Nature Pays the Price

Animal and plant life in streams and rivers suffers badly when the water is confined and made to flow faster. Natural river banks are luxuriant places, with abundant vegetation and plenty of nooks and crannies providing shelter for a multitude of different forms of life. Canalised river banks, on the other hand, are steep, barren and uniform, affording practically no viable habitat. In any case, the current is too swift for aquatic invertebrates or the small animals and birds that rest, reproduce or feed at the calm, shallow edges of rivers. Fish have no chance of survival in a river like this, even if they have not already been driven elsewhere or killed off by industrial pollution. The vast majority of fish species native to European streams and rivers have long since disappeared. Food is short because the small animals and the aquatic plants which form the bases of the food chain will have perished. Many insect larvae, for example, can only survive in the stagnant pools that are temporarily created when flood waters subside.

Many species that live for all or part of the year on flood plains find there the special conditions they need to reproduce. Birds like the stone curlew (or thicknee) and the little ringed plover, for example, will only lay their eggs on the bare gravel bars that appear after flood waters recede during the short time when they are free of vegetation.

The impoverished biology of regulated and straightened rivers reflects a human mania for uniformity: all that is left are a few stubborn fish that persist against the odds in an otherwise wrecked and largely barren environment where once a rich ecosystem existed.

The drying-out of the land through drainage and ditches happens gradually and almost imperceptibly, but this does not make its consequences any less drastic. According to an extensive survey, 201 plant species were in danger of extinction in Germany by 1988 as a direct result of drainage. The worst-hit areas are moors and lakeshores, where ecosystems are particularly diverse and on which farmers and construction companies regularly set their sights. Even in Latin America, 20 per cent of the wetlands internationally classified as worthy of conservation are directly threatened by agricultural planning.

A meander on the River Warnow near Schwerin in north-east Germany. A river is much more than water flowing between two banks; it creates a kind of corridor of biodiversity, sustaining the whole landscape through which it passes.

Opposite page. The Mississippi River flooding at Portage Des Sioux, near St Louis, Missouri, in August 1993.

Chat Moss in Lancashire, northern England – drainage before peat-cutting. Many gardeners who use peat as a soil enricher have no idea that their splendid horticultural achievements are supported by the destruction of unique, irreplaceable ecosystems.

Undoing the Damage

In many countries, people are beginning to become aware of the fate of their rivers. Movements like 'Adopt-a-river' in the United States and *Bachpatenschaft* (Stream Sponsorship) in Germany bear witness to a growing public reluctance to accept the straitjacketing of their rivers, and a desire to find out more about what is going on and to become involved in the water authorities' decision-making. In Switzerland, for example, large numbers of people protested against plans to increase the height of existing embankments along the small River Thur, following flooding in the late 1970s. They demanded, instead, a strategy for flood control that was more in keeping with the natural environment, and would thus give fish and other river fauna a chance. After ten years of argument, the authorities and the environmentalists finally agreed on a scheme of creating irregular, rather than dead-straight, riverbanks, with

overflow troughs that the river would fill at high water, allowing the flora and fauna to regain a hold.

Attempts to allow nature back can be the salvation of rivers and streams that have been banked up and straightened almost to death; the same is true for wetlands. Various trials are currently underway that are attempting to return dried-out marshes or moors to their original state. Often, all it takes is for drainage ditches to be filled in or drainage pipes to be blocked off and the groundwater level will start to rise again. Nevertheless, it may take decades for the ecosystem to recover and for vegetation typical of the habitat to recolonise.

The Everglades in southern Florida stand as an excellent all-round model for this kind of restoration. Large tracts of these apparently endless swamps, the natural habitat of numerous species of birds and of the American alligator, have been destroyed by water exploitation. Canals chop through the watery landscape draining it for citrus plantations and tourist developments and to provide drinking water to the cities for their rapidly growing populations. Where once the Kissimee River, which feeds the Everglades, meandered its way through jungle and swamp lush with water-loving plants, a dead-straight canal was cut by the US Corps of Engineers in the 1960s. Now, the Corps has been given the task of converting 35 kilometres of their canal back into 69 kilometres of Kissimee River. The fate of other rehabilitation projects will hang on the success of this US$ 372 million project.

Hydraulic engineering is an art which demands more than just the ability to calculate the speed of current and to read flow statistics. In the 20th century humanity has interfered in countless ways with the water cycle, but rarely with a full understanding of how it actually works. For decades, hydraulic engineers have stubbornly backed land reclamation and the straightening of rivers without worrying about what the consequences might be. It is characteristic that this manipulation is publicly criticised only when rivers begin flexing their muscles. Perhaps the floods of recent years will teach us that hydraulic engineering is much more than canalisation of the landscape and involves sensitive interaction with a living organism.

Above. Corkscrew Swamp in Florida, the United States – a luxuriant, triumphantly diverse corner of sub-tropical swamp forest.

Right. Ducks, mainly pintail (Anas acuta), resting and feeding at a waterhole in Waza National Park, Cameroon.

CHAPTER SEVEN

WATERING THE LAND

The heat of the sun shining on the oceans causes water at the surface to evaporate, and moisture is taken up into the air. When this virtually distilled water returns to the earth in the form of rain, it is (unless the atmosphere is polluted) pure and fresh. And free. This – the water that drops out of the sky – is the source of all fresh water on earth: in lakes, springs, rivers and the natural reservoirs that lie beneath the earth's surface. And it is these supplies of water that sustain all life on the planet, be it human, animal or plant.

In the course of evolution, the plant life on earth has adapted to a wide variety of habitats. Some species survive only in continuously wet conditions; others can cope with very dry climates or even sustained drought. Plants like the shrub *Flacaria vulgaris* that grows in the Steppes have roots that can extend to a depth several times their height in order to reach reservoirs of water deep underground. Varieties of acacia trees typical of the African savannah have been introduced in areas of desertification because their extremely long roots

Four images from the Namib – a coastal desert in south-western Africa.

Opposite page, bottom. Fog bank clearing over sand dunes near Gobabeb. Plants and animals that live in arid places make use of every drop of water that comes there way, even if it is only atmospheric moisture — in this case coastal fogs that have been blown inland after forming above the cold Benguela current. Top. The fog-basking beetle (Onymacris unguicularis) – note the water droplets condensing from the fog.

This page, above. It is said that more people drown in the desert than die of thirst – the Kuibeb river in spate at Gobabeb, on one of the few days (if any) that it flows each year. Right. These leguminous flowers remain dormant in the gravel plains of the Namib Desert until the ground is drenched by rain, then, with great speed, flourish, deposit their seeds and disappear until the next good soaking.

can reach the water table. Succulents, such as *Aloe vera*, have leaves with a very thick surface layer that minimises loss of water through evaporation. Cacti are true masters of the art of collecting and rationing tiny amounts of moisture. During the night they take up carbon dioxide which their special biochemistry allows them to store until daylight returns, when it can be used in photosynthesis. Some plants even contrive to remain viable in the desert in the form of dry, dormant seeds. A sudden brief shower – even after years of drought – can be enough to make the dormant seeds burst into life and an apparently barren landscape fill with the bright colours and scents of thousands of flowers. It usually takes only a few days for the scorching heat of the sun to put an end to this miraculous spectacle, but by this time the desert plants will have produced new seeds that dry out to wait for the next shower, however long it may be in coming.

Farmers attempting to plant and harvest crops on a regular basis cannot of course wait long periods for unpredictable rainfall. Moist soil, together with plenty of sunshine and warmth, are the most important prerequisites for good, reliable harvests. As a general rule, a minimum of 300 to 400 mm of rainfall is needed per year to make arable farming possible. Even this may not be enough if it all falls during a short, heavy rainy season, leaving crops to dry out in the remaining months of the year. Farmers

in monsoon countries such as India, Bangladesh and Thailand have traditional and well-tested methods for dealing with this: monsoon rain is stored in shallow reservoirs surrounded by earthen walls – known as *jheels* in India – and is then used to water the fields during the long dry season. In spite of the vagaries of climate, the greater part of cultivated land on earth is watered solely by rainwater. Exact figures are hard to come by, but best estimates come out with a figure of around 84 per cent; rivers or groundwater are used to irrigate the remainder.

Unforeseen Consequences

Irrigation with river or groundwater can carry with it serious risks, which may ultimately have catastrophic results. Rivers and groundwater always contain dissolved salts; this is often simply ordinary salt (sodium chloride), but there may also be various sulphates or carbonates which have dissolved as the water has passed through rocks and sediment. When this water is used for irrigation, there is a substantial possibility, especially in hot, dry climates, that salts will accumulate in the soil. After anything from weeks to decades, depending on conditions, the earth will become infertile and have to be abandoned.

Soil salinisation is an inevitable side effect of irrigation using anything other than rainwater. As the water evaporates, the salts

Above. Farmers from Chittagong in south-eastern Bangladesh hastily plant paddies before the onset of the monsoon floods.
Left. Once the rains have arrived, ploughs are

discarded in favour of fishing nets as the fields are turned into gigantic lakes where fish come to feed and spawn. 80 per cent of Bangladesh is made up of flood plains, large parts of which are regularly inundated by water pouring in from the vast river system of the Ganges, Brahmaputra and Meghna. Fertile silt is deposited on the land, ensuring that farmers consistently produce bumper food crops, in spite of using no artificial fertilisers and only traditional tools.

contained in it remain in the soil. Evaporation can be considerably reduced by transporting the water directly to the level of the plant roots via subsurface pipes, but in the long term the soil's salt content will still increase.

Waterlogging, a frequent occurrence on irrigated land where the water cannot drain away easily, causes rapid salinisation. In a dry, hot climate, as the soil becomes saturated and the water evaporates at its surface, capillary action, working rather like blotting paper, draws up more water from deep in the soil. This evaporates, depositing its salts, and more groundwater rises, only to evaporate in its turn. Soon the surface of the fields is covered with a thick crust of crystalline salt. Desperate attempts to rinse out the salt using large amounts of water merely exacerbate things: the ideal precondition for the salinisation cycle is soil saturated with water.

Land is not always wrecked by people watering it. Successful irrigation has been achieved in some parts of the world for centuries, but only where there is good, natural drainage. In terraced fields, for example, any water absorbed into the soil can easily drain away. Inevitably, where river or spring water is used, slight salinisation occurs, but a single heavy shower is usually enough to wash away the salt. Flooding rivers can also work wonders in removing salt from fields – one of the less well-known, positive effects of the annual monsoon floods in India and Bangladesh. Where natural correctives of this kind are absent or cannot be relied upon, artificial drainage – usually with subsurface pipe systems – is the only option. The water drains away quickly, so that at least capillary action from the groundwater is prevented. The huge drawback of schemes of this kind, however, and the reason why they are

The south of China is an area of high rainfall and large rivers; for over 6,000 years the people living here have benefited from farming on the fertile floodplains, often using highly effective techniques of controlled flooding.

Opposite page. In Egypt, it is only in the area made fertile by the River Nile that people have been able to settle. On the left is a traditional boom or shaduf of a type used for the last 3,000 years to bail water out of the river when it is low, and into small, carefully maintained fields like these (right) near the Temple of Kom Ombo.

unlikely ever to offer a practicable solution, is the enormous cost of installation and maintenance. For most of the world, they are not even an option.

Ancient Irrigation

Water-related structures such as Roman baths and aqueducts are among the most impressive surviving architectural achievements of ancient civilisations, but there is also less spectacular evidence in many places of highly effective systems of water management dating back hundreds, even thousands, of years. Canals and ditches, weirs and sluices all bear witness to engineering and construction schemes or irrigation systems that were remarkably elaborate, even by modern standards.

Traces of some of the earliest known urban societies have been discovered on the fertile plains of large rivers. Rivers both provided water for irrigating the soil and regularly flooded the surrounding land, leaving fertile topsoil on the fields. Year in, year out, this free boost to fertility guaranteed excellent harvests. The soil's fertility was inexhaustible, providing ideal conditions for feeding fast-growing populations.

There is no record of when the beneficial effect of flooding was first used to help in the cultivation of food. It may have been on the banks of the Huang Ho (Yellow River) in China, or by the Indus in what is now Pakistan. The most detailed information about this form of agriculture comes from the Nile Valley, where it was widely practised well into this century. Egypt, with almost no rain, would be as infertile as the Sahara were it not for the River Nile – and even this huge watercourse can bring to life only two per cent of the country's area. In mid-June, the heavy monsoon rains from Ethiopia and Uganda reach Lower Egypt as the Nile floods, carrying the prized red earth on to the surrounding fields precisely when it is needed.

This simple but effective natural cycle was put to good use for thousands of years. When the river rose, the farmers opened up small breeches to allow the water to flood basin-shaped fields. There the water remained at a depth of a half to three metres for about six weeks. Gradually, the rich mud settled out, and as the river's water level began to drop, the water in the basins slowly trickled away through the earth back towards the river. Basin irrigation scarcely affected the natural flow of the Nile; it was said that the river gods rewarded the farmers' care by enhancing the fertility of the soil. Thanks to the relatively steep gradient of the river and the enormous amounts of water it carries, any salts deposited in the fields were thoroughly rinsed out each year.

In 1971, Egypt decided to seal off the Nile Valley with the Aswan High Dam, hoping to make even more intensive use of the river. Certainly, it meant that the water could be distributed over a longer period: new areas have been cultivated and in some places a second harvest has even been possible. But damming up the water has of course involved damming up the fertile mud too, and while it settles uselessly behind the dam, expensive artificial fertilisers have to be used in its place. Farmland is now steadily being lost through salinisation for the first time in Egypt's history – 30 per cent of cultivated land has already been affected.

Ancient Egyptians worshipped the Nile as a deity. Everything depended on its floods. A few metres' variation in the river's height when it flooded could make the difference between a failed harvest and ideal irrigation. Ancient high-water markers can still be seen all along the river – these not only made it easy to assess its height, but were also a measure of taxes to be paid by farmers. The higher the water, the better the harvest to be expected, and the higher the taxes demanded by the Pharaohs.

Things were not quite so simple for the inhabitants of Mesopotamia (now Iraq and

Rice terraces in northern Luzon, Philippines, where the humid climate is ideally suited to rice cultivation. This method of farming, however, is time- and labour-intensive, and cash-crop oriented development schemes are more likely to approve ultimately unsustainable mechanised rice-growing in dry regions supported by expensive artificial irrigation – with all the environmental and human risks this entails.

Syria), which lay between the Euphrates and the Tigris, where the land was particularly fertile and the Sumerians settled over 6,000 years ago. Here, the seasonsal floods were not as fortuitous as in Egypt and did not suit the crops, coming too late for the summer sowing and too early for the winter sowing. So the Sumerians developed a technique of taking water from the rivers all the year round and storing it to allow them to produce two harvests a year. The other problem they had to contend with was the sheer unpredictable power of the water. Water coursing down from the mountains sometimes made the rivers swell to huge proportions and overflow in unexpected directions – so much so that both the Euphrates and the Tigris have altered their courses many times over the centuries. Flash floods can cause huge damage, bringing with them topsoil and other debris, and depositing a layer of mud so thick that it stifles the fertile soil. To counter this a system of dykes was established to protect farmland and dwellings from uncontrolled flooding.

In spite of the difficulties, the Sumerians (and after them the Babylonians and Assyrians) succeeded in turning Mesopotamia into a garden of plenty. The original crops were tough strains of barley and emmer (a particularly robust variety of wheat), which were soon joined by other cereals. Flax was grown for linen, and sesame seeds were pressed to make oil. Date palms provided shade for vegetable gardens where onions, cucumbers, garlic, dill and caraway were grown. Even lilies and roses were planted and thrived. This richly cultivated landscape required continuous extension of the irrigation network. Large main arteries fed smaller ancillary canals which ultimately led into the farmers' storage basins. This kind of infrastructure would have required constant care and attention, and, above all, protection against flood damage. The extensive work involved could only be organised in the context of a well-functioning community.

Early water legislation was accordingly strict, as we know from the water law of the Babylonian King Hammurabi (BC?1728-?1686 BC). A standing stone slab inscribed with a long text in cuneiform script was discovered during archeological excavations

Maintaining terraces perched precariously on the sides of hills and mountains involves devising ways of preventing the hard-won little fields being washed into the valley by heavy rain. The diagonal storm channels cutting across the cultivated strips in the background are the ingenious solution used here, in Java, Indonesia.

As soon as farmers give up repairing and taking care of terraces, the results of generations' worth of labour very quickly start to deteriorate. When they were cultivated, the only source of water for these coffee fields on the western slopes of the Haraz mountains in Yemen was dew condensing at night and occasional rain showers.

elaborate irrigation.

Whether the decline of Mesopotamia was ultimately due to a breakdown in law and order or to insurmountable agricultural problems is a matter for historical and sociological debate. What seems certain is that the land's unfavourable topography accelerated its fall. Unlike the flood waters of the Nile, which drained off fairly rapidly, the flooded fields of Mesopotamia drained slowly, if at all. In the scorching summer heat, the water gradually evaporated, leaving only salt on the earth. Year by year the soil's salt content increased relentlessly, and its yield steadily dropped. In 2400 BC, Babylonian farmers were able to harvest as much as 1.7 tonnes of wheat per hectare, but by 2100 BC this figure had fallen to 1 tonne. Barley, being more tolerant of salt, gradually became the region's main crop until it, too, failed because of salinisation.

Successful cultivation was of course not limited exclusively to areas around large rivers; methods of farming evolved to cope with differing conditions of topography, soil and climate. Terracing is a notable example, rendering even the steepest mountain slopes fertile, and has been widely used in, for example, Syria and Palestine, China, India and pre-Columbian America. This method produces the largest possible surface area for farming on a hill

in 1902 in the ancient Elamite capital of Susa, near the modern town of Dezful in western Iran. Comprising 282 Articles, it was found to be a complete legal code over 4000 years old – the oldest known legal text. Article 53 of the Code of Hammurabi stated that anyone failing to take care of his section of the canal was liable to compensate with his own harvest any farmers adversely affected if the dyke burst. If the offender did not have enough grain, all of his possessions, including land, would be confiscated and divided up among the injured parties. The harshness and strictness of laws of this kind moved the American sociologist, Karl Wittfogel, to write a study of 'hydraulic despotism' and subscribe to the theory that only a centralised state power with unconditional control over construction and maintenance of the water infrastructure, could be effective in communities dependent on

or mountainside, as well as successfully retaining the rain or spring water so essential for raising crops. It also prevents valuable soil from being washed away, and by catching rain, protects the valleys below from flooding.

The Treasure of the Sabaeans

As far back as 4,000 years ago, people were contriving ways of getting the most out of land where rainfall was extremely sparse. There is no better documented example of early, but nevertheless sophisticated, knowledge of water than the irrigation system of Marib, a city with a population of approximately 30,000 and the capital of the Sabaean Empire in southern Arabia from c.1000 BC.

Normal farming is inconceivable in the southern part of the Arabian peninsula because of the lack of rain. When the monsoon rains fall in the mountains nearby, however, river valleys or wadis that have been arid for most of the year suddenly turn into raging torrents. The catchment of the Wadi Dhana near Marib covers around 10,000 square kilometres. Small wadis feed into it in the same way that streams run into rivers. Close by the ancient capital, the Wadi Dhana passes through a gap in the rocks just before it opens out into the plain. Here, in around 800 BC, the Sabaeans erected a massive earthen dam, sealing off the valley. The beauty of the system they operated was that as the water was stored so briefly, most of the sediment did not have a chance to settle behind the dam. During the rainy season, the water poured in at colossal speed, filling the the dam at a rate of up to 1,700 cubic metres per second. Slowing the water down and allowing it to dissipate its energy, while making sure that it reached fields up to 21 kilometres away before the fertile mud it contained could settle, presented a considerable challenge.

The water was channelled as fast as possible into an elaborate network of canals leading to an oasis covering 1600 hectares. There, small enclosures surrounded by low earthen walls were filled with 60 to 70 cm of water, saturating the soil. As soon as the water had drained away, sowing could begin. Like the Mesopotamians, the Sab-

aeans practised a method of farming which involved shading one crop with another: barley, millet, vegetables and fruit were all grown in the shade of date palms, which were also used to protect pasture for sheep.

Every year, around seven millimetres of sediment remained on the soil once the water had soaked in. The farmed land grew higher and higher, and the canal systems and dam in the wadi had to be periodically raised. Finally there came a time when the old earthen dam could be raised no further, and in 520 BC the foundation stone for a new construction was laid. The remains of this later dam can still be seen in Marib – 600 metres long and 18 metres high, it must have taken the entire Sabaean workforce to build it.

At the time, Saba (or Sheba) was ruled by priest-kings known as the *mukarribs*; for centuries, control and care of the irrigation system remained in their hands. The richness and fertility of Marib were legendary, and the town, baking under the hot southern Arabian sun, became an important staging post on the old spice route leading from India to the Mediterranean. The dam, the source of the Sabaean empire's wealth and high standard of living, was inspected, repaired and raised at regular intervals. The removal of the mud deposited behind

Part of the complex irrigation system (now in Yemen) built by the Sabaeans, whose technical expertise in managing water over 3,000 years ago remains highly impressive. By contrast with modern dams, which simply trap heavy rainfall or floods, the purpose of the Marib Dam was to redirect storm water as fast as possible so that both it and its precious cargo of fertile soil could be used on fields nearby.

the dam must have been a mammoth task: workers employed on the job consumed in the space of a single year some 200,000 sheep and goats, 50,000 sacks of flour and 26,000 cases of dates.

Nonetheless, the dam finally burst, probably as the result of a particularly heavy storm, in around AD 570. It had secured Saba's wealth for a thousand years. Hardly any other event of the pre-Islamic age has so often been the subject of fantastic description, or been recounted in as many different versions, as the bursting of the Marib dam. Its legendary destruction is even mentioned in the Koran as a warning of how Allah can punish non-believers like the inhabitants of Marib.

Irrigation Crusades

Wadi irrigation was used by a number of ancient civilisations, and developed to a state of perfection in the Negev Desert by the Nabateans. When the long-awaited rain fell, it washed down the wadi and was caught, together with sediment, by a series of small stone walls built across the wadi. Gradually the spaces behind the walls filled up with sediment to form small terraces capable of retaining the precious moisture. When they were filled to capacity, a further series of wadi walls would be built.

Opposite page, top. In dry areas, the first priority of agriculture is to find ways of husbanding the sparse rain so that it doesn't just trickle away unused. Water and top soil gather behind these crescent-shaped diguettes in Burkina Faso and gradually form fertile beds for crops such as millet – a plant highly resistant to drought.

Opposite page, bottom. If it were not for the barren hillside in the background, one might never guess that these blossoming apricot trees are growing in the Negev Desert. The secret of this astonishing success (in the Wadi Mashash) lies not in dammed-up rivers, or pumped-up groundwater or even canals, but exclusively in rainwater which is caught by a network of low walls in the wadi.

The Romans, who were greatly impressed by the Nabateans' wadi irrigation when they invaded the Negev Desert under Trajan in AD 106, introduced the technique in each area of North Africa that they colonised, turning the Maghreb into the Roman Empire's granary.

In the second half of the 20th century, studies of the economic success of the Nabataeans prompted Israeli scientists to take a closer look at these ancient methods. An attempt to grow grain and vegetables in the virtually uninhabited Negev Desert based on the Nabataean system of wadi irrigation was so successful, that it has proved hard to improve upon, even with the aid of modern agricultural technology. Good yields were obtained simply by making intelligent use of the conditions in the desert and by husbanding soil and the scarce rainwater.

As Islam expanded, in the seventh and eighth centuries, it took with it the techniques of irrigation. In territories as far east as Samarkand (in what is now Uzbekistan), and as far west as the Iberian peninsula, the invaders – from Syria, Egypt, Persia and Iraq – introduced the traditional farming systems of their homelands.

The highly developed agricultural system set up by the Moors during their almost 800-year presence on the Iberian peninsula contrasted sharply with practices in the rest of Europe. The Arabs were extremely successful farmers, ready always to adapt their methods to suit local soil, climate and rivers. In Valencia, for example, water was transported to the fields by means of small dams in primary and secondary canals, while the entire irrigation area of Murcia was supplied by a single large dam on the Rio Segura. In spite of substantial climatic and hydrological differences from region to region, Moorish farmers successfully introduced cultivated crops such as rice, sugar cane, cotton and oranges to Andalusia. Numerous Moorish weirs, sluices and canals have survived and even today are in perfect working order.

Colonialism and Irrigation

Spain's efficient, high-yield systems of irrigated agriculture undoubtedly made a significant contribution to the country's rise as a world power in the 15th century after completion of the Reconquista, when Christian armies finally expelled the Moors from the Iberian peninsula. When the Spanish subjugated Latin America in the 16th and 17th centuries, any irrigation systems they found there were mercilessly destroyed and replaced by Spanish technology. In 1492, when Christopher Columbus arrived in the Americas, the continent was home to one third of the people on the planet – as many as lived in China, and considerably more than in Europe. The majority of the population obtained food from methods of irrigation agriculture that were no less sophisticated than those in Spain and indeed in many respects superior to them. Irrigation systems dating back to the pre-Columbian period are still being discovered in Latin America, often proving to have been better suited to local conditions than the Spanish models and significantly more effective than modern cultivation techniques. In a pilot project on Lake Titicaca run by the University of Pennsylvania with Quechua farmers, the 3,000-year-old technique of growing potatoes on raised fields seemed to enhance the crops' chances of surviving frost, drought and waterlogging. Harvests from these fields were three times greater than those in neighbouring fields using western techology (see p.146).

Colonising powers have always tended to assume that military and technological superiority go together. This presumptuousness was particularly evident in India, where the British attempted to improve irrigation in order to develop the country's agriculture. The British engineers, who, not surprisingly, knew nothing about irrigation, set about studying the relevant Spanish and Italian literature, but entirely ignored local knowledge of farming dating back some 2,000 years.

Many Indian irrigation systems were indeed in a poor state at the time of British colonisation. The 200-year-old canals on the Yamuna River in northern India, for example, which had operated satisfactorily into the 18th century, were in ruins. The complex task of rebuilding this irrigation system, carried out under the guidance of British engineers between 1820 and 1830, proved a complete disaster: the gradient of the canals was too steep, so the water ran in rapids and underwashed banks, sluices and bridges. In a subsequent project, the reconstruction of the 1,800-year-old irrigation system in the Cauvery delta to the south of Madras, the new dam was so unstable and ineffective that another had to be built upriver only seven years later.

British engineers slowly learned from their mistakes and a number of projects were successful, at least in financial terms. Once they had finished renovating old structures, however, and began implementing plans of their own, new problems arose. The Ganges Canal, the world's largest on its inauguration in 1854, was intended to provide a solution to the periodic famines that bedevilled northern India by irrigating the fertile plain between the Ganges and the Yamuna. Yet, a well-functioning agricultural system already existed here, irrigating the land with water from shallow wells. The canal caused the groundwater level to rise, rendering the wells unusable. Field drainage also worsened, and it was not long before the stagnant water that collected led to outbreaks of malaria. Thousands lost their lives. Scandalously, the malaria was not unexpected: at the planning stage of the canal project, doctors had emphasised that good drainage was essential to the area. That the Ganges Canal was nonetheless regarded as a success by the British was due to the lucrative new harvests of export products such as cotton and indigo. Profits made on these raw materials back home more than covered the costs of the Canal. Few people even raised an eyebrow at the changes forced on the formerly independent farmers who now had to work the fields for rich landowners, or at the concomitant destruction of traditional social groupings.

The British Empire left behind it over 100,000 kilometres of canals in the Indian subcontinent; it spent roughly as much on them as on railway construction. The area of land irrigated by the time the British withdrew was larger than the whole of England. It is impossible to judge whether this massive conversion of Indian agriculture has ultimately been of benefit. Certainly, India has to live with its legacy.

Wherever people have needed to cultivate crops in extreme climatic conditions – whether in the Negev Desert, on Lake

Every drop of the Indus is spoken for. From its upper reaches in the Himalayas – here near Leh in Ladakh in northern India – to the lowlands in Sind province in Pakistan, there are monumental dams and vast canals dedicated to delivering the entire flow of this mighty river to cotton, rice and grain plantations.

Titicaca or in India – irrigation has always played a key part in traditional agriculture. In many places, it would have been impossible to survive without intelligent methods of storage and distribution of rain that fell only in a particular season. What all traditional irrigation techniques had in common was that they were perfectly adapted to local conditions. Developed and improved over many generations, they achieved crop yields which continue to impress agricultural scientists today. No matter how detailed studies of nutrient cycles, soil microbiology or plant physiology are, they can never replace the wisdom accumulated over centuries of experience.

Sadly, it is likely that an immense wealth of valuable knowledge has been irretrievably lost over the past century. Remains of ancient agricultural techniques are being discovered all the time, but it is usually possible only to guess at how they worked, unless some local knowledge of them survives. In southern France, in the dry region around Gordes and Apt, the remains of strange, beehive-like structures known as

bories can be seen which act as cooling towers for surrounding plots of land. The *bories* have thick, dry-stone walls through which air can freely pass. At night, the towers cool down; in the early morning the air outside begins to warm up and is therefore sucked into them, cooling on contact with the stone inside. Because cool air is denser than warm, it flows out through door-like openings at the base of the *bories*, supplying the surrounding dry-stone-wall enclosures with pools of cool air that cause generous amounts of dew to form and inhibit transpiration. In this way moisture is

For a long time, bories like this one, in Provence, southern France, were taken to be ancient shelters or wine stores, but it is now known that they produce a cooling effect on the plots of land around them. Built in pre-Roman times, it is thought that these curious towers were erected to make cultivation possible in areas without rivers or streams.

supplied to the enclosed fields even at the driest times of year.

That cultivation is possible (given sufficient knowledge and patience) even in regions with little or no rainfall is clear on Lanzarote in the Canaries. This island, the northernmost in the Spanish archipelago, lies 100 kilometres off the coast of Africa and is effectively a continuation of the Sahara desert. It has very little natural vegetation, and the mountains are not high enough to cool the clouds of the Atlantic (which would bring rain). Farmers in Lanzarote instead make use of dew. Whenever a new field is cultivated, the fertile earth is covered with a layer some ten to twenty centimetres thick of coarse black volcanic ash. Every night, the cool wind deposits dew, which seeps down through the layer of sand, providing moisture for the soil. The lava sand inhibits evaporation during the day. This is, however, not a system for the impatient: it takes ten years for the soil to become sufficiently moistened by the dew for cultivation.

Drip-feeding the World

Irrigation agriculture today bears little resemblance to earlier traditional systems, and much of the transformation has taken place over the last 40 years. Of the world's irrigated surface area, two-thirds dates from after 1950. With the aid of large dams, water pipelines and high-power pumps, modern projects have interfered with landscapes and natural water systems on a scale unimaginable in previous centuries. At any place and any time, it would seem, water can be made available. The ultimate objective of all this technology is the intensification of agriculture through the use of high-yield, high-performance crops. Humanity's ambition to become less and less dependent on the unpredictability of nature hangs on the use of artificial fertilisers, chemical insecticides and weed killers, bigger and better machines, monocultures and ultimately genetic engineering – with agriculture as a branch of industry and fields turned into biological reactors. Crucial to all development of this kind is water acquisition: agriculture accounts for some 70 to 80 per cent of today's worldwide water consumption.

Country	Domestic	Industrial	Agricultural
USA	10	49	41
USSR	8	29	63
UK	23	76	1
Spain	7	22	72
Switzerland	30	65	5
Argentina	9	18	73
Venezuela	37	4	59
Mexico	5	7	88
Turkey	7	9	85
India	3	4	93
Algeria	13	6	81
Ghana	44	3	54
Uganda	43	0	57

Water consumed by agriculture compared with other sectors in 1988/89 (as percentages of total consumption)

Water for modern irrigation can be obtained in three ways – by diverting river water, by installing dams, or by pumping water from groundwater resources – all of which have serious and far-reaching repercussions. Groundwater is affected even at depths of over 100 metres; whole microclimates change as a result of increased atmospheric humidity; the hydrology of entire river systems is altered. Once powerful rivers now reach the sea as mere trickles, because their water has been drawn off into canals. Dams block the natural course of rivers, invariably causing unexpected ecological problems, not to mention social upheavals. Groundwater resources are exhausted far faster than they can be replenished by rain, fundamentally changing the hydrology of whole regions.

For many modern projects, the accumulation of salt in the soil is a growing problem, just as it was in Mesopotamia. Many of the irrigation projects established in the past 40 years seem slowly but surely to be resulting in irreversible salinisation. Research by the United Nations' FAO (Food and Agriculture Organisation) indicates that 20 to 30 million hectares of land worldwide have been severely affected by salinisation, while the productivity of another 60 to 80 million hectares has been reduced because of salty soil. More than a million hectares (or at least 0.5 per cent of the world's total irrigated surface area) is irrevocably lost each year. This means

If water for agriculture everywhere were managed as carefully and effectively as on Lanzarote, one of the Canary Islands, where there is no water source and scant rain, there would never be any need for artificial irrigation – even in very dry regions.

The dew that forms in the early hours of the morning is trapped by black volcanic ash which has been diligently spread over the top soil by generations of farmers. The hollows around these vines and low walls built of lava (called lapilli or picon) enhance dew formation and provide shelter from the drying winds that sweep the island. Crops raised in this extraordinary landscape include vines, figs, citrus fruits, potatoes, maize, onions, tomatoes and melons.

Salinisation of previously fertile land can happen in a number of ways. Irrigation commonly causes the water table to rise, but this may also happen as a result of replacing forest with arable land. In this case, near Perth, Western Australia, both factors coincided: eucalypts, which draw strongly on the groundwater, were replaced by irrigated farmland, the water table rose to the surface, bringing with it deadly quantities of salt.

The dream of making the desert miraculously productive with the introduction of irrigation is as elusive as it is seductive. It is in exactly these conditions that waterlogging so easily turns the desert to useless salty earth. Many times more water than is used by the crops would be needed to wash out the salt. Opposite is part of a huge tract of land in Pakistan that is effectively dead because of salinisation.

food supplies: the fertile Sind region in the Indus Valley could be lost for cultivation in its entirety. In the United States, too, salinisation is causing major problems: crops are affected on 25 to 30 per cent of irrigated land.

Groundwater At Risk

Salinisation is not the only problem to strike apparently without warning. Many farmers seem to have been just as shocked and surprised by their wells drying up. But it stands to reason that even the largest groundwater resources will come to an end if they are pumped off more rapidly than they can be replenished by rainwater. People have been sinking wells to find drinking water and for field irrigation for thousands of years without posing any serious threat to the supply. It was the introduction from the 1960s of tube wells

that, in all, one third of the total area of the world's irrigated land has already been blighted by salinisation.

The problem has reached disastrous proportions in the Central Asian Republic of Turkmenistan. At least half the cotton fields which used to be irrigated are covered with a thick crust of salt or have turned into salty bog after less than 30 years of irrigation. In Pakistan, the soil in many areas is threatened with salinisation as a result of waterlogging, which ultimately endangers

(which extract water from unprecedented depths with motor-powered pumps) that triggered large-scale overexploitation of groundwater resources. As more farmers seek to increase their yield by drawing on resources far below the earth's surface, the groundwater silently and invisibly falls. On the Saurashtra coast in the Indian state of Gujarat, for example, it has taken a mere 20 years of irrigation with groundwater to cause complete and utter catastrophe. Before the installation of tube wells, record harvests of oilseeds, groundnuts and bananas were being achieved; now, subsurface groundwater aquifers are so depleted by pumping that they have been penetrated by sea water. Coconuts grow to only half their previous size. The brackish water is undrinkable and ruins crops. In the village of Talodara, as in many other places in Gujarat, the now-salty groundwater from the irrigation pumps was supposed to have

been for drinking too. But farmers are now forced to make a laborious journey by ox and cart to find the nearest well still free of salt water to obtain water for themselves and their animals.

Groundwater further inland in Gujarat is still unaffected, but it is clear to everyone that sea water seepage is continuing deep underground. In spite of this, there are no attempts to save water or to use less of it. Traditional irrigation systems, drawing water from rivers or canals, allowed everyone to see how much water there was, and could ensure fair distribution as well as preventing overexploitation. Power-driven tube wells, however, mean that nobody can see what is happening so that no controls are exercised: all users pump off as much as they can as long as supplies last.

Since 1960, India's irrigated farmland has been expanded almost exclusively at the expense of groundwater resources. The

total surface area irrigated by tube wells went up from only 0.6 per cent in 1960/61 to over 30 per cent in 1988/89. The rapid drain on groundwater reserves is indicated by the increasing depth of wells: in places where only 20 years ago farmers obtained ample water supplies from a depth of 90 metres, today they have to drill down as much as 450 metres. It is easy to imagine the tragic but inevitable consequences if India's food supply remains this dependent on its rapidly diminishing groundwater.

The United States, the world's largest food exporter, is also having to face the consequences of misguided irrigation policies. The scene of the American irrigation débacle is the High Plains, an arid plateau to the east of the Rocky Mountains. Here, one of the world's largest groundwater reservoirs, the Ogallala aquifer, stretches from South Dakota, through Wyoming, Colorado, Nebraska and Kansas, and as far as

Texas. Farmers have been making copious use of this groundwater for decades. Over 150,000 irrigation wells have turned the region into a luxuriant agricultural belt. Fifteen per cent of America's grain production is dependent on Ogallala water; agricultural revenue in the area amounts to $20 billion – around a fifth of the total for the United States.

But this farming miracle is running into difficulties: groundwater resources have already been decimated by subsurface pumping. Twelve billion cubic metres of water are drawn off annually, causing a drop in the groundwater level in some places of between one-and-a-half and two metres a year. It will take at least 100 years for rainfall to replenish what is currently consumed in a single year. If pumping continues at the present rate, experts predict that the High Plains irrigation landscape could come to a dry end in just 20 years'

time. Some farmers in Texas and Kansas have already had to abandon land because groundwater has dropped to an inaccessible level.

Despite imminent shortages, farmers in the High Plains appear to be using water as wastefully as ever. The most obvious crop to cut down on or abandon is fodder grain for livestock, which provides an ultimate nutritional value to humans over ten times less per cubic metre of groundwater than that from wheat for bread. The most thirsty crops still predominate: Texas, for example, produces over two million bales of water-intensive cotton a year from irrigated land. Generous subsidies make even corn (maize) a viable option for irrigation farmers despite the fact that it requires more than twice as much water per hectare as wheat. Increasing the cost of groundwater could help to check such absurd misuse, but the farming lobby is strong,

and there is little hope of a tax on water being introduced. Despite the fact that 90 per cent of Ogallala water is used by agriculture, most farmers object fiercely even to having meters fitted to their pumps.

If agricultural production in the High Plains is to continue in the long term, there will have to be a radical rethink. Replacing high-pressure sprinklers prone to heavy evaporation with low-pressure technology can reduce water consumption, but an even more effective method is the conservation of soil moisture by ensuring that the land is well covered with some sort of vegetation during the driest months. The cultivation of drought-resistant varieties is another measure that can help to effect dramatic reductions in the consumption of groundwater, or even make its use unnecessary. At present, however, without proper legislation, any advice to farmers on saving water seems merely to

Every pump, every water pipe cuts people off from water and knowledge of where it has come from. This dislocation greatly increases the tendency to waste water. Artificial irrigation in areas that enjoy plenty of rain, as here in northern Germany, is used solely to boost harvests.

The Coto Doñana in southern Spain, an important wetland and valuable haven for wildlife, has suffered more than its fair share from the ill effects of modern agriculture.

Right. Water redistribution. In order to irrigate arable land, neighbouring areas are often unceremoniously pumped dry. This former marshland has been sacrificed in the name of strawberries grown for export.

Far right. Monocultures depend on constant applications of artificial fertiliser. Particularly where sprinklers are used, a lot of this ends up not feeding the crops but going straight into rivers, and from there into the sea. The Guadalquivir Marshes that border the Coto Doñana in Spain show the all too common result – eutrophication.

Below. Irrigation stanchions watering asparagus – an inappropriate crop for the warm, dry climate here. When sprinklers are used, far more water is lost through evaporation than is used by the plants.

encourage the spread of irrigation. Once they are aware of how to get by with only half as much as before, farmers simply double the size of their irrigated fields. And the future for groundwater looks if anything even bleaker.

The Perils of Monoculture

In the American plains, nothing is keeping the law courts busier than disputes over the distribution of the farmer's most important resource. It is said that no matter where you find yourself in Denver, Colorado, there will be water attorney a stone's throw away. Acrimonious legal arguments ensue every time restrictions are placed on the amount of groundwater a farmer can pump out. And, in the end, nature is almost invariably the loser.

The catchment of the Platte River in the High Plains consists of a network of smaller

rivers and extensive marshy areas that are largely dependent on the Ogallala groundwater which surfaces here. These wetlands, now threatened with dehydration from the drop in groundwater level, are essential stopping-off points for millions of migrating birds which, twice a year, feed in the rich bogs and ponds of the High Plains. The groundwater plays a pivotal role, especially in spring: it is relatively warm when it surfaces, and so thaws the earth as early as mid-February, ensuring that a large and varied insect menu is ready and waiting for over 100 species of hungry birds that arrive in spring, among them sandhill cranes, white-fronted geese and least terns. The interdependence of the various species here and their reliance on this particular habitat are striking. Sand-

hill cranes, for example, cannot produce viable eggs unless they feed on snails and other invertebrates that thrive only where there is an ample supply of water.

Irrigation projects that involve diverting river water are usually just as ecologically harmful as those exploiting groundwater. In many places, the agricultural lobby treats rivers as if they were simply the first section of the water main and not a living part of the natural environment. Their exploitation is planned down to the last drop. The aim is to re-route as much water as possible, making it 'useful', rather than 'wasting' it by letting it flow into the sea. It is not uncommon for most, if not all, of a river's water to be removed and transferred to another river's catchment. In Turkmenistan, for example, fourteen billion cubic metres

Simultaneous triumph and tragedy. The so-called Hunger Steppe in Kazakhstan, virtually uninhabited until the 1950s, was transformed into an immense grain- and cotton-growing region by large-scale irrigation, supported by the waters of the Syr Dar'ya, one of the two main rivers feeding the Aral Sea. This once-vast lake has paid a heavy price, catastrophically losing two-thirds of its water in only 30 years. Ironically, the future of food production in the region is far from secure as more and more land is being lost to salination.

Spraying paraquat in New Guinea. Intensive monocultures are prone to pests and diseases, and each year hundreds of thousands of tonnes of pesticides are used worldwide. Quite apart from the toxic effects of these on the environment, the World Health Organization estimates that 220,000 people (principally farm workers in the developing world) die annually from pesticide poisoning.

of water from the Amu-Dar'ya are diverted every year into the 1,300 kilometre Kara-Kum Canal to the west. The consequence of such extreme manipulation is that the Aral Sea into which the Amu-Dar'ya flows, once the fourth largest lake in the world, is now quite literally drying up.

Even large rivers like the Nile or the Indus, which carry such huge volumes of water that in the past they drove powerful wedges of freshwater into the sea, are not safe from permanent damage resulting from irrigation. Each year, less and less water emerges at the mouth of a river, and sea water penetrates a few metres further into the river deltas. This is leading to the destruction of mangrove forests, which are irreplaceable ecosystems that support a huge diversity of fish and bird species, acting as breeding grounds and nurseries for many of them, but also providing fishing grounds essential to the survival of the local human population.

Some of the water taken from rivers for irrigation purposes does find its way back into the rivers from the fields. But by the time it does, it is full of salts, fertilisers and pesticides. If insecticides and weedkillers do not finish off the fish and invertebrates, fertilisers ultimately will. Dense growths of algae develop that require so much oxygen to decompose that even the most resistant fish species either leave the area or die. This of course means that any birds or animals that feed on the fish will also vanish.

The Human Factor

Interference on this scale, which amounts to trying to redraw the landscape, will inevitably rebound on humanity in the long term. When schemes for transporting large quantities of water into an area are proposed, for example, there is rarely any talk of the dangerous diseases that may follow in their wake, yet this is a demonstrable and significant risk. One of the most tragic instances is to be seen in El Gezira, once a semi-arid plain between the Blue Nile and the White Nile in the Sudan. Here, thousands of people have paid with their lives for the cheap cultivation of cotton, and hundreds of thousands more have been permanently disabled. The failure of the 1909 cotton harvests in the USA and Egypt led the British to look for new cultivation areas in El Gezira. Following successful tests, a dam and an extensive canal system were built at Sennar on the Blue Nile. The project was expanded after 1950, with almost one million people settling in the two-million-hectare irrigation area.

Today, 80 per cent of the population of El Gezira suffer from bilharziasis, a blood fluke infection caused by the flatworm *Bilharzia* (or *Schistosoma*), which has a life cycle that includes humans and the water snail, *Biomphalaria*. The snails flourish in the warm and shallow stagnant water of irrigation channels. Anyone in contact with the water where the snails live is vulnerable to

Drought

Reports of people starving in Africa underline how dependent agriculture is on water. News stories about catastrophic drought are often presented in the same terms as earthquakes and volcanic eruptions, giving the impression that all such disasters are caused by the capricious and unpredictable powers at work in nature. But this is not the case. Significant fluctuations in rainfall are a natural phenomenon in arid and semi-arid climatic zones, and in the past people living in these areas had highly sophisticated strategies to cope with droughts lasting as long as three or four years.

In areas of semi-desert, there is usually, despite appearances, enough water to support traditional ways of life. Often these subsistence economies involve nomadic or semi-nomadic lifestyles.

Raising animals is usually pivotal to the survival of nomadic peoples. Herds of cattle or goats are driven from pasture to pasture, which, in dry years, can mean covering hundreds of kilometres, while grain and vegetables are grown in small plots near villages. When crops fail, beasts are sold for cash or bartered against staple food. Crucial to this lifestyle is knowledge, garnered over generations, of where pastures and water can be found – where and for how long the cattle can be allowed to graze, where to dig in a dried-up river bed for enough water for a herdsman and his stock to drink.

It was not until nomads were forced to settle, and farming (mainly with the help of development aid) was made dependent on deep wells and crops needing far more water than those traditionally grown, that hunger, even famine began to follow the periodic droughts. Where in dry years harvests had been poor, crops now fail completely. Much larger herds of cattle, fed and watered thanks to motorised pump wells, cannot possibly survive when the now-fixed sources of water dry up. Where this all-too-common sequence of tragic events ends in disaster, the ideal relief programme would include abandoning inappropriate technology and farming methods, and readopting tried and tested local systems.

On most of the islands of Cabo Verde, effectively an outpost of the Sahel in mid Atlantic, maize (the staple food) is raised in dry-field cultivation. The seed is planted after the first summer rainshower in the hope that further rainfall will materialise in the next three months. This is far from predictable, and, on average, only about a third of the maize survives to be harvested. Here, beans have also been planted so that, even if the maize fails, it can act as a support for them.

the flukes that can penetrate human skin and pass into the blood, usually ending up in the wall of the bladder. There is no vaccine, and the disease is resistant to treatment. The lack of any sanitary facilities for agricultural workers – cotton investors decided such provision was unnecessary – means that the eggs of the fluke are passed back into the irrigation channels via the urine and faeces of those infected. The tragic cycle is complete: further infections are unavoidable; a man-made disease has been created. The World Health Organization estimates that around 200 million people suffer from bilharziasis today, and most of them live in the vicinity of large dams or irrigation canals. Only a small proportion of those who contract the disease die, but it causes terrible suffering and pain.

Dangerous Ambitions

Despite all the problems, agricultural ministers and irrigation experts still set their sights on gigantic new projects. Satellites scan the earth's surface in search of still undiscovered groundwater, and drawing boards are piled high with plans for river diversions and dam construction. Since the early 1990s, the upper courses of the Euphrates and the Tigris have been dammed up in eastern Turkey and the waters channelled off – all to realise the dreams of the late Turgut Özal, a water engineer and ex-president of Turkey. The intention is for water from the two rivers to bring fertility to 1.6 million hectares of new farmland in Anatolia, the barren, arid upland to the east of the Mediterranean, thus making this poor and politically unstable region rich – or so the plan goes. Such a move is almost guaranteed to destabilise relations between countries in the region. Turkey is now appropriating the lion's share of the two rivers' natural riches. Syria and Iraq, the two countries downriver, have to survive on what little water remains.

In Indochina, international development banks and investors are viewing the prospect of a final peace settlement in Cambodia with greedy anticipation. Civil war, which has raged there since the end of the Vietnam War, has prevented the industrialisation of the entire Mekong region. The catchment of the Mekong, the

Above. The colossal Atatürk Dam on the Euphrates, and right, the Sanliurfa Tunnel – built to service 700,000 hectares of irrigation agriculture in the dry region of Anatolia. Turkey's enormously ambitious plans to construct 22 dams on the Euphrates and Tigris is unusual in attracting almost universal international disapproval. Much of the anxiety stems not from reservations about the inevitable social and ecological consequences of diverting much of the flow of these two huge rivers, but from fears about the effects that this will have on the dry countries of Syria and Iraq that lie downstream of the plundered waters.

tenth largest river in the world, is home to 30 million people, whose survival depends largely on fishing and traditional farming; the Mekong Committee (comprising government representatives from the four countries bordering the lower Mekong) intends to turn the area into a high-performance agricultural region. The development model is a familiar one: large dams, exerting firm control over the Mekong and its tributaries. The theory is that in future, there will be no seasonal fluctuation in the river's water level, enabling the creation of new and more extensive farming areas that can be irrigated all the year round. Instead of a single harvest, farmers are being led to believe that they could enjoy two, three or even four harvests a year.

In reality, things usually work out a bit differently. In north-eastern Thailand, for example, in the province of Kalasin, the Khlong Lam Bao (Bao River) was dammed in 1968 to provide year-round irrigation of an area covering 48,000 hectares. At the same time, 27,000 hectares of excellent farming land disappeared beneath the waters of the new lake, and 4,000 families had to be compulsorily resettled – on farmland with no irrigation. To date, less than half the land created for cultivation by the new reservoir has been put to use, because farmers now need tractors and insecticides, which they can afford only if they are able to sell large amounts of produce further afield. But the nearest town is far away, and transport costs are often beyond their means.

Then there are the ecological consequences: even the Mekong Committee's irrigation experts believe that dry-season irrigation should never have been introduced to many parts of north-eastern Thailand. They pin the blame for 'waterlogging, salinisation, proliferation of water-borne diseases, increased incidence of crop pests and diseases, pollution of waterways and fishery losses' on projects like the one on the Lam Bao. Nevertheless, the Mekong Committee continues to pursue irrigation projects in order to achieve 'a smaller but modernised and market-driven agricultural sector.'

The markets they are aiming for have little in common with the bustling, colourful, weekly markets of Indochina. Food grown by the farmers will not go to feed the population, but to the export industry: tomatoes for tomato purée, pineapples for canning and cassava destined to be livestock fodder in the European Union. Experience elsewhere in Thailand has already shown that the only way farmers will be able to produce sufficient quantities to make a living is by purchasing high-performance seeds, insecticides and artificial fertilisers. These expensive supplies will force them to take out bank loans, and the pressure of repayment will compel them to intensify their farming methods further. Many of the farmers will be unable to cope with the intensification spiral set in motion by new irrigation projects and will be forced to seek a living in the cities.

Yet this is all in line with the overall economic plan. Migrants from the countryside will be eagerly awaited in the urban areas – after all, the ultimate purpose of the new dams is to generate cheap electricity for industry, which will need labour. This, it is hoped, will aid the transition from an agrarian to an industrial society. Whether this crude imitation of European history will make any sense in the 21st century remains to be seen. Far more important is the fact that the Mekong and its fertile delta are now home to one of the world's most productive agricultural and ecological systems. If it is destroyed, the region will suffer for centuries (see page 152).

Dicing with the Future

Modern, high-tech irrigation is liable to cause severe environmental damage, not least because it has expanded rapidly and projects have become so much more extensive since the Second World War. In brief: valuable farming land is being destroyed by salinisation, irreplaceable groundwater is being overexploited and rivers are drying up. The short-term increases in crop yield proffered by such systems can in no way justify their potential ecological and social consequences.

Numerous research projects have shown that irrigation based on traditional systems is highly productive as well as providing an essential basis for people's survival in inhospitable and arid regions. The long-term success of agricultural methods of this kind has always rested on careful and wise adaptation of farming to suit soil, climate and local population requirements. The naive belief of modern planners that they can conjure up productive agriculture simply by providing water is one of the biggest obstacles to enlightened development.

Most agricultural experts claim that only an expansion of irrigation will ensure adequate food supplies for the world's growing population in years to come. In fact, quite the contrary is the case: if statistics provided by the United Nations' Food and Agriculture Organisation are accurate, 30 per cent of world food supplies are now reliant on artificial irrigation, a level of dependence that is potentially fatal for large numbers of people. Many irrigation areas are likely to be lost as a result of salinisation and wells drying up, so the cultivation of foodstuffs in these areas will not be sustainable for long. In many areas a well-ordered retreat from dependence on artificial irrigation is urgently required together with an abandoning of the ambition to mimic methods used in rainy countries by practising entirely inappropriate intensive farming in semi-desert or during the dry rainless season.

Every drop of water counts, even more so in dry regions than elsewhere. Judging from the huge cotton monocultures and lush pastures thriving under the burning desert sun, this knowledge has evidently passed the people who run such projects by. Politicians and farm managers are increasingly having to ask themselves whether it is acceptable to use water to irrigate cash crops rather than growing food for subsistence or providing drinking water, or even leaving the water for the exclusive use of nature.

Farming experience gathered over four or five thousand years led to successful production methods even in the most unpromising regions on earth. The secret of these successes – apart from care of the soil and use of natural water resources – was the choice of crops: a wide variety of species appropriate to local soil and climatic conditions ensured that our ancestors had enough to eat. In 1930, around 60 per cent of the world's cultivated surface was still planted with moderately drought-resistant grains and particularly tough varieties of

Rice paddies in Bali, Indonesia. Countless varieties of rice are raised in traditional cultivation across the world, chosen for their suitablility to specific climatic and geographical conditions.

flax, sunflowers and sugar beet. Even less water is required by millet, lentils, groundnuts, olives, grapes, almonds, pistachios and figs – all traditional staple foods in dry countries. But crops of this kind are in decline. Since the 1950s, crops have been selected largely on the basis of how their yield can be boosted by the use of fertilisers, and it is rare for drought resistance and high yield to go hand in hand. Robust varieties are increasingly disappearing from the world's farmed landscape. There used to be 30,000 varieties of rice grown in India, but the rice planted in three-quarters of the country's rice-growing areas today is drawn from only twelve varieties. Farmers are left with little option: continuing falls in world prices force them to produce more and more and to grow new, thirsty, high-performance varieties.

Native food crops that are well adapted to local conditions are far better suited to satisfying the population's basic needs.

They require no artificial watering or expensive aids such as artificial fertilisers or pesticides. The yield per hectare may be more modest than it is when the entire arsenal of modern agricultural technology is used, but they are still the best guarantee of a full stomach and a maximum degree of independence.

85 per cent of farmland on the planet requires no more than natural rainfall. It would be disastrous if the supply of food for the world's human population came to depend on an expansion of irrigation. Places where crops do not grow naturally should be left as they are. Supplies of food to a steadily growing world population must be based on intelligent schemes to get the best out of local water resources. The necessary knowledge still exists, though it is fast being forgotten. It is high time to rediscover that the earth voluntarily feeds its people, and that nothing has to be torn from it by force.

CHAPTER EIGHT

AN END TO THE DAM AGE?

Every day, millions of cubic metres of water evaporate from the oceans and the water vapour is carried miles up into the atmosphere to be distributed by the wind systems before returning to the earth's surface in the form of precipitation. This global dynamo is bursting with energy. The thunder and lightning that sometimes accompany rainstorms are perhaps the most potent reminder of the vast forces at work delivering the water that will set streams and rivers on their courses towards the sea for as long as the sun continues to warm the earth. The energy dissipated by a large river is astonishing: it has been calculated that every half hour, as it flows from the mountains to the sea, the Columbia River, in the north-west of the United States, releases energy equivalent to that of the nuclear bomb dropped on Hiroshima.

Twenty per cent of the electricity generated worldwide (or six per cent of total energy consumed) is obtained by harnessing this global water cycle. The price paid for hydroelectricity, however, is high. Entire regions are being deprived of their life source: natural river systems. As people become increasingly aware of this, resistance to such massive intervention in the landscape is growing. Almost all plans to construct large dams now run into fierce opposition; hydropower has become one of the most controversial forms of energy.

Early Water Power

Waterwheels equipped with buckets that lifted water out of the river to feed irrigation canals were probably the first devices to make use of the power of running water. Much later, the Romans were probably the first to convert water power into mechanical energy to mill grain. The water wheels used by the Romans in about 100 BC were installed in a horizontal position, so that the axle could be connected directly to the millstone. Later mill wheels were vertical: in the vicinity of Arles in southern France, the ruins are still clearly visible of a series of grain mills dating from the fourth century AD, which supplied 300 to 500 kilogrammes of flour per hour for the Roman garrison.

But for centuries mills were relatively rare. Whenever labour was cheap (for example, from a ready supply of slaves), there was little motivation to make the substantial investments necessary to build them. Men could grind grain far more cheaply than any mill.

From the early Middle Ages, water-wheels were increasingly used in northern Europe to facilitate and speed up particularly strenuous tasks. According to the Domesday Book, as many as 5,624 grain mills were already in operation in England in 1086. Around the end of the 12th century there was a surge of industrial activity, which would not have been possible without water power. Water wheels were the source of mechanical power in forges, both for forging irons and to work bellows for the smelting hearths. They were also used to drive the chains of buckets that extracted water from coal mines. Even paper manufacture was revolutionised by water power: stamping presses turned rags into a watery pulp from which paper could ultimately be made. A similar process was used in the

Opposite page. Dettifoss, Iceland – the most powerful falls in Europe.

Right. Long before waterwheels were employed to mill grain, they were used to lift water. This one on the River Regnitz bears witness to a 500-year-old tradition of field irrigation in the Bavarian countryside near Möhrendorf in southern Germany; similar arrangements existed in Egypt and Mesopotamia 3,000 years ago.

woollen industry to strengthen cloth by making it denser and heavier.

Soon grain mills could be found on every stream and small river in the British Isles, even in the remote Hebridean Islands. Once landowners grasped that mills could provide them with a steady source of income, they had their own grain mills built and rented them out to millers. They then stipulated that tenant farmers must use the landlord's mill for milling the grain; the landowner was to receive part of the flour produced as payment. This was not a popular development, and it was only when hand-operated grindstones (called querns) were banned that farmers reluctantly gave in and used the mills.

Water power was the only alternative to the muscle power of man or beast and a far superior option to the less reliable wind-mills. But it was restricted to operations that could be carried out on the riverbanks, because whatever machinery was used had to be connected directly to the water wheel. The invention of the steam engine liberated industry from this limitation, and coal-driven steam engines (with all the air pollution they produced) were able almost entirely to replace water power as the energy of industrialisation in the first half of the 19th century.

Hydroelectricity

It was not until late in the 19th century that water power began to regain some of its importance with the invention of the dynamo, which allowed the power from water-driven wheels and turbines to be converted into electricity. This meant that the energy no longer had to be used near rivers, but there was a new technical problem. Electricity cannot be stored, but has to be used as it is produced. Demand for electricity is seldom constant, fluctuating between day and night and between summer and winter, but no surplus can be retained against periods of peak usage. It quickly became obvious to the engineers that if electricity could not be stored, water would have to be. The age of dams had dawned.

Starting in the 1920s and 1930s, hundreds of rivers in Europe, North America and the young Soviet Union were blocked by hydroelectric dams, so that their waters could be saved up for periods of peak demand. By 1950, around 5,000 dams over fifteen metres in height had been built; in the short time since then, a further 30,000

of these major dams have been constructed. In the United States alone, artificial reservoirs have been created behind a total of 75,000 weirs and dams; their collective area is larger than the states of Vermont and New Hampshire put together. Only nine per cent of the total length of rivers in the United States – excluding Alaska – is still regarded by planners as undeveloped. Across Europe, from the Atlantic coast to the Urals and the Black Sea, there are only a few major rivers whose free flow has not been interrupted by man-made structures.

Engineers now have rivers under their control and are able to dispose of their waters as they see fit. Fertile river valleys have been turned into reservoirs, the seasonal patterns of high and low water are subjugated to fluctuations in demand for electricity. Instead of the water being low in autumn and winter and high in spring, the flow cycle is completely reversed. In spring, when vegetation all along the original course of the river is dependent on the melted snow and ice that would normally come down from the mountains, the sluices are closed so that the reservoir can fill up, replacing the water that has been used during the winter months, when huge amounts of electricity are used for heating.

Little or no effort has been made to devise an efficient technology for storing electricity, and until this problem is seriously addressed the desire to exploit the full power-generating potential of rivers will focus exclusively on dams. If power stations were constructed that made use of the river's current, or only part of the river's water were diverted for exploitation, water power could be employed without the need for the expensive storage reservoirs that cause such damage to nature. This, however, does not fit in with the planners' aims of total exploitation. But just how environmentally sound is water power? What sacrifices are absolutely essential if it is to be used, and what damage can be avoided?

Opposite page. Sprawling lake created by hydroelectric scheme on the Tana River, Kenya. Advocates of huge hydroelectric dams often point to their additional benefits for transport (stemming from controlled water levels) as well as for irrigation and drinking supplies. In fact, most dams of this kind are dedicated exclusively

to power generation. The sacrifices they exact are rarely mentioned by the planners: whole towns, rich farmland, forests or, at the very least, the natural courses of rivers are inundated to create reservoirs for hydropower schemes.

Above. The Colorado River, which over millions of years created one of the great natural wonders of the world – the Grand Canyon – is now reduced to providing power for toasters, computers and air-conditioning systems. Glen Canyon Dam, 70 kilometres upstream of the Grand Canyon on the Utah/Arizona border.

Left to themselves, most rivers develop luxuriant margins providing shelter and sustenance for numerous insects, small mammals, birds and fish. Rich vegetation of this sort usually depends on seasonal fluctuations in water level – a rhythm that would be destroyed by the construction of a hydroelectric dam upstream.

*Opposite page. Female kingfisher (*Alcedo atthis*) resting with her catch from a river in southern England. Kingfishers, the most brilliantly coloured of all European birds, depend for much of their diet on small river fish, whose numbers are frequently decimated in dammed rivers. They also need a perch above the water from which to fish – an impossibility when the river has been reduced to a trickle well away from its original banks.*

Ecological Collapse

The airy observation platforms of large dams afford the worst conceivable perspective from which to judge their impact. With a gigantic, often clear blue reservoir on one side and the water rushing white and frothy out of the turbines far below on the other, it is difficult not to be awed by the technical and engineering achievement it represents. Power lines stretching as far as the eye can see are a reminder of the dam's benefit to society. In this tidy, park-like scenery, it seems churlish to point to ecological damage.

The extent of the changes wrought by any dam will become evident only through study of the river. Detailed research on Swiss rivers has revealed that even the slightest change in the volume of water carried by a river – whether as a result of diverting it or of building a dam – causes huge upheavals in the ecology. The lower level of the water means that fish suddenly find their hideaways and shelters high and dry, and the much reduced body of water is far more susceptible to fluctuations in air temperature. If the water volume is reduced by half, the current will slow down to such an extent that silt is no longer rinsed away from the river bed and begins to accumulate, making it likely that a thick layer of algae and bacteria will develop to the detriment of the insect larvae on which many fish feed. The regulated water level typical of rivers harnessed to hydroelectric power stations, which only fluctuates very slightly, means that many water creatures, whose development depends on water levels that change with the seasons, will die. A great many species, such as the moth-like caddis flies (Trichoptera) and stone flies (Plecoptera), so called because their larvae live under stones in rivers, simply disappear from managed waters or survive only in greatly reduced numbers.

The economic and social consequences of this kind of ecological collapse are particularly serious in Asia, where hundreds of thousands of people are dependent on fishing in large rivers for their food. While the impoverishment of river biology and the displacement of traditional fishing are considered a price worth paying by development planners, even the keenest proponents of technology are starting to get nervous at the prospect of what is happening at the mouths of rivers that have been dammed further upstream. Where millions of tons of sediment once settled, ensuring that the land was extended further into the sea, the sea is now rapidly conquering the land. Calm reservoirs behind dams act as gigantic sediment traps, so little of the sediment is carried to the mouth of the river where it would previously have been deposited. The borders between salt and fresh water are moving further inland, destroying biologically rich mangrove forests and posing a threat to farmland near the coast. In the delta of the River Nile, which has now been dammed up for almost 100 years, the Mediterranean has so far snatched over four kilometres of land. Egypt can only attempt to slow down further coastal erosion by constructing an expensive system of dykes.

Clear Skies – Calm Waters

When the clear blue waters of the reservoirs that come with hydro power stations are dotted with sleek, brightly coloured sailing boats and washed by the frothy wake of speedboats, their recreational potential seems like a wonderful bonus on top of the blessing of cheap electricity. But spare a thought for what lies beneath the sparkling surface. Many reservoirs have been created over large tracts of valuable land; all too often, hydro power has been pursued at the expense of any other consideration.

In 1966, the building of the Akosombo Dam in Ghana involved the flooding of an area the size of the Lebanon, yet its

turbines generate a mere 0.9 kilowatts of energy per hectare. When, in the 1940s, the Volga and Kama rivers at Rybinsk, 300 kilometres north of Moscow, were dammed to form an enormous reservoir, 455,000 hectares of best-quality arable and meadow land disappeared – for the slim electrical gain of 0.7 kilowatts per hectare.

It is not only the land that gets in the way of dam-builders – people do, too. 40,000 had to make way for the Kainji Dam in Nigeria, and 80,000 for the Akosombo Dam in Ghana. The conversion of the Volga and Dnepr rivers into a chain of shallow reservoirs forced the resettlement of hundreds of thousands of people from the fertile plains that had bounded the river. Rarely do refugees of this kind hit the headlines,

but whether they are in Nigeria, the Sudan or Thailand, they invariably face grave economic and social problems as a result of their displacement. Only gradually is it beginning to dawn on international agencies that it is virtually impossible to predict or manage the social consequences of uprooting people in this way and moving them *en masse* to new areas. In 1993, the Canadian government justified its withdrawal from the world's largest dam project, the Three Gorges project on the Yangtze River in China, by stating that it was impossible to accept responsibility for resettling well over a million people, most of whom did not want to move.

Most large-scale dams are planned in tropical countries and would entail the

A picture postcard view in Spain of the Riaño reservoir in the thin light of early morning, with the outcrops of the Picos de Europa behind. The construction of the dam here for hydroelectric and irrigation purposes involved moving the old town of Riaño from the valley floor to a new site on the bare mountainside.

flooding of large areas of natural rainforest. Clearing these huge forests before flooding the reservoirs would make gigantic projects of this kind unprofitable, and the forest is simply left to rot under water. The gases emitted from rotting reservoirs like this – in particular, methane – contribute much more to the greenhouse effect than the emissions of a coal or oil-fired power station producing a similar amount of electricity. Hydroelectric power's reputation as a source of energy which does not contribute to global warming is certainly not justified in the case of rainforest dams.

Who Gains?

Large dams are extremely expensive to build. The amounts borrowed by Brazil on the international capital markets between 1973 and 1983 – over US $30 billion dollars – add up to to one quarter of the country's crippling foreign debt. The alluring economic benefits of extremely cheap energy that hydro power seemed to offer have largely failed to materialise, especially in developing countries. The grandiose schemes initiated by President Roosevelt in the 1930s for the Hoover Dam on the Colorado River and the Grand Coulee project on the Columbia were for a long time seen as models for economic development (namely, the industrialisation of California and Washington State) but countries like Brazil, Ghana and Mozambique have hardly benefited at all from their large-scale dams. Almost all of the borrowed capital is used to pay foreign construction companies, and to buy turbine technology and engineering know-how that are unavailable in the country concerned. Frequently the industries that benefit from the cheap electricity are also foreign and invest their profits abroad, with the result that little advantage accrues to the host country.

The aluminium industry plays a key role in all of this. Enormous amounts of electricity are required for the manufacture of raw aluminium from bauxite ore – around 15,000 kilowatt hours per kilogram of aluminium. The industry can compete with the iron and plastics industries only if it receives electricity at a preferential rate. Numerous large hydroelectric power projects are used primarily for the manufacture of

aluminium, and some are built solely for this purpose. Ghana's Akosombo Dam is one of the most striking examples of this: in a country blessed with countless natural advantages including rich mineral deposits, what was originally intended to mark the beginning of comprehensive industrialisation became a classic economic disaster. The US aluminium company, Kaiser, negotiated a deal which guaranteed it half the total supply of electricity produced until 1997 at one twentieth of the world market price. Ghana's bauxite deposits remain unused because Kaiser prefers to import it from Jamaica. The fertile Volta Valley has been lost beneath Africa's largest artificial lake, and no money is available to implement new irrigation projects. After almost thirty years, Ghana has profited so little from the dam that it is not even able to repay the loans taken out to build it.

Many dams have proved to be much shorter-lived producers of electricity than had been hoped for by their operators. Particularly in mountainous regions and in other areas subject to erosion, rivers carry enormous amounts of sediment, which are trapped by dams and gradually accumulate in the reservoirs behind them. Numerous hydroelectric power stations are out of operation because their reservoirs are choked with silt. Little can be done to save a large dam once its reservoir in this condition.

The enormous costs of large-scale hydroelectric power schemes and the fact that economic success is far from guaranteed have led many international development banks to withdraw their support for such projects. In April 1993, for example, the World Bank withdrew a $170 million loan for the Sardar Sarovar Dam on the sacred Narmada River in India; the American government's Bureau of Reclamation, which has always been obsessed with hydroelectric power, like Canada, withdrew from the Chinese Three Gorges Dam in 1993, and subsequently doubt has even been cast on World Bank involvement in the project.

Advocates of large dams are becoming increasingly rare; the hard core of support that remains emanates almost exclusively from vested interests. Discussions have been taking place in Zambia about whether to construct a further large dam – the Batoka Dam – on the Zambezi. While a broad

raft of opinion has rejected the Batoka Dam as unnecessary and damaging to the environment, its champions – headed by the state electricity company and the powerful mining lobby – shake their heads and predict a national energy crisis. In fact, Zambia uses less than twenty per cent of the electricity it already produces: twelve per cent is exported to Zimbabwe, and 70 per cent is consumed by a single company, Zambia Consolidated Copper Mines. It is quite obvious that the new dam would not benefit the country's people, but only the energy-hungry mining industry. (See also p. 129.)

Squandered Energy

Large-scale development of hydro power is always justified in terms of demand for more energy, usually on the basis of forecasts made by interested parties such as electricity boards or oil companies. Yet when the energy industry is contemplating new projects, no account is taken of possible energy-saving strategies that could be adopted by both producers and users. There is no longer any significant potential for expansion of the market for energy in the industrialised world. The cheapest way forward is efficient use of energy. Economists have coined the expression 'negawatt' to express the idea that electricity saved – through the use of energy-saving lightbulbs, heat insulation or more efficient electrical appliances – is electricity gained for another use. Making available 500 megawatts by saving power is obviously cheaper than building a brand new power station to generate the same amount. This negawatt potential should be exploited to the full before any further expansion of power station capacity is contemplated. In the United States in the 1980s, seven times more energy was provided by saving electricity than by constructing new power stations.

First the world should find out how little energy it can manage with. Only then does it make sense to generate more. New energy provisions must threaten neither local nor global ecological systems. This is not a utopian ambition: the target must be to base total energy supply on renewable resources, primarily the exploitation of solar energy. Energy use in most countries is still highly inefficient and unecological with

Solar Energy – The Cure-All?

Unlimited energy is still the ultimate goal of most development planners. One of the possibilities under consideration is the use of vast solar farms to convert sunlight into electricity, in other words, using the sun as a gigantic socket to plug the planet into. Hopes are again being raised (by the very experts who regularly predict ever-increasing energy demands) of a new, cheap and, better still, never-ending source of energy. Other scientists, however, believe that the discovery of an inexhaustible source of energy, no matter how environmentally sound, would mean that humanity could face problems it has never even imagined.

To date, or so their line of argument runs, the sun has determined what happens on earth: when its rays meet the earth's surface they set in motion life-giving biological and meteorological processes and create the extraordinarily complex ecosystems that thrive on the planet, starting with the plants that use its light to convert carbon dioxide and water into energy-rich substances such as sugar and starch by photosynthesis. While sunlight supports a vast global network of constructive processes (or syntropy), the sum total of human activity, on the other hand, inevitably has destructive effects. Radical though this assertion may seem, it has a sound physical basis in the Second Law of Thermodynamics. No matter how environ-

mentally friendly the method of production, any increase in the availability of energy to humanity runs the risk of allowing the human population of the planet to achieve such levels of activity and therefore destruction that we could undermine the very structures and processes that allow life to exist on earth.

This may sound like the apocalyptic vision of a mad scientist, but some people believe that there is already evidence of it happening. The greater the amount of energy available in a particular place, the higher the piles of refuse, the larger the number of cars and trains, the more the countryside is under attack or sealed up – in other words, the greater the 'side effects' of civilisation. Our technological opportunities have multiplied through the tapping of new sources of energy, far outstripping our control of the consequences. It is probably no coincidence that the Brazilian industrial city of Cubatão, with its virtually unlimited supplies of hydroelectric power, has become a symbol of ecological destruction. Cubatão is a wrecked, poisoned patch of earth, the victim of human exploitation with no holds barred.

All efforts to clean up the industrial city of Cubatão in Brazil for the 1992 environmental summit in Rio de Janeiro were in vain. The whole region is saturated with the toxic residues and by-products of the chemical, fertiliser and aluminium industries attracted by cheap hydropower.

a high reliance placed on electricity to generate heat, which is environmentally damaging, wasteful and costly. Around two-thirds of domestic energy requirements are for warmth – for space and water heating and cooking. The technology already exists to satisfy a large proportion of this demand with solar heating. Electricity should be used only for functions for which it is indispensable, such as lighting, machine operation and refrigeration. The key to energy-saving is to use the right energy for the right purpose. Running an electric shower for three minutes, for example, uses up as much electricity as it takes to light a room uninterruptedly for three days. If the whole gamut of energy-saving strategies were incorporated into a newly built house (including energy-efficient light bulbs and appliances, insulation and shading instead of air-conditioning), average

consumption could easily be halved.

Using more energy than necessary clearly makes no sense. Yet energy-wasting is the hallmark of modern industrial society. Manufacturing industry uses three or four times as much energy as domestic consumers. In other words, we consume most energy indirectly – in what we buy. Most domestic refuse (particularly packaging and disposable products) takes a lot of energy to manufacture, only to be turned into rubbish after generally brief usage. Every rubbish bin contains several kilowatt hours of wasted energy, and no recycling can bring them back.

Development concepts for poorer countries in Africa, Asia and Latin America are still based on this opulent Western model of waste. High energy consumption is still seen as a sign of progress and modernity. For almost all developing countries, the

aim is to double consumption within the next ten years. A major part of the forecast demand is to be covered by large-scale dam projects, even where the potential for tapping solar power is impressive. Brazil, for example, intends to invest another US$75 billion in dams by the year 2000.

The energy consumed by a typical household in the developed world is susceptible to a reduction of 50 per cent using existing technology. If the same potential were exploited to the full in poorer countries in the southern hemisphere, the desired improvement in living standards could be achieved without building numerous new power stations.

Governments in Africa and Latin America need to be extremely cautious in their choice of energy consultants: hydroelectric power experts believe that only five per cent of exploitable sites have yet been

Who owns the Iguassu Falls, and who has the right to exploit their hydrolectric power potential has been a matter of some controversy, as they lie on the borders of Brazil, Argentina and Paraguay. Brazil and Paraguay currently share the output of the largest hydroelectric power station on earth – the Itaipu Dam on the Rio Paraná, a few kilometres away from here – making Paraguay the largest exporter of electricity in the world.

used in Africa, and only eight per cent in Latin America – a seductive prospect for international construction groups, energy companies and industries that benefit from cheap electricity.

Water Power in the Future

The exploitation of water power – however reckless – is still generally regarded as clean and environmentally friendly. The German city of Hamburg, for example, plans to import 'clean' hydroelectric power from Norway or even Iceland via gigantic, long-distance cables, in order to be less dependent on nuclear power stations. Who would seriously wish to doubt that hydroelectric power is preferable to nuclear energy? So far public concern has been focused on how electricity is being produced, but not on what it is being used for.

Innovative energy-saving techniques and the direct use of solar energy will necessitate a re-evaluation of all energy sources, including hydroelectric power, as well as the use to which it is put. The assessment of how far water power should be used will vary from region to region: less recourse will be made to it in places with plenty of sunshine than in temperate or polar zones.

It seems likely that before long, the twentieth century's mass transformation of rivers into suppliers of electricity will be regarded as a huge and dreadful mistake. It is time to realise that flexing our muscles at nature to extract ever more energy is not going to work in the long term. The more intelligently we deploy energy, the lighter our touch on nature will be and the more rivers will be allowed to follow their natural course and enrich the areas through which they flow.

CHAPTER NINE

WATERWAYS

Rivers, lakes and oceans have offered the means to transport people and goods since humanity first discovered how to float craft on water. For centuries, boatmen with detailed knowledge of the watercourses on which they worked used their skill to take advantage of currents and winds and make it possible to travel and transport goods over distances that would have seemed unimaginable by any other means. Indeed, until the mid 19th century, water transport was far superior to any other means of transportation. Today there are still parts of the world where rivers and lakes are the most frequently used or even the only method of access to remote inland settlements or to sources of food or raw materials. But it is generally only in regions saturated in water, such as parts of Siberia, the Amazon and the delta of the Ganges and Brahmaputra rivers in Bangladesh, where it is physically impossible or prohibitively expensive to build roads or bridges that water transport still predominates.

For the most part, the barges that used to ply their trade on the rivers of the industrialised world have been pushed into the background, their role taken over by rail and road transport. In a world where urgency has become a way of life, barges and ships simply seem too slow. Nevertheless, inland waterways remain competitive for bulk transport of heavy materials such as coal and steel, grain and fertilisers, oil and certain bulk chemicals, of which millions of tonnes are still carried annually, because barges use far less fuel than trucks or trains.

Until the second half of the 20th century, most international trade (and domestic trade in areas where roads were poor or non-existent) took place by sea, and towns and cities on the coast or on rivers navigable from the sea were the main centres of economic and political importance. Regions remote from navigable rivers were opened up by the construction of man-made canals, and other canals were built to link rivers. Some canals had immense economic and strategic significance: heavy loads being transported from the French Mediterranean coast to Bordeaux on the Atlantic, a distance of only 200 kilometres by land, had to be sent on a lengthy sea journey around the Spanish coast and through the Straits of Gibraltar. It was a move by the Spanish to impose huge tolls on ships sailing within their waters that prompted the French king, Louis XIV, to have the 240-kilometre Canal du Midi built in 1670, linking the Mediterranean and the Atlantic. England's network of waterways – navigable rivers linked by canals – facilitated the industrial revolution of the late 18th century that gave Britain a considerable economic advantage over the rest of Europe. However, canals are not a modern European invention: one thousand years before the construction of the Canal du Midi, the Chinese Emperor, Yang Ti, had a 1300-kilometre canal built connecting the two largest rivers in his Empire, the Huang

Left. Building the Rhine/Main/Danube Canal in Bavaria involved encasing a whole river – the picturesque Altmühl – in a concrete channel. Along its entire 171-kilometre length, including the area around the medieval town of Berching in the picture, the groundwater level sank by several metres, destroying all the wetlands in the vicinity.

Opposite page. The Elbe, which for 40 years marked the border between East and West Germany, is one of the few major rivers in Europe to have escaped large-scale embankment and channelling. Groynes, like these at Hitzacker, Lower Saxony, are designed to strengthen the current in the middle of the river, thereby deepening the navigable channel as well as protecting the river banks from erosion.

Ho and the Yangtze. Today, the Grand Canal extends some 1800 kilometres, making it the world's longest.

In the early 19th century, rivers, lakes and canals were still the only viable routes for inland transportation in most areas, though long journeys by road or track from one system of waterways to another – over the Alps or the Pyrenees, for example – could be extremely arduous, or, in severe weather conditions, impossible. The introduction of the steam engine, followed by the combustion engine, heralded a new era in inland shipping. It solved a long-standing problem of transportation – the lack of hauling power – and unleashed a huge increase in the movement of goods around the industrialised world. The ambition to carry larger loads faster meant that the old canals were soon judged to be far too small, and rivers too meandering,

shallow and variable in depth to accommodate the new heavier traffic. Removing these obstacles became one of the guiding imperatives of European and American economic policy – expansion and improvement of inland waterways was seen as the key to progress.

By the early 20th century, Europe was criss-crossed by a tight network of canals and rivers, most of them straightened and equipped with weirs to guarantee a minimum depth for larger boats. Perhaps the most striking example of the effect water transport could have in the heyday of industrialisation was New York. When in 1823, the city was directly connected to Lake Erie, and therefore the resources around it, by the construction of the 580-kilometre Erie Canal from Albany on the Hudson River to Buffalo, freight prices between Buffalo and New York dropped by

85 per cent, from $120 to $14 per tonne. This gave New York a big advantage over cities such as Boston and Philadelphia as a terminal for international trade and established it as an important metropolis. The construction of the St Lawrence Seaway over a century later had a similarly striking effect, providing a navigable watercourse for ocean-going ships from the Great Lakes to the Atlantic, and facilitating the export of iron ore, wheat and coal from Canada and the United States.

The canal networks of countries such as Britain, France, the Netherlands and Germany took several centuries to develop, but in the 1930s, Josef Stalin decided that the young Soviet Union had to be equipped with a modern water transport system in the space of a few years. Overseen by Stalin's notorious political police agency, the GPU, a canal system was built linking the White

Sea in the north to the Baltic, the Black Sea and the Caspian Sea, involving, among other things, the conversion of the Volga and Dnepr rivers into a chain of navigable reservoirs. Countless thousands of political prisoners and prisoners of war perished in the process. 200,000 people are thought to have lost their lives during the building of one part of the new transport system alone – the 700-kilometre White Sea Canal.

For the engineers planning and working on large-scale canalising projects all over the world, the task seemed ambitious but straightforward – a good technological challenge. Existing waterways simply had to be brought up to standard – in terms of depth, flow and straightness – so that they could serve as efficient water highways. The prospect of dyking up, damming and straightening rivers was all too enticing: not only were transport capacity and speed increased, there were also the attractions of two other major aids to economic growth – land acquisition and cheap electricity. Thousands of hectares of former flood areas were drained, and then newly settled or ploughed for farming. Weirs were installed to regulate the river's depth and remove seasonal variability; some were also equipped with turbines to provide hydroelectric power.

The Taming of the Rivers

Waterways in Europe's heavily industrialised landscapes look very different from natural rivers. A river that has been left to its own devices does not usually flow in a straight line along a single course, but branches off from time to time, forming smaller channels separated by islets and sandbanks. It chooses its path where the geology of the land offers least resistance. Rivers carry immense amounts of mineral and organic sediment, some of which is deposited along calm stretches, and then caught up again at high water and carried further downstream. New courses are continually drawn across the land, creating rich and varied ecosystems. The river forms a broad corridor of biological diversity within the landscape. The groundwater lying beneath the river's floodplain is an integral part of this system. If the landscape is undisturbed by human intervention, the

river, when it is full, constantly replenishes the groundwater beneath it; in periods of drought, when the river is low, the groundwater will, in its turn, help to feed the river.

Anything that is done to change the physical features in and around a river will upset this balance. Straightening a river may seem to the casual observer to be simply a matter of removing obstacles, but it will react to the removal of its bends by flowing faster down the now steeper gradient. Suddenly, far from being sustained and enriched by the river, its banks start to be eroded. This prompts engineers to shore them up with rocks or concrete, which in turn means that all the water's energy is now directed at the river bed, cutting it deeper and deeper and washing away the natural accumulation of sediment. As the volume of water remains pretty much the same, but the channel is now deeper, the level of the river falls in relation to the land around it. This causes the groundwater level to drop, leaving plants and trees on the riverbank high and dry.

When the water level of a river is raised to make it suitable for shipping, weirs are constructed, which slow the current to a virtual standstill, creating large pools that look more like elongated lakes than rivers. Downstream of a weir, which is usually several metres high, the river finds itself unnaturally accelerated again and free of sediment, and may dig its way down with great force. Experience has shown that vertical erosion of the river bed can occur at the rate of up to two metres a year over a 20-kilometre stretch. This effect can be prevented only by constructing another weir further downstream. On the Upper Rhine in southern Germany, for instance, more and more new weirs have become necessary. There are already ten, and it looks as though an eleventh will be inevitable if further erosion of the river bed is to be prevented.

For a variety of reasons, the construction of weirs quickly leads to a drastic impoverishment of a river's ecology. As the river's level no longer varies between high and low water and shallows have been destroyed, many river dwellers disappear for want of a suitable habitat; other species lose their feeding and breeding places, especially those dependent on particular,

seasonal conditions. In addition, the low oxygen level of the river (caused by reduced flow which in turn means less air mixing with the water), makes it impossible for most species of fish to survive, particularly in summer.

In some places, where the authorities are aware that fish migration routes have been interrupted, fish ladders have been installed; this may work for salmon, but smaller species are often incapable of climbing them. In fact, weirs have been held directly responsible for the extinction of all so-called anadromous fish in the vast majority of Europe's rivers. Anadromous fish, which include the Atlantic salmon, the sea trout, the allis shad, the lampern and the sturgeon, start their lives in rivers, migrate to the ocean when young, then return to the same rivers to spawn. For crayfish, too, weirs usually present insurmountable obstacles; even if they manage to climb them, they then end up in the thick carpet of mud and sediment on the upstream side of the weir and are trapped. Inevitably, rivers engineered for shipping compromise the whole ecology that would naturally thrive around them, becoming sterile waterways where wildlife is at best hugely reduced, and at worst entirely absent.

Boats for Rivers or Rivers for Boats?

A small number of navigable river courses in industrialised countries have remained relatively intact, but even they are not safe from development. German and Czech business associations, for example, want to canalise the River Elbe, one of the few large rivers in Europe that is not yet fully controlled. One of their aims is to make the river navigable for large craft on an average 340 days per year, rather than the 240 to which they claim to be limited at present. The European Union is planning to spend billions subsidising the expansion of waterways, claiming that ship transportation is ecologically sound. As boats and barges emit less carbon dioxide per tonne of goods than road or rail vehicles, so the argument goes, it is possible that they could help to cut down the deleterious

Moving bamboo and straw up-river near Dhaka. Bangladesh is a country with no cross-country main roads or railway lines; building bridges over the huge, powerful Jamuna and Brahmaputra rivers, even given the most up-to-date technology, is not practicable. Almost all transportation happens by water. Making use of the wind and the flow and currents of natural rivers involves skills that can only be learned over many years. Often this kind of knowledge is passed from one generation to the next.

Morning rush hour on the Perfume River at
Hué in Vietnam.

effect of carbon emissions on the world's atmosphere. But it appears that nobody has considered the hugely damaging effects that will be caused by further transformation of rivers into water highways in the absence of any coherent strategy for their protection.

Most people realise that transportation cannot continue to grow at the rate it has done over the last few decades – expansion of the transport infrastructure is no longer the guarantee of economic growth that it was 50 years ago. In Europe and North America, there is less and less heavy and manufacturing industry – the big users of transport – and more emphasis on services and high-technology products such as electronic goods. Even the monumental St Lawrence Seaway has not been able to curb the decline of heavy industry along the shores of the Great Lakes over the past decade. Any economic policy that is based on endless construction of new transportation routes is caught in a time warp – what worked in the 19th century will most certainly not work now.

As reuse and recycling of materials become more widespread, (decreasing the need for importation of large quantities of raw materials), transport volume will drop still further. And finally, as governments are forced to react to the reality of global warming, strategies will have to be adopted to curb pollution by reducing traffic. Today's transportation depends almost exclusively on fuel-intensive road, and to a lesser extent, rail vehicles. A substantial increase in fuel prices would make water transportation highly competitive.

Even then, contrary to the opinion of some planners, rivers would not necessarily have to be rebuilt. It is still possible to transport goods along shallow and windy rivers – this was, after all, how transportation was effected for hundreds of years. There is a long history of building boats to suit particular rivers (one example is the stern-wheelers of the Mississippi with their wide hulls and shallow draught) and of special skills employed by boatmen to negotiate variable conditions. At low water, for example, a vessel's draught can be reduced by the simple expedient of loading less cargo.

Boats should be customised for rivers, rather than rivers being customised for boats. Ecological river transport of this kind might well be a bit more expensive, and it would certainly rule out ambitions to render any given river navigable 365 days a year. It might be necessary, for example, to introduce the idea that transport costs would vary according to the season. Ultimately we have to decide whether nature is to continue to shoulder the whole burden of our transport policy, or whether we will share it. The ways in which water has been used for transport reflect what has happened in other areas of people's interaction with water. For most of human history, this usage was low-impact, causing very little environmental damage. There is no reason why this should not again be the case in the 21st century.

Public transport on Lake Victoria. Crowds waiting at Homa Bay in Kenya to board boats which offer the fastest and shortest – as well as the most relaxing – way of crossing the lake.

CHAPTER TEN

THE DEMANDS OF INDUSTRY

A scene unthinkable anywhere that industry has polluted a river: fishing among swathes of water crowfoot, an aquatic buttercup with white flowers, in the River Dee, Clwyd, Wales, with a party of mute swans in the background.

It has taken society only a hundred years to accustom itself to the presence of industrial outfalls and polluted rivers, and, after twenty years of protest, many environmentalists have come to regard them as a necessary evil. But it is crucial that fundamental questions be asked about the right of industry to continue to load rivers and lakes with waste, and, indeed, how much water needs to be used in industrial production in the first place.

Industry's uses of water are legion. Many things are soluble or can be suspended in water – salts, organic substances and even minerals such as metal ores. The materials used in industrial processes like chemical production, mining and metal refining often have to be in solution before they react with each other. Water is also an essential wetting agent in treatments like textile-dyeing and leather-staining. A large proportion of the water used in industry is for washing, cleaning and rinsing purposes to remove unwanted matter such as fats, salts and dust, usually with the help of soaps and detergents. Almost every product, whether metal or glass, paper or plastic, is cleaned with water at some stage in its manufacture. Unlike organic solvents, notably chlorine-containing chemicals such as chloroform or trichloroethane, water leaves no unwanted residues, making it one of the most important processing materials in the food industry.

Another important industrial water use is for heat transfer. In steel production, especially, huge amounts are used to cool the newly cast red-hot metal – anything up to 280,000 litres per tonne. In the chemical industry, water dissipates the heat produced by chemical reactions, and in oil refining it cools down distillation columns. Some industrial processes produce excess heat, and steam provides the means to dispose of it or recycle it. Figures for industrial water consumption often list cooling water separately; as it is not polluted, goes the argument, it cannot really be said to be consumed. But

Industrial Water Consumption in 1990				
	Total Industrial Consumption in thousand million cubic metres per annum	Industrial Consumption in litres per capita per day	Domestic Consumption in litres per capita per day	Percentage of total water consumption accounted for by industry
Argentina	5.0	522	261	18
Australia	0.36	72	2326	2
Austria	2.3	834	217	73
Bangladesh	0.2	6	17	1
Belgium*	7.7	2135	276	85
Brazil	6.0	99	250	17
Canada*	33.8	3840	528	80
Chile	0.8	223	267	5
China	32.2	89	76	7
Denmark*	0.4	214	238	27
France*	27.7	1376	319	69
Germany (former FRG)*	28.9	1281	183	70
Germany (former GDR)*	6.2	1015	209	68
India	15.2	67	50	4
Iraq*	2.1	627	376	5
Israel	0.1	61	196	5
Italy*	15.2	727	377	27
Japan*	35.6	834	430	33
Netherlands*	8.8	1710	140	61
New Zealand	0.12	104	478	10
Norway	1.4	965	268	72
South Korea	1.5	114	90	14
Spain*	11.8	836	386	26
Sweden*	2.2	722	472	55
Switzerland*	2.3	1004	316	73
Turkey	3.0	165	208	19
United Kingdom*	21.8	1070	278	77
USA*	214.8	2725	711	46
USSR (former)	102.4	1057	219	29
Worldwide	745.2	416	145	23

*includes cooling water for industry, which may or may not take account of cooling water for power plants. The figures above, which are extracted from government statistics, normally exclude water used in mining and always exclude water used for hydropower.

even if the water does not come into direct contact with the product being manufactured (as it does in the steel industry), it is still not necessarily free of chemicals after use. Insecticides and other poisonous chemicals are added to it to prevent the growth of algae and molluscs in cooling systems – a substantial problem for industry and power plants – and these end up in rivers, often without even passing through a treatment plant. Even unpolluted cooling water does not leave rivers unscathed, as it is much warmer than the river, causing thermal

pollution which has far-reaching effects on the ecosystem. The rise in temperature reduces the amount of dissolved oxygen in the water, affecting trout, for example, which can only live in a cool, well-aerated river. In some European rivers, thermal pollution has thrown river ecosystems so far out of balance that tropical species of snail are thriving, while native species have disappeared, especially near the outfalls of large power stations.

By far the biggest boon that water offers industry is the ability to dispose of waste

cheaply, easily and legally. Although historically water has been the preferred means of disposal for industrial waste, it is certainly not the only way. Waste-water discharge is therefore not a precondition for industrial activity – only relatively small quantities of water are necessary for actual production processes. But instead of removing the impurities from production water for recycling, most industries discharge it – and with it the bulk of their waste – after a single use. This practice requires a continuous flow of fresh water, and is largely responsible for industry's enormous consumption. Simply reclaiming and reusing the water used in production would cut consumption drastically and would ultimately allow the rivers (no longer burdened with industrial waste) to return to their natural state.

Water as a Location Factor

Almost every branch of industry takes for granted unlimited access to water supplies and resists any restriction of what it regards as a right. Water is regarded as a decisive location factor for industrial plants. The water-intensive chemical, paper, textile and steel industries have traditionally grown up along the banks of large rivers or the shores of lakes. The Volga and the Rhine, the Dnepr and the Rhône, the Mississippi and the Danube – all rivers carrying large volumes of water – have become focuses for industry. The Great Lakes in North America, the Caspian Sea and Lake Baikal in Russia, are prime locations for industrial planners searching for plentiful water resources.

The table on this page shows that 23 per cent of the water consumed worldwide is used by industry, whose share of national consumption is usually regarded as an index of industrialisation. In many developing countries, like Bangladesh, total water consumption by industry can be as low as one per cent, while the average for Europe is 54 per cent. Countries such as Israel, with limited water resources and strict legislation to conserve them, show that industry can operate successfully without having to use vast amounts of water. Israel's industrial water consumption – which works out at 61 litres per member of the population per day – stands as an impressive model for the rest of the world.

California has proved that it is almost always possible for industry to get by with substantially less water than it has become accustomed to using. When water began to run out on America's West Coast in the late 1980s after years of drought, industry had to face the real possibility of production grinding to a halt. With surprising promptness, manufacturers contrived to reduce water consumption by almost a fifth without any cuts whatsoever in production. How little effort has been made to date to employ even the simplest means of saving water is clear from the experience of an American sporting goods manufacturer in Massachusetts: placed under pressure by continuing drought, he hit upon the not particularly original idea of recycling the cooling water for his machinery. His water consumption dropped by 96 per cent within three years.

The secret of successes like this one lies in the simple recognition that, with care, water can be used more than once. Some water is essential for certain manufacturing processes – paper, for example, requires around 250 litres per kilogramme. This water is, however, not used up in production, apart from what is lost through evaporation and what remains in the paper as residual moisture. Used responsibly, the water in modern paper manufacture can be recycled more than twenty times.

This reduces net consumption to well below ten litres per kilogramme of paper, and some firms even manage with as little as 1.1 litres per kilogramme.

Up until the mid-'seventies, increased industrial water consumption in developed nations went hand in hand with growth in economic capacity. Since then, however, it has stabilised, despite a further upward trend in production. In 1989, for every cubic metre of water used, Japanese industry produced $77 worth of goods, as compared to $21 worth in 1965. This was due not to ecological awareness on the part of Japanese managers, but to the introduction of hefty charges for each cubic metre of polluted waste water discharged into lakes or rivers. There is a long way to go before all possibilities for saving water are exhausted. Bulk consumers still pay little or nothing for the water they use, and it therefore plays a minor role in manufacturers'

Water-intensive Industries Figures for West Germany in millions of cubic metres (1987)		
	Annual Consumption	Amount taken from groundwater
Chemicals	4169	764
Iron and Steel	1163	119
Cellulose/Paper	673	115
Foodstuffs	426	208
Oil	291	53

cost accounting. On the whole industry assumes that anything it can get for nothing has no value, and so there is no need to conserve it.

In spite of the odd hopeful sign, all the indications are that in global terms industrial water consumption is set to expand enormously. Wherever large-scale industrial development is planned, unlimited water acquisition becomes a main priority. According to UN forecasts, the volume of water used for industry and mining will increase from around 745 billion cubic metres in the early 1990s to 1200 billion cubic metres by the year 2000.

What Uses Most Water?

It is well-nigh impossible for the ecologically aware consumer to work out which products use most water in their manufacture and so to make informed judgements

Cement plant on the Cuyahoga River in Ohio, United States; in the background is a steel works. In the 20th century there has been an explosive increase in industrial activity all over the world, with ever more water being used and bigger and bigger expanses of riverbanks and lakesides being colonised by industrial plants.

Two Centuries of Industrial Abuse

A mere 250 years ago, the River Mersey and its estuary were abundantly stocked fishing grounds. But since British industry first began to boom in the late 18th century, Merseyside, often considered the cradle of European industrialisation, has been a byword for industrial pollution, providing shaming evidence of one of modern society's worst habits: the abuse of rivers as cheap disposal systems for production waste, conduits to the dumping grounds where it will be least visible: the sea. By the mid 1980s, and probably well before that, the Mersey was judged to be to all intents and purposes biologically dead.

The British government, stung by pressure from environmental groups and galvanised into action by mounting public concern, initiated the Mersey Basin Clean-up Campaign, heralding it as a ground-breaking step in undoing industrial damage to the environment. Sadly, any hopes that this might prove to be more than a cosmetic exercise have long since been dashed.

120 manufacturers empty their waste water either directly or via sewers into the Mersey estuary, and hundreds more dump waste into the river's tributaries. Far from putting an end to dumping, the government has merely encouraged industry to dump waste differently. To save companies the expense of investing in costly treatment plants or new production systems, they have been invited instead to divert their waste water from the rivers and into municipal sewers. Some enlargement and re-equipping of municipal treatment plants has been carried out – paid for by a combination of domestic consumers and a £4 billion grant spread over 25-years provided partly by the British government but principally by the European Union. The fact remains that the treatment plants were designed to cope with domestic waste, and the majority of highly toxic residues from industrial waste evade treatment, and are still eventually discharged into the Mersey, albeit further downstream and through longer outfall pipes. Sewage sludge, now heavily contaminated with industrial chemicals, can no longer be used as fertiliser on the land and is dumped directly into the Irish Sea – a practice uniquely continued by Britain and scandalously condoned by the North Sea Conference (which represents governments around the North Sea and rules on environmental issues).

A few fish have now returned to the Mersey, but this is little cause for comfort. The annual discharge of heavy metals and persistent chemicals into the Irish Sea has continued unabated, although the outfalls are less visible. Five years ago, research showed that grey seals were suffering reproductive failure as a direct result of industrial pollutants. Record levels of toxic substances originating in industry continue to be found in fish and seals. Everyday practice in industrial plants remains unchanged. Even those which publicly support the clean-up campaign still have no idea of the total amounts of chemicals discharged by them because there is no legally binding duty to carry out environmental waste audits or to adopt genuinely clean production methods. No moves are being made either to install waste-water-free production, known in the jargon as 'zero discharge', or even to avoid the use of substances known to be persistent and harmful to the environment. One can only ask how long industry will be permitted to benefit from this cynical 'environmental' policy. It would be welcome news indeed if the government could one day reverse its urgent advice to fishermen that they eat nothing they catch in the waters of the Mersey.

Stream polluted with chemicals pouring into the Mersey.

about which to buy. How, for example, do you begin to calculate the amount of water used in making a car? Do you count mining of the ore, or the steel production? Or the refining of raw materials for the plastic parts? Or the manufacture of the paints? For a middle-of-the-range car made in Germany, the production of the steel and aluminium alone takes 78,000 litres of water, without allowing for the extraction of raw materials or other stages in manufacture that are extremely water-intensive but virtually impossible to quantify.

It is not even possible to produce reliable figures for the water consumption involved in the production of a frozen chicken. In an American slaughterhouse, processing

Minimum Water Consumption in the Production of Selected Products	
Frozen chicken	26 litres
One litre of beer	2.2- 10 litres
Car	78,000 litres
One tonne of steel	14,000-280,000 litres
Paper (with water recycling)	1.1 litres per kilo
Paper (no water recycling)	250 litres per kilo
One tonne of cement	160-2,000 litres

alone uses up an average of 26 litres per broiler, a figure that does not allow for the irrigation water used in growing the chicken feed, the rinsing out of chicken pens, or the water used by refineries to produce the petrol required to transport the

Cooling water combining with iron-oxide discharge into a river next to a steelworks at Aviles in Spain, while steam (and with it entirely unused energy) is puffed uselessly into the atmosphere. If both water and steam were recycled, the environment and the company's bank balance would both benefit.

chickens. In 1989, the water consumption of American slaughterhouses processing five billion chickens amounted to 132 billion litres, equivalent to the annual water requirements of a European city of two million inhabitants.

Controlled Pollution?

The greater part of water used by industry – on average 86 per cent – returns to the water cycle polluted. This waste water is full of by-products, materials used in processing, rinsed-out dirt, detergents and anything else industry wishes to dispose of or does not consider worth reusing. In many cases, the waste water passes through a treatment plant where a proportion of the harmful substances are removed with the aid of sophisticated technology. In the 1960s and 1970s, following the sudden catastrophic deaths of fish and the appearance of huge quantities of foam in Europe's rivers, governments lit upon the treatment of waste water as a miracle cure, making it the cornerstone of their environmental policy, and threw money at it. The foam disappeared, some of the fish returned; the plan seemed to be succeeding.

The money spent on industrial waste water treatment along the Rhine, which acts as a drain to the North Sea from Switzerland, Germany, France and finally the Netherlands, must exceed the expenditure on any other river in the world. And yet it is filthy. Every day, it carries 35,000 tonnes of salts and several thousand tonnes of non bio-degradable and persistent chemicals across the German border into Holland. When drinking water is produced from the Rhine for the 20 million or so people who depend on it, the rich brew taken from the river, containing water that has already passed through the treatment plants of the paper, chemical, textile and metal industries, must then be put through as many as eighteen further processes. The polluters, however, refuse to improve their waste-water treatment, claiming that it would be technically impossible and financially prohibitive to do so.

Treatment plant of chemical works in Litvinov, the Czech Republic. The treatment and recycling of industrial waste water is a hopeless undertaking if chemicals resulting from different processes are mixed together. Waste water can be reused only if it contains substances that can be easily extracted from it.

The production methods of the industrialised nations have so far been adopted generally without question by developing countries, often because the necessary capital derives from multi-nationals. Waste is simply got rid of by the back door. Lakes with no drainage are particularly vulnerable – Lake Magadi, a natural soda lake in Kenya, has been brought to the point of ecological collapse.

important nursery for many Atlantic fish. Heavy metals, nutrients and organic chlorine compounds are some of the substances contributing to disastrous changes in the North Sea. The scale of the problems in rivers like the Rhine is now so striking that more and more scientists, politicians and ordinary citizens are questioning standard industrial practice and, more importantly, the legal right to pollute rivers and seas.

Quite how absurd today's production systems really are can be seen in places where industry has ruined the very water on which it depends. A number of rivers are so polluted with industrial effluent that their water cannot be treated to a sufficient standard for use in production. In the Donbass region of the Ukraine, steel and chemical factories have to obtain water via a canal from the Dnepr River some 263 kilometres away because they have turned the Siverskij Donets River, which flows by them, into a dark stream of black gunge. For similar reasons, large chemical factories on the Rhine opted a long time ago to use groundwater: BASF, the chemical multi-national, for example, pumps it up from 180 metres beneath the surface at Ludwigshafen in Germany.

Despite this idiocy, industrial planners seem wedded to their conviction that water is just a cheap, all-purpose material for disposing of waste. This attitude has long been passed on to so-called emerging economies, that is, nations with economic growth rates high enough to worry Europeans and Americans. The price that these countries are paying for their rapid economic success is, however, much higher than that paid by First World countries. What seems at first glance to mirror the industrialisation of Europe 100 years ago is by comparison a nightmarish scenario. Today's production processes and the waste they generate are far more damaging than those of a century ago, and the volume of production is many times larger. Emergent nations are also victims of the dubious practice of some Western multinationals which move high-risk production such as that of pesticides and plastics away from the environmentally conscious northern countries into parts of the world where people are less aware of the dire implications of the production processes involved.

If we continue to depend exclusively on end-of-the-pipe clean-up technology, the water in the Rhine will remain undrinkable and the North Sea will continue to be a dumping ground. Fortunately, some of the river's poisonous cargo settles in Rotterdam's harbour basin, from which, each year, ten million cubic metres of it are dredged up and transported to the Slufter, a man-made island of poisonous waste. But most of it ends up in the sensitive ecosystem of the shallow North Sea – an

The Chlorine Problem

Chlorine is one of the most commonly used industrial chemicals and is produced in vast quantities. It is relatively cheap to produce, and since the 1930s has been used in a vast and ever-increasing range of products, among them solvents, pesticides, wood preservatives, plastics and paints. 40 million tonnes of chlorine a year are used in industry worldwide.

Chlorine may be cheap, but the true, long-term cost of its widespread use is colossal. Organic chlorine compounds do not occur naturally, and the metabolic systems of plants, animals and even bacteria are poorly equipped to deal with them; they are broken down only very slowly, if at all – in other words, they are not biodegradable. Chlorinated hydrocarbons are now turning up in even the most remote parts of the globe – traces have been found in the far icy landscapes of Antarctica, in glaciers, and in rain and groundwater across the world. Chlorinated hydrocarbons are among the most toxic chemicals both for human health and for the natural environment; many of them are now known to be carcinogenic or to trigger genetic mutation. One of their most dangerous characteristics is their persistence – we cannot hope for them to be diluted or to disappear; they are retained in biological systems, accumulating slowly but surely in the food chain, including humans, resisting all attempts to dispose of them.

Rivers in industrialised nations carry enormous loads of chlorine-based organic chemicals. It has been estimated that the waste water discharged by major chemical companies contains in excess of 100,000 different substances, whose chemical structure and toxicity are usually unknown, and a large proportion of them are chlorine-based. Once they enter the lakes, rivers and groundwater, not to mention the oceans into which the water ultimately drains, these chemicals become extremely difficult to detect or to analyse. Only substances which do not readily dissolve in water and are thus susceptible to being extracted from it with activated carbon, can be examined. It is into this class of products that most chlorinated hydrocarbons fall and to which almost all the names associated with environmental scandals belong – Lindane, DDT, PCBs and dioxins. But huge numbers of chemicals remain unaccounted for.

Environmental policies, and particularly the rules and regulations that should underpin them, can be formulated only around the small group of chemicals that can be extracted with activated carbon – it is hard to draw anyone's attention to something that cannot be identified. Whenever pressure has been applied to the chemical industry to deal with the chlorine compounds in its waste water, it has reacted by installing activated carbon filters; these remove only the chemicals that will show up in tests, a perfect way of demonstrating the industry's new 'clean' policies and of extracting maximum good publicity in the process. What is missing is any attempt to tackle the root cause of the problem, the heavy reliance that continues to be placed on chlorine in chemical production as a whole. The industry's image benefits, but there is little overall improvement in the state of its waste water.

Thousands and thousands of chemicals, many of them containing chlorine and some of them highly toxic, continue to enter our rivers and oceans with no possibility of being detected in an environmental laboratory. If the chemical industry were compelled to recycle its used water and to stop discharging into the world's waterways, this highly controversial waste would begin to pile up on land, and it would become only too obvious why the industry has been making it disappear into the rivers. And if chemical companies had to confront their own toxic production waste rather than always sending it somewhere else, they might be more likely to concede that harmless substitutes have to be found for the chemicals on which they currently base their business. Chemical production must be modified so that both its waste and the products themselves are biodegradable and can be harmlessly absorbed into the planet's natural cycles.

Greenpeace activist blocking the outflow of ICI Hillhouse into the River Wyre at Fleetwood in the north west of England in September 1992.

The Mining Industry

In mining, water is used principally to separate ore from rock and to wash away the spoil (rubble, stones and earth). Worldwide, more debris is washed into rivers from mining enterprises each year than from the natural process of erosion. Large quantities are also used as a solvent for the chemicals that release precious metals from ore. Polluted with metal residues and the chemicals used to aid extraction – such as the highly toxic cyanides – the water is then fed back into rivers.

Acute problems of this kind have occurred since people first learned how to extract metal from rock. In Ancient Greece and Rome entire mountain ranges were hollowed out, waters polluted and rivers diverted into mines in the search for mineral resources. In north-western Spain, remains are still visible at Las Medulas of Roman aqueducts that were up to 50 kilometres long, and enabled the daily transportation of 34 million litres of water for the exclusive use of the gold mines there. Entire regions were deforested to obtain the charcoal required for working the ores. The Isle of Elba was already stripped of trees in the time of the Emperor Augustus (63 BC-AD 14), and the rich deposits of iron ore on the island had to be shipped for processing to Populonia on the Italian mainland, near the present-day town of Piombino.

From the moment that it became possible to pursue mining by mechanical means, the assault on nature began to escalate. In the past, most underground mineral extraction had been carried out by hand. Since the 1920s ever more powerful machines have been introduced to remove the rock overlying mineral deposits. As the deposits dwindle, more and more rock has to be removed and is likely to be dumped in rivers for less and less mineral return. Today, 1,000 tonnes have to be excavated to produce a single tonne of copper.

Waste-water-free

Water cannot be limitlessly exploited. Every region has a maximum level for sustainable water extraction determined by rainfall, hydrology and climate. This amount has to be shared by all users – be they domestic, agricultural, mining or industrial. If it were taken as read that water management had to work within these limits, the true price of water would suddenly become very clear, and industry's profligacy would be exposed for the utterly unacceptable practice that it is. Simple, basic rules are being ignored: in most industrial regions, water in the environment is consistently overexploited. Rivers, lakes and oceans are under attack, year in, year out, from tens of thousands of tonnes of industrial waste. Even the ancient, fundamental principle of

drinking water always taking priority is being ignored. It is common for industry to make prodigious use of pristine groundwater, while the general population has to drink treated river water.

Environmental policies limited to wastewater treatment are never going to solve these problems. Implemented at enormous financial cost, they mainly shift the problem to dumps and incinerators. Rivers and seas do not really benefit either, as the really tough chemicals resist any treatment. Water companies and authorities supplying drinking water from rivers warn that not even the chemical structure of most of these substances is known, let alone their effects on humans. Cleansing drinking water of substances about which little or nothing is known is not an easy task.

Enlightened and ecologically tenable industrial policy would prescribe a number of radical changes. Waste water would no longer leave the factory site but would be treated and then reused in the production cycle. There are now growing numbers of industrial concerns across the world which manage to operate successfully without any waste water. The paper manufacturing industry leads the way in this respect, but the metal and textile industries are also gaining ground. What usually triggers the development of manufacturing processes which

do not discharge waste water is recognition of the ecological impact on the rivers and lakes into which waste has been allowed to flow (see p.150.)

Waste-water-free does not, of course, mean water-free. But the water needs to be used in such a way that it can be returned to its original state after use in production. To achieve this, manufacturing processes have to be designed so that whatever ends up in the water is biologically degradable, and any residues are not just dumped, but are dealt with in an environmentally suitable way. In the chemical industry, there are the beginnings of a move away from raw materials derived from oil (which tend to be highly persistent) and towards the use of biodegradable plant products.

Dumping on Land

The threat posed to groundwater by the dumped left-overs of industrial production is often underestimated. 250 million tonnes of solid industrial waste are produced every year in the European Union. Most of it is deposited in landfill sites, and almost five times that amount of rubble and excavated material ends up on spoil heaps. Waste water treatment plants have added to the piles of solid industrial waste. Part of what was once carried away by rivers now

Both workers and the natural environment sustain injury from the mining of raw materials. In the ironically named Bom Futuro (Good Future) mine in Brazil, 2,500 garimpeiros, or prospectors, mine tin ore; 80 per cent of them have malaria. The devastation of the land is only too evident.

accumulates as sludge, which is either dumped or incinerated (together with other waste). Incinerator waste and the dust filtered out of incinerator chimneys are then taken to dumps where, despite all the safety measures in place, they continue to pose long-term risks to groundwater.

In its search for ways and means of disposing of solid waste, manufacturing industry has frequently been given a helping hand by the mining and oil industries, which have made available redundant workings. Abandoned oil and gas boreholes and salt mines are all highly sought after for waste-dumping, and huge sums of money change hands in their acquisition. In the United States, there are 181 projects in which around 40 million tonnes of chemical waste and other toxic substances a year are disposed of by deep well injection – pumped down far below the earth, in the hope that they will never be seen again. When they will enter the groundwater is anyone's guess: in 40 years of deep-well injection in the USA, 39 cases of toxic substances penetrating the groundwater have been recorded. All of the deep wells concerned had been assessed by scientists as being safe for at least another 10,000 years. But nobody has precise knowledge of geological structures so far underground.

In former East Germany, several decades of intense mining and chemical industry have left the soil saturated with chemical solvents and waste, and the groundwater under large tracts of land is in great danger, if it has not already been affected. Privatisation of industrial complexes has stalled, because no-one is prepared to assume liability for contaminated soil or groundwater. Other countries are in exactly the same position: in the Netherlands, official sources estimate that the soil is polluted on over 280,000 industrial sites.

A Better Future

Waste-water-free industry would mean not just that rivers and seas would be kept free of harmful industrial substances, but also that vast amounts of water would be saved through recycling. An industrial strategy of this kind would benefit not only regions with a shortage of water; in temperate zones, too, where there is plenty of rain,

As well as making use of waste-water lagoons like this one at Runcorn, the British chemical concern ICI has gained access to abandoned brine cavities (or salt mines) near Northwich in Cheshire into which it dumps 35,000 tonnes of highly toxic chlorine-based chemicals every year.

ecosystems profit from every drop of water that is left in the natural environment.

Advance planning is essential: industry must be given clear-cut, quantifiable outlines of the objectives that society wishes it to aim for, so that it has an opportunity to develop the requisite products and technologies. Avoidance of waste-water discharge should become mandatory in the manufacture of goods worldwide. The amounts of water required to produce a microchip or a tonne of paper are the same everywhere. If the best processes so far developed were to become the norm for every production line in the world – free of waste water and conserving raw materials and energy – it would remove the advantage enjoyed by countries which today owe their competitive edge to lax environmental legislation. Eco-dumping, however, currently brings in big profits for a great many powerful companies. Any attempts to have ecological outline conditions included in world trade agreements such as GATT (General Agreement on Tariffs and Trade) have so far been roundly rejected and successfully blocked by industrial lobbies.

It is sometimes said that poor countries simply cannot afford waste-water treatment. But in fact, waste-water-free and thus water-saving industrial manufacture may in the end prove to be a money-saving strategy. For many developing nations, a waste-water-free policy is in any case essential because their urban populations are utterly dependent on rivers as their sole source of drinking water, and purifying river water for human consumption after it has been polluted by industrial waste is way beyond their financial and technological means.

The world may just have time to change its habits and stop dumping waste in rivers, lakes and seas, even though doing so has been regarded as normal for the last century. Waste-water-free production is now viable; it is an option to which there is no defensible alternative.

Outfalls like those in Bitterfeld in former East Germany (top) and Yorkshire, England (right) must become a thing of the past. Industry has to be persuaded to revamp its production technology, so that it can reuse its waste water rather than dumping it.

CHAPTER ELEVEN

OVEREXPLOITATION & NEGLECT

This book has so far revealed how all major uses of water – be they agricultural, industrial or domestic – must be re-examined and changed if their negative impact on the planet's life-support systems is to be checked. A crucial key to good water use, however, must also lie in the development of a sense of mutual responsibility among those competing for the same, limited resources. The pattern of use typical of the industrialised world derives from an assumption on the part of all consumers, be they individual householders or multi-national companies, that they have an unlimited 'right' to use as much water as they please, regardless of anyone else's interests.

In this and the next chapter, a series of examples drawn from across the world shows, on one hand, the disastrous consequences of failure to address the complex issues surrounding rival claims to water, and on the other the glimmers of hope where courageous attempts have been made to respond to ecological crises or to preempt them. These are, of course, merely a sample of the countless struggles over water that can be identified almost anywhere on the globe. The example of Botswana, the last stop on this whistle-stop tour and one of the world's poorest countries, provides the exceptionally optimistic precedent of a government adopting a strategy of coordinated water management. It is to be hoped that many more countries will follow Botswana's lead.

SOUTHERN AFRICA
Storm Clouds over the Zambezi

Most large rivers flow through more than one country, and governments have to come to mutually acceptable arrangements for the distribution of their water. Elaborate water legislation is common at a national level, but binding international agreements are still the exception rather than the rule, in spite of the fact that for any country water is crucial to social or economic development. In most cases, the wealthiest riparian states (those through which a river passes) have long since secured more than their fair share of water, often leaving poorer or politically weaker seriously short of water.

Across the world, countless competing claims to water have been at the root of dangerous international disputes and many more have been smouldering for decades. A classic imbalance in water distribution and a correspondingly high potential for conflict exist along the Euphrates and the Nile, where Turkey and Egypt respectively claim the majority of the annual discharge. Syria and Iraq, downstream of Turkey, fear that their water supplies will be severely compromised, and Egypt is threatening to bomb any dam that Sudan tries to construct. This potentially explosive situation is far from being resolved.

In the case of southern Africa, confrontations are likely to emerge from a shift in the geopolitical balance of power. Powerful economic growth is expected across the whole of southern Africa following the collapse of apartheid in the Republic of South Africa. Every government in the region believes that it must secure extensive rights to water if it is to participate in the expected boom.

Water is certainly scarce in southern Africa. The northern part of the Republic of South Africa, and the whole of Botswana and Namibia as well as western Zimbabwe are very arid areas with extensive regions of desert and savannah such as the Namib and the Kalahari Deserts. Almost all the large rivers south of the Zambezi – the Orange, the Vaal and the Limpopo – are already being exploited or polluted beyond an ecologically viable level. In addition, a densely populated, highly industrialised zone has been allowed to develop in the Transvaal, centred around Johannesburg and Pretoria, without any account being taken of water availability in the region. Shortages are triggered not by the natural aridness of the climate but by the huge demands made by all manner of industrial concerns, notably gold and diamond mining, by irrigation agriculture, and – to a lesser extent – by the excessive quantities taken by a small proportion of domestic consumers.

South Africa has been successful in its search for water for the time being, having found what it was looking for in Lesotho. This tiny mountain state, nominally independent but entirely surrounded by South Africa, is blessed with plentiful rainfall, and it is here that the Orange River has its source. The South African Lesotho Highlands Water Project is currently developing this rich resource at a cost of 9 billion rand ($2.45 billion). The project centres around the Katse Dam, which, at 180 metres high, is the largest of its kind in Africa; its waters are transported directly into the Transvaal along a tunnel 48 kilometres long. One can only guess at the political pressure exerted on Lesotho to go along with this project: the agreements were signed only after the 1986 military coup, which had followed economic sanctions imposed by South Africa. Six million cubic metres of water per day – practically all of the tiny nation's water – will be taken when the four phases have been completed

in 2020, leaving virtually none for the country's own use and development. In return, Lesotho will receive annual payments of $80 million, making water by far its most lucrative export. It remains to be seen. Whether this will be adequate recompense in the long term remains to be seen.

Meanwhile, in the Transvaal, growing demand threatens to exceed the amount of water obtainable from Lesotho. Greedy eyes have already been cast in a northerly direction towards the Zambezi, the largest river in southern Africa, which carries water from the rainy tropical zones to within 1,300 kilometres of the Transvaal before heading east to flow into the Indian Ocean. A canal could be built to transport an estimated 2,500 to 3,000 million cubic metres of water a year to Johannesburg. Apart from the technical difficulties of pumping as much as three billion tonnes of water at least 1,400 metres uphill, there are legal problems: neither the Zambezi nor even its catchment fall within the Republic of South Africa. Strictly speaking, therefore, South Africa has no entitlement to any of its water – unless, of course, it manages to obtain the share of a neighbouring state.

There is little chance of this happening, however, since most of the nations through which the river flows need all the water they can get. According to Article 4 of the Helsinki Rules (drawn up by the International Law Association in 1966), any nation bordering an international river is entitled to a 'reasonable and equitable share of the beneficial uses of the waters'. Nothing beyond this has been discussed, but a number of states have been attempting to establish claims unilaterally. All the elements are present for a classic water conflict.

Zimbabwe, for example, already extracts two million cubic metres of water a month from the Batoka Gorge to cool its coal-fired power station 45 kilometres to the south at Hwange. Bulawayo, a centre of industry in arid western Zimbabwe, makes even greater demands on the river. The city

Above. At 2660 kilometres long, the Zambezi is the fourth largest river in Africa, with a catchment eight times as big as that of the Rhine. If all the countries through which it flows took the water they claim to be entitled to, there would be nothing but an insubstantial trickle by the time the river arrived at its lower reaches in Mozambique's Tete province, where this photograph was taken.

Opposite page. Shepherd minding his flock in the so-called 'water castle' of the Lesotho kings where the mountains are high enough to cool the moisture-laden winds blowing in from the sea and thus to cause rain to fall.

would like to triple its water budget and obtain an extra 100 million cubic metres a year by installing a water pipeline some 360 kilometres long and 1.4 metres in diameter. However, the project faces huge technical and financial difficulties: the water from the Zambezi would have to be pumped almost 1,000 metres uphill, and the estimated cost of at least one billion Zimbabwean dollars (about US$200 million) is at present unthinkable for such a poor country – Zimbabwe's entire national budget for water and energy in 1991 totalled only one tenth of the sum required (Z$ 102 million).

Namibia's boundaries were drawn at the end of the 19th century when it was German South West Africa. They took in a narrow strip of territory, much of it only 30 kilometres wide but 500 kilometres long, which became known as the Caprivi Strip (after Bismarck's successor as German Chancellor). This effectively gives Namibia access to all the major watercourses in the region – the Cuito, the Chobe and the Zambezi rivers. The sugar-cane plantations in the Caprivi Strip are soon to be expanded by several thousand hectares. Thirsty monocultures of this sort depend on artificial irrigation and use huge quantities of water: the International Union for the Conservation of Nature and Natural Resources, IUCN, estimates that 2,500 hectares of sugar cane in this climate will need at least 50 million cubic metres of water annually.

To date, the most modest demands made on the Zambezi are by Botswana, the driest of the countries bordering it. This nation's 1.3 million inhabitants make a living almost exclusively from copper, nickel and diamond mining, which accounts for 87 per cent of the country's exports. Up to now, Botswana has not removed any water from the Zambezi, but it intends to secure water rights stretching beyond the year 2020. It remains to be seen whether these rights will then be sold off to South Africa. After all, South African plans for obtaining water from the river hinge on the construction of a canal right through Botswana, from which 60 million cubic metres of water would be diverted for Botswana's needs – a mere two per cent of total volume.

The impression that many people evidently still have of the Zambezi River as an inexhaustible water supply is quite simply false. Since 1982, the river has been carrying considerably less water than it has in the past. The planned canal from the Zambezi to the Transvaal would be enough to cause a serious shortage of water in the river: if Johannesburg were, as contemplated, to take 2,500 million cubic metres a year upriver of the Victoria Falls, this would be equivalent to 80 cubic metres a second. That amounts to six per cent of the river's average annual discharge, but as much as 24 per cent of the average flow during the dry season. The lowest level of discharge recorded to date at Victoria Falls was 142 cubic metres per second – which would leave only 62 cubic metres a second in the river after Johannesburg had removed its supply. This would not even be enough to allow the Kariba Dam power plant downstream to function, let alone to satisfy all the other interested parties.

As yet, however, no water management plan has been agreed upon by the various countries involved. Instead of commissioning building contractors and engineers for ever more ambitious prestige projects, every possible effort should be made to economise on water use. In mining and other industrial enterprises, in particular, there is huge potential for saving water. Agriculture, too, could switch to less water intensive crops and methods of cultivation. Approaches such as these could greatly alleviate water shortages in southern Africa in a very short space of time.

In southern Africa, rainfall and rivers dictate a type of development based on limited reserves of water. Only if legally enforceable regulations are established for sensible and economical water use in all countries can an uncontrollable conflict over water be avoided in the region. The foundation for all future international water treaties should be based on similar principles to those applied in national water legislation: any infractions of such treaties by governments or multi-national companies ought to be severely dealt with. If rivers were regarded by all riparian states as a resource to be protected and shared fairly rather than as a commodity for which there are rival claims, a decisive step would have been taken towards pre-empting future water conflicts.

THE CASPIAN SEA
Caught Out By Nature

The fickleness of the weather is legendary. Being drenched by a sudden shower after a forecast of fine weather may be irritating, but it is not surprising – it is well known that complex and unpredictable processes are responsible for the weather systems that catch us out. Far less common is a recognition of the effects that human activity might have on these elaborate natural systems, and yet, even apparently slight changes in the balance of natural cycles can have devastating repercussions. As physicists have put it, the flapping of a butterfly's wings at the right time and in the right place has the potential to change the weather of a whole continent.

Interference in the water regime is likely to produce far-reaching, unexpected results because a whole network of tightly interlaced processes will be affected. The possible consequences of reshaping the landscape, which of course includes rivers, can be seen in what has happened around the Caspian Sea, the world's largest inland sea. This huge, closed body of water has no drainage; its water level is determined by the balance between evaporation and the amount of water flowing in from rivers or falling as rain. If the rate of evaporation is faster than the replenishment of water from rain or rivers, the water level will drop.

The Caspian Sea suffered grievously at the hands of Soviet hydraulic engineers. In the 1950s and 1960s, the Volga, once Europe's largest river, was turned into a string of shallow reservoirs. The net result for the Caspian Sea, which used to receive up to 80 per cent of its water from the Volga, was the loss of much of its supply. The supposed benefits of this mammoth project are questionable in the extreme, as it has involved the flooding or turning into swamp of immense areas of farmland and the resettlement of hundreds of thousands of people. Up to one quarter of the water from the Volga is now diverted for the irrigation of arid areas, and the huge surface area of the nine shallow reservoirs

Children playing in the valuable but heavily oil-polluted waters of the Caspian Sea in Azerbaijan. Fishing has always played an important part in the economies bordering the lake, most famously in the production of caviar (the salted roe of the sturgeon). But no-one knows how long this lucrative trade will be able to survive. Dams on the Volga (the main river feeding this salt lake) block the sturgeons' path to their spawning grounds upstream, and pollution from a range of industries poses serious threats to the lake's ecology.

(the Kuybyshev Reservoir alone is more than eleven times the size of Lake Geneva) means that the river now loses even more water through evaporation.

Until recently, the level of the Caspian Sea had risen and fallen in response to fluctuations in climate, but since 1929 it has dropped almost continuously. By 1976, it was more than two metres lower, leaving an area of land the size of the Netherlands (over 40,000 square kilometres) high and dry. What cannot be proved is the relative extents of the losses from the reduced flow of water from the Volga and evaporation as against those caused by a drier climate. Certainly the increase in water extraction from the Volga led scientific observers un-

animously to predict that the level would continue to sink. The area above water level, which only a few decades before had been under water, was developed: houses were built, farmland and industrial sites extended towards the new shoreline; even a nuclear power station was constructed.

In 1976, in order to prevent the water level of the Caspian Sea from falling any further, the Supreme Soviet followed recommendations made by the Academy of Sciences to block off, with a massive concrete dyke, the Kara-Bogaz-Gol Gulf, a closed bay-like continental lake of some 12,000 square kilometres on the eastern flank of the Caspian Sea. It was assumed that the particularly high evaporation from the surface of the shallow Kara-Bogaz-Gol was partly to blame for the loss of water from the Caspian Sea. By 1978, just two years later, the Kara-Bogaz-Gol was already beginning to dry up, developing a thick crust of Glauber salts and sodium chloride, and the level of the Caspian Sea rose by 38 centimetres for the first time in 50 years.

The planners were delighted: their engineering feats seemed to have achieved the desired result. But in 1992, the water level rose dramatically, by almost a metre in twelve months, and threatened to engulf the oil fields, the fast-breeder reactor on the Mangyshlak peninsula, and a nuclear power station. Suddenly the warnings were recalled of scientists from Turkmenistan in the Academy of Sciences who in the 1970s had voted against the Kara-Bogoz-Gol plan. Their opposition was based on knowledge of ancient Islamic records, according to which the water level of the Caspian Sea is subject to long-term natural fluctuation following a 70-year cycle.

Prompt action was necessary to cope with the rising water, and in 1992 the dam blocking off the Kara-Bogaz-Gol was opened up. Scientists now hope that the water level will drop again – on the assumption that this powerful water system can be regulated in much the same way as pulling a plug out of a bath tub. Without having the remotest knowledge of the complex natural mechanisms governing the waters of the Caspian Sea, their (not uncommon) knee-jerk reaction is to rectify problems caused by their large-scale projects by pursuing even more far-reaching plans that will cause still greater damage.

Monuments to misguided hydraulic planning can be seen all over the world. Highly sensitive natural systems – such as closed lakes with no drainage – are often the first to suffer. Humanity has to take into consideration the fact that, even with the best will in the world, natural systems cannot be entirely understood and regulated. Natural water cycles must not be tampered with because they are intimately linked with the biological and meteorological cycles of the planet. Any large-scale manipulation of rivers, lakes and groundwater will compromise the balance of a system that is the very basis of human survival.

THAILAND
Pernicious Role Models

Over the last fifteen years, while the industrialised nations have increasingly been confronted by unemployment and loss of economic power, south-east Asia has, by contrast, acted as a cradle for economic growth. Feared by Western competitors and praised by international economists, a handful of states, headed by Taiwan and South Korea, have blossomed into so-called emergent nations.

Their success, generally expressed in terms of a growth in gross national product supported by export figures, has been possible only at great cost to the environment. The damage is vast: deforestation, devastating erosion, traffic chaos, cities choking in fumes. Rivers have suffered grievously: not only are they polluted with ever greater loads of waste discharged by the chemical, steel and food industries, but many of them have also been turned into chains of man-made lakes through the construction of hydroelectric dams.

In Thailand, a recent member of this exclusive club of industrialising nations, it is the food industry that leads the field in despoiling the environment. Canning factories for tropical fruit and fish, sugar refineries and cattle and pig feed manufacturers have the highest growth rates. Because of their importance to the nation's export trade, and therefore the balance of payments, they are able to do almost entirely as they please as far as the environment is concerned. Thus, no-one was particularly bothered when a sugar factory in Khon Kaen, a provincial town in the Isan region in north-eastern Thailand, greatly increased its capacity without making any plans for the disposal of the extra waste products. In late March 1992, 9,000 tons of molasses, a by-product of sugar processing, slowly drifted down the Nam Pong in the form of a sticky, smelly mass some 70 kilometres long, sapping the river of oxygen and killing off all its fish. The Khon Kaen 'accident' shook the nation. Suddenly the destructive potential that had been put in place along the banks of

rivers all over the country became alarmingly apparent.

Attempts by the authorities to dissolve the dense, viscous mass with water taken from the nearby Ubolrath Reservoir simply moved the disaster further downstream: now it was the turn of the fish in the Nam

While the industrialised countries of the north have long since turned most of their rivers into polluted drains, in south-east Asia, many people still rely directly on rivers for food, for washing, for drinking water, often living right at the water's edge, as here near the border town of Mae Sai in the north of Thailand. Perhaps this accounts for the deep-rooted belief in these countries in the need to preserve the life of rivers and protect them from the abuses of industry. Any fouling of the waters has an immediate impact on the quality of life of those living downstream.

Chi, of which the Nam Pong is a tributary, to be suffocated by the molasses. By the time the huge lump had passed more than 300 kilometres down the Nam Chi, and then a few days later into the Nam Mun, it was still eight kilometres long, over 200 metres wide and two metres thick. No more than five per cent of the fish in the three rivers, the Pong, the Chi and the Mun, survived. According to the Ministry of Fisheries' estimates, it will take at least ten years for the rivers' ecology to recover. And many of the 141 species of endemic fish will never return. The Director of the Thailand State Fishery Department described the extent of the damage as fish genocide: 'We cannot measure the extinction of fish species in terms of money.'

The molasses disaster of Khon Kaen dominated the headlines in Thailand for several weeks, but it was by no means unique. 23,000 companies are registered in the capital city of Bangkok alone; almost all of them discharge their waste products into the city's rivers. The side effect of the expansion of Thai industry was a total discharge in 1991 of over two million tonnes of toxic industrial waste. Where these immense amounts of waste finished up is not at all clear. The Ministry for Economic Development is also responsible for environmental protection, and – in the name of progress and development – the subject has thus far not been up for discussion in Thailand.

Rapid and highly visible deterioration in environmental conditions and thus in the quality of life has moved many in south-east Asia to question what is happening. In spite of industrial expansion being presented as the single most likely route to higher standards of living, protests are beginning to be heard throughout the region against further destruction of nature. For the many people who still feel themselves to be a part of the natural world, rather than divorced from it, the deforestation of the jungle and pollution of rivers represent serious and clearly recognised threats. It is not just that fishermen lose their livelihoods when the fish in the rivers die; there is a sense that the entire natural order is being thrown out of balance. Little faith is placed in technological solutions to alleviate environmental destruction on

this scale. In South Korea, for example, even industrialists can be heard calling for a 'radical spiritual change', in other words, a whole new attitude to the exploitation of natural resources.

Many of those responsible for environmental problems in south-east Asia realised long before their counterparts in Europe, Japan and the United States that the solution to the problem of industrial pollution lies not in treatment plants and incinerators, but in rethinking whole systems of production so that the waste is not produced in the first place. The Thai Ministry for Economic Development has recently declared, for example, that, starting with the pulp and paper industry, efforts will be concentrated on modern, waste-water-free processes.

Ideas of this kind are particularly unwelcome to competitors in First World countries. For one thing, they have no wish to see ecologically exemplary production methods in the emergent nations which might shame them into adopting similar strategies. For another, the environmental technology market is on the verge of expanding into the Third World and is worried that potentially lucrative markets for conventionally re-equipping infamously dirty industries with treatment plants and filters might be spoilt.

If the current growth rate of the world's emergent economies is sustained, their industrial plants will double in number over the next ten years. There is no reason why new plants should not be resource- and energy-efficient and waste-water-free. However, in order to prevent an estimated one in every two industrial plants in south-east Asia becoming ecologically more advanced than First World factories by the year 2005, Western companies supply these countries with outdated equipment or set up subsidiaries that still use damaging production techniques. This strategy is doubly harmful: in transferring environmentally polluting technology, Western industry gets round increasingly stringent requirements at home by passing on the potential for damage to newly industrialised economies, effectively blocking any global strategy for genuinely ecological production.

BEIJING
A Pressing Need for Integrated Planning

Human societies have always had regulations governing the use of water and stipulating priorities. In the 20th century, however, it has generally been forgotten that all users of water owe one another mutual consideration. Individual sectors – public water suppliers, agriculture, industry – take an interest only in their own needs, and in many countries responsibility for water is divided between several ministries. So, different users exploit water resources without any co-ordination of their divergent and often growing demands.

What this can lead to, even in a country with a centralised administration, can be seen in China. Man-made water shortages are particularly acute in the relatively arid northern Chinese plateau bordering the Mongolian steppes. The population of Beijing and its environs has increased tenfold since 1949 to the current 11 million, and there has been consistent growth in industrial production and intensification of agricultural irrigation. As a result, water consumption has shot up, even though resources are limited. If the present levels of consumption are not tackled, the region's natural water reserves will be able to satisfy only 60 per cent of predicted demand by the year 2000.

The scarcity of water cannot be attributed exclusively to lack of rain in the region, (the average annual rainfall is 600mm); it has been provoked primarily by economic targets set by Mao Ze Dong in the 1950s. For centuries Beijing had been supplied with rice and grain from vast, fertile floodplains in southern China via the Grand Canal, which runs from Hangzhou to Tianjin, but Mao stipulated that 'parasitic Beijing' should now, like all the other regions, feed itself. This led in the 1960s to almost every stream in the Beijing district, however small, being dammed up so that water could be allowed to collect for the cultivation of rice in paddies. In the 1950s, only ten per cent of fields were irrigated; by 1990, this figure had risen to over 80 per cent. In rural districts of the capital, agriculture now uses ten times as much water as domestic and industrial consumers put together.

In the early 1980s, a long period of drought provoked Beijing's first serious water shortage. Water from some of the irrigation reservoirs was reallocated for domestic use, but for a short period in 1981 even these dried up, and the municipal authorities had to resort to groundwater. A mere twelve months later, the groundwater level had dropped by three metres, and it was clear that the demands made by agriculture would be impossible to satisfy in the long term. But agrarian planners continued to ignore the warning signs and encouraged farmers to use groundwater for irrigation. The number of electrical pumps in the region increased steadily, and by 1990 there were over 43,000.

Industrialists in and around Beijing paid just as little attention as the farmers to the water situation. Over 4,000 new industrial sites were established, including some for the water-intensive steel industry. Since 1949, the region's industrial water consumption has risen from 49 million cubic metres to over a billion. The recycling of water is only just beginning to be practised, and waste-water-free production remains an unknown concept. Like its Western and Soviet counterparts before it, Chinese industry disposes of its production waste in the most convenient fashion, by washing it away in rivers. Any water downstream of industrial regions is thus unfit for human consumption or for use in irrigation.

It is not just the rivers that have been contaminated – pollution has also taken its toll on the groundwater. In the Fang Shan district south of Beijing, waste water from a refinery has made its way via the Niukou Valley Reservoir into the groundwater, which is now unsuitable either for use as drinking water or for irrigating fields, and all supplies now have to be imported to the region via a 100-kilometre pipeline.

If the water in Beijing were used sparingly and sensibly, there would be no water shortages. What is crucial is that the city does not entrust its resources to the kind of system used and purveyed by northern industrial countries that are rich in water. Water-saving measures are beginning to be demanded by the water supply authorities.

Overexploitation and pollution by industry of the water regime could be stopped by the introduction of water recycling and low-waste production methods. In agriculture, consumption could easily be cut by half, simply by reintroducing traditional, drought-resistant varieties of grain, such as gao-liang and millet and using more effective irrigation.

The need for integrated water planning was painfully obvious in the early 1980s, when entire districts had to manage without water for weeks at a time. In recent years, rainfall in Beijing has been above average, temporarily allaying the worst fears of water shortages, but in 1994, the drought returned to northern China. The strategies that are being adopted to reduce industrial and domestic consumption in and around the city are a step in the right direction, but future crises will be averted only if radical steps are taken to cut agriculture's colossal usage.

In the arid regions of northern China, vast water conduits like this one near the Ming Tombs, have been built to transport practically every drop from the rivers via vast reservoirs constructued to support irrigation agriculture.

MEXICO CITY
Quenching the Thirst of the Megalopolis

During the last hundred years, towns and cities across the world have expanded rapidly. In developing countries, the scale of migration into urban areas has made countless cities grow explosively, sometimes in the space of only a few short years. In Asia and Africa, an average 33 per cent of the population live in urban settlements, but the figure for Latin America is an astonishing 72 per cent, and the cities are bursting at the seams.

The combination of too many people crammed together and the infrastructure (however basic) that accompanies them multiplies the burden on the environment and on the people themselves: noise, traffic chaos, rubbish, smog and an explosion in the consumption of natural resources and energy. The availablity of water is inevitably a crucially limiting factor to urban development. Provision has to be made for the supply of drinking water, the disposal of sewage and the diversion of rainfall.

Mexico City, with its enormous growth rate, has turned into a water management nightmare. Since 1970, the population of the Mexican capital has increased by over eight million to its 1994 level of 25 to 30 million. Mexico City is situated some 2,200 metres above sea level in the high-lying Anahuac valley on a fertile plain, fed by plentiful mountain streams but with no river to drain it. Where once almost 2,000 square kilometres of shallow lagoons covered the land and the Aztecs tended their legendary floating gardens or *chinampas*, endless rows of towerblocks now stretch as far as the eye can see. The lagoons have long since been filled in or drained, and the climate of the high-lying valley has become significantly drier as a result.

Despite the fact that the rivers flowing into the Anahuac valley carry water all year round and that there are huge reserves of groundwater, those responsible for maintaining the supply of drinking water to Mexico City are now facing insurmountable difficulties. For decades, the groundwater has been pumped off at twice the rate at which it has been replenished by rain and river water, and in the near future it is likely to dry up entirely – a typical scenario in late 20th-century mega cities, where consumption usually greatly exceeds natural supply. Importing water from elsewhere is prohibitively expensive and in any case against the interests of neighbouring regions which need every drop of water for themselves. Already around 800 million cubic metres of water are being imported annually into Mexico City from rivers in neighbouring areas, and soon supplies from as far away as the coastal regions will be exploited. Transportation costs are astronomical, as the water has to be pumped up to the plateau from 1,500 metres below: the Mexican Centre of Ecological Development estimates that one third of Mexico City's entire energy consumption is expended on water pumps, at a cost of approximately a billion dollars a year. And the demand for water is set to rise still further. At least two million of Mexico City's inhabitants have no running water, and migration to the city continues apace.

Paradoxically, Mexico City suffers not only from a shortage of water, but also from flooding. Rainwater goes into the same sewers as domestic and industrial waste water, and the sewage system is barely able to cope with the immense volume of waste water, even during the dry season. Consequently, every summer, when there is heavy rain, the waters force their way to the surface at the lowest point in the city, leaving the slums on its eastern periphery knee-deep in foul-smelling mud.

The problem arises from something that is common to all cities: rain is unable to drain into the soil because it is covered with asphalt and concrete and has nowhere

Collecting water in an old chemical drum in Mexico City. It is estimated that 1,000 people arrive in the city from rural areas every day.

Opposite page. Nowhere is the draw of the city stronger than in Latin America. La Paz, the largest city of Bolivia, has long since grown out of the basin-shaped valley where the town was founded in 1548. The slums now stretch right up to the cold and exposed Altiplano over 4000 metres above sea level.

to go but the sewers. Getting rainwater out of the city as quickly as possible is still one of the prime objectives of water engineers. The larger cities become, the less feasible it is in both financial and technical terms to install the necessary infrastructure. In Tokyo, attempts are being made to conduct storm water away from the huge urban area and drain it straight into the sea by constructing a vast sewer 30 kilometres long and twelve metres wide – twice the diameter of an underground railway tunnel. In Mexico City, however, both rainwater and waste water got out of hand long ago: it is generally agreed today that such heavy settlement of the valley should never have been allowed in the first place.

It remains to be seen whether the right lessons have been learned from the experiences of megalopolises such as Mexico City, Caracas, Shanghai, Bangkok and Tokyo. Given the desperate state of so many metropolitan areas, it is perhaps time to question the economic ideology which for decades has recognised only urban centres as the exclusive focuses of progress and improvement.

If current forecasts are to be believed, almost half of humanity will be living in cities by the year 2000. This trend should be halted or at least slowed, and incentives provided to persuade people to live in rural areas or in smaller towns. The myth that vast cities are the most desirable and efficient way to accommodate large numbers of people, offering the best chance of a high standard of living, must be challenged.

QUEBEC
Mega-Projects for Mega-Profits

Watching rivers flow by makes people pensive. Some people regard them as a symbol of life itself, some wonder at the richness and diversity of their ecosystems, others again see them as historical paths along which civilisations and ideas took root. Supporters of hydroelectric power have a very particular view of rivers, summed up by Robert Bourassa, long-serving Prime Minister of the Canadian province of Quebec (succeeded by Jacques Parizeau in late 1994). In his opinion, the water in the province just begs to be transformed into hydroelectricity, 'and every day millions of potential kilowatt-hours flow downhill and out to sea. What a waste!'

Bourassa is a man not just of words, but of action. A huge area of land in the north of Quebec, which until the 1970s remained unbroached by a single road and was inhabited exclusively by members of the Cree and Inuit tribes, has been turned into a gigantic electricity plant by the state hydro-electric power company, Hydro-Québec. Here, where the pine forests of the taiga

slowly give way to the Arctic tundra, La Grande, the most powerful river running into Hudson Bay, has been converted into a chain of shallow reservoirs by hundreds of kilometres of dykes and a series of colossal dams. Several other large rivers – the Eastmain, the Opinaca and the Caniapiscau – have been dammed up and diverted into the La Grande reservoirs. Over 10,000 square kilometres of forests and river courses have disappeared beneath the reservoirs. Quebec now enjoys an abundance of electricity; three gigantic power stations generate a total output of around 10,300 megawatts, and new plants will by 1995 expand the capacity of the James Bay complex to 15,500 megawatts.

When an area almost the size of Britain no longer has a single river following its natural course, there are inevitable consequences for the environment. The seasonal rhythms of freezing and ice melt at the mouths of rivers are entirely disrupted; dams prevent fish from making their way upstream to their habitual spawning grounds; caribou find their traditional migratory routes under water. Most changes happen slowly in this cold, barren landscape. The long-term consequences for James Bay and Hudson Bay are entirely unknown: the reservoirs have, for example, reversed the seasonal pattern of nutrient and heat supply from the rivers. In the

past, when the spring came, snow melt water in the rivers warmed the coastal sea waters, allowing the algae to develop early in the year under the ice, thus providing ample food for fish. Nowadays, the spring flood waters are held back to refill the reservoirs after the heavy consumption of energy over the winter, leaving the rivers with only a fraction of their natural spring flow. If the provinces of Ontario and Manitoba put into action similar hydroelectric plans to those of Quebec on the west coast of Hudson Bay, the entire sub-Arctic ecosystem of the huge bay – with its rich fish life, beluga whales and its unique bearded seals – is likely to collapse. The ice melt on the bay will happen far later and the beginning of the marine food chain – usually stimulated by the nutrients and the higher temperatures of the river's spring floods – will be delayed; the devastating effects on the ecology that this is likely to have can only be guessed at.

Bourassa's plans went still further. His next project was to convert into artificial reservoirs the Great Whale River, which lies to the north of the James Bay complex, and ultimately the entire catchments of three rivers further south – the Nottaway, Broadback and Rupert. The plan was to tame these untouched rivers for the sole purpose of generating electricity. The battle over these new projects has been fierce: a

Opposite page. Caribou crossing Eau Claire, a hitherto unspoilt river in northern Quebec. Each year, caribou migrate hundreds of kilometres to their breeding grounds, often across quite large rivers, but the vast artificial hydrolakes are effectively impassable to them.

Left. La Grande II – over 150 metres high and five kilometres wide – is the main dam in the James Bay scheme. 83,000 kilometres of natural riverbanks and 12,000 square kilometres of forest have disappeared under the waters of newly created reservoirs in the area.

broadly based coalition of Cree and Inuit, scientists, environmentalists, economists and growing numbers of the population are opposed to Bourassa's project. He is, however, not alone in his enthusiasm for the Great Whale scheme. What may have seemed like the power fantasies of a lone hydromaniac have actually been supported (more or less openly) by a number of other parties.

Common to almost all advocates of the 3,200 megawatt Great Whale project is the financial advantage they might win from it. SNC-Lavalin, for instance, Canada's largest engineering consultancy with over 6,000 employees (thanks to its involvement in Bourassa's hydroelectric projects), has been promised 85 per cent of prospective contracts for Great Whale. Engineering companies of this size purvey a wide variety of engineering schemes such as dams,

underground railways or refineries, and need large contracts to keep their gigantic planning machinery ticking over. SNC-Lavalin also has a major role in the world's largest hydroelectric power project, the controversial Three Gorges Dam on the Yangtze River in China.

No electricity is sold more cheaply than hydropower. The main beneficiaries are energy-intensive industries such as paper mills and fertiliser manufacturers, and, notably, aluminium smelters. Quebec has for years attracted energy-hungry industries to the province by offering super-cheap electricity. Today, one third of the province's power is used by industry, and the share is rising. Recently, Hydro-Québec agreed to make its sales price dependent on its customers' selling prices. If the price of aluminium drops – as it did in 1993/94 when excess production from Russian

arms factories appeared on the world markets – Hydro-Québec receives from the aluminium industry less than half the cost price of the electricity consumed. Any trading losses made by industrial users of electricity are thus effectively compensated by the state. Industry has long shown its gratitude for such unbeatable terms by providing guaranteed support for Bourassa's plans.

Behind the scenes of the global energy market, powerful investment banks pull the strings. It is they who arrange the huge loans required by companies like Hydro-Québec to finance the construction of dams or of coal or nuclear power stations. Hydroelectric power is regarded as a safe and profitable investment – investors in the La Grande project are said to have received a collective return of 17 per cent per annum. However, in industrialised economies, such as North America, which are saturated markets for electricity, capital loans are dependent on evidence of demand. If the Great Whale project is to be the monument to his hydroelectric achievements that Bourassa wanted, Hydro-Québec will have somehow to conjure up more bulk consumers. The latest scheme seems almost to smack of desperation: using electricity to extract hydrogen from water and then exporting it by ship to Europe as an allegedly environmentally friendly petrol substitute.

While a number of large companies have profited from Quebec's hydroelectric power projects, there has been no sign of the wealth creation that was promised for the province itself. Unemployment has risen, and the per-capita income in Quebec is lower than the Canadian average. The construction of the dams created new employment, but it was transient and cost the taxpayer Canadian $208,000 per job per year. The metal industry that was lured to Quebec by the promise of cheap power has also failed to trigger the anticipated upswing, as raw aluminium is exported before it has undergone the lucrative stage

of further processing. Again, there is a handsome state subsidy of up to Canadian $200,000 per job in the aluminium industry.

In a mature energy market such as Canada's, extra electricity can be made available far more easily by saving energy than by building new power stations. Opponents of the Great Whale project claim that heat insulation programmes alone would be enough to make it surplus to requirements, calculating that programmes of this kind would be 60 per cent cheaper and create four times as many jobs as a new hydroelectric power project. If the Great Whale Scheme goes ahead, plans are in position to increase Hydro-Québec's current debt of Canadian $33 billion (or Can $10,038 per customer), which accounts for approximately 45 per cent of the province's total public debt, by a further Canadian $35 to 40 billion between 1996 and 2010. Hydro-Québec pays off the interest it accrues (over Can $3 billion in 1993 alone) out of citizens' pockets: it is estimated that the cost of electricity for domestic use could double by the end of the decade.

These plans can be implemented, however, only if Hydro-Québec succeeds in identifying major bulk customers for its surplus electricity. Following the visit to Europe by Robert Bourassa in 1992, a consortium of high-tech companies and engineering syndicates expressed an interest in using Canadian hydrogen as a fuel substitute, in spite of the fact that its overall energy efficiency would be devastatingly low. If the Canadians succeed in offloading excess electricity by supplying hydrogen to the European market, Bourassa may get his monument after all.

Recently there has been a glimmer of hope for campaigners against the scheme. In November 1994, Bourassa's successor, Jacques Parizeau, announced that all further developments had been put on ice. How long this moratorium will hold is currently unknown.

Cree hunter on the Great Whale River – central to Cree and Inuit culture and traditional economies. Its enormous power is all too obviously tempting to hydroelectric engineers.

EUROPEAN UNION
Shielding the Polluters

Given the excellent economic position of Europe and its high technical and living standards, one would expect its water courses and drinking water to be protected to the highest possible levels.

In 1992, the European Commission presented an impressive water programme promising, among other things, the 'prevention of pollution to surface and fresh water' and 'more rational use and management of water'. When the draft legislation appeared, however, it was couched in somewhat different terms, particularly as far as the regulation of industrial emissions was concerned. Instead of establishing uniform minimum standards for industrial emissions in Europe, the Commission is taking a line that effectively sanctions a contest between member states for the lowest ecological standards. There is no mention at all of recycling water used in industry. All that the Commission is prepared to prescribe is the 'best available technology' for treating waste water – and even then companies will have to use it only if this can be 'economically reasonably expected'. In other words, whatever industry pumps through its outfall pipes into the rivers is legal – no matter what its effect might be. The relevant legislation is entitled *Directive on Integrated Prevention and Pollution Control*, but it is in fact more likely to be used to shield polluters from public protest than to protect the environment.

Water protection is anathema to industry, because almost all industrial activities are likely to affect water in some way or other. It is not surprising, therefore, that – even at the planning stage – industry is mobilising to influence European water legislation so as to exclude any ecological strategies; these would include: a) the precautionary principle, which sanctions only those practices known to be harmless to the environment, b) the idea that when environmental damage occurs, the polluters pays to put it right, and c) the preventative principle, which shifts the emphasis from treatment of waste water to zero discharge. So far,

industrial associations across Europe have managed to block any moves to phase in mandatory ecologically sound production standards, such as those that have already been established in Denmark. Even the introduction of year-on-year progressively

The Po in northern Italy is in many ways an object lesson as to the fate of European rivers. Above. The clear fresh headwaters of the river near Crissolo in the Italian Alps; virtually untouched for its first 20 kilometres, it is then abruptly dammed up for hydroelectricity.

rising fees for the discharge of waste water (a system successfully implemented by some member states for many years) appears in the draft legislation only as an optional clause.

A second piece of legislation, the *Directive on the Ecological Quality of Water*, aims to improve the quality of rivers and lakes (surface water) in the Union. Once again, the industrial associations, perceiving a threat to their hitherto inalienable right to dispose of waste water in rivers, lobbied hard. As a result, an opt-out clause allows member states to exclude entire regions from the directive at will, simply by declaring that the water in a specific region is already in such poor condition or is subject to such heavy demand that it cannot be restored. Clearly, little now remains of the legislation's declared aim to protect water.

The reason for the huge discrepancy between original intent and current practice lies in the European Union's history as a group of trading partners. Any legislation drawn up by the EU is closely vetted for its possible effect on industry in lengthy negotiations with industrial associations. No examination of directives is made in terms of their suitability for the environment, nor is there any serious consultation with environmental organisations.

Directives recently proposed by the European Union do not constitute protective

Above. The Po near the Casale Dam, so low that much of the river bed is exposed – largely as a result of water extracted for the irrigation demanded by intensive agriculture.

Opposite page, top. Dusk outside Turin with foamy effluent being discharged directly from sewers into the river; bottom: the Po near Pavia. Artificial banks, often reinforced with concrete blocks, and straightened courses speed up the flow and increase the force of the river, making surrounding land even more vulnerable to flooding, as recent disastrous events have shown. Across the embankment streams the outfall from a chemical factory.

Left. Gravel mining in the Po has carved deep channels in the river's bed, contributing to speeding up the flow, as well as lowering the groundwater, so that surrounding farmland and any surviving wetlands dry out.

legislation for water; on the contrary, they allow water users to proceed as before without let or hindrance, promoting high-tech water management aimed at satisfying all conceivable demand and allowing pollution up to a 'just-tolerable' level. In other words, the EU Commission is preparing to abandon any serious attempt to restore or protect European waters.

The concept of just-tolerable levels of pollution has already turned out to be a failure: treatment of steadily more polluted water resources to turn them into drinking water has become so complicated and expensive that consumers are beginning to demand that the polluters should bear the spiralling costs. People are at last beginning to wake up to what is happening, but growing public unease at the effects on water of industry and agriculture is now to be countered by the EU Commission with a weakening of its drinking water stipulations. There are plans to replace the strict drinking water directive that has been in effect since 1980 with considerably more lax standards, notably where pesticides are concerned. This, says the Commission, would bring about savings for consumers in the cost of water treatment; it would also liberate industry and agriculture from any obligation to introduce expensive, ecologically sound production methods.

But Brussels may have another think coming: in 1994 hundreds of thousands of citizens from all over Europe petitioned against any lowering of drinking water standards. The new directive has still not been approved. It remains to be seen whether the European Union will be driven by the interests of industry or of its citizens. The battle over Europe's water has only just begun.

CHAPTER TWELVE

HOPE FOR THE FUTURE

PERU
The Raised Fields of Lake Titicaca

The atmosphere on the High Plateau of Lake Titicaca is rarified, and the roads are dusty. Some 3,800 metres above sea level, cold winds blow across the plateau and the slate-grey lake; night frosts can strike at any time of year. Farming in this climate is extremely tough work. The Indio farmers wring sparse potato harvests from the soil, which alternates between being too moist and too dry for successful cultivation. It is almost impossible to make a living from arable farming here, and large numbers of llamas and alpacas, whose wool represents the main source of income for the Indios, graze the bare slopes near the lake.

Despite the spartan conditions, a civilisation had already developed on the Altiplano long before the Incas conquered the region in around 1450. There are signs that this area was settled uninterruptedly from around 1,000 BC until AD 400, first by the Qaluyu people and later by the Pucara. The number and distribution of archaeological finds dating from that period indicate that the population living on the shores of Lake Titicaca was much larger than that of today, and dense settlement of this kind would not have been possible without large and reliable harvests. Quite how several hundred thousand people managed to live off the land on a plateau waterlogged in some places and arid in others, was until a few years ago a complete mystery. Only recently did archaeologists discover the secret; in doing so they may have stumbled upon a farming technique which could radically improve present-day living standards around Lake Titicaca.

In the 1960s, strange ridges that could not be of natural origin were noticed in the land surface around Lake Titicaca over an area of some 80,000 hectares. These were identified by archaeologists as the eroded remains of centuries-old raised fields. The fields, it was discovered, had been arranged in rows up to 100 metres long and about ten metres apart, and between them, canals about one to one-and-a-half metres deep were dug. These fulfilled a number of functions. When there was heavy rain, there was ample opportunity for the fields to drain, thus avoiding waterlogging, and in dry years the canal water was used for irrigation. From time to time the fertile sediment which collected in the canals was spread on the fields, making them a great deal more fertile than the surrounding land. Gradually the American team of researchers built up a picture of a system of agriculture that was perfectly suited to the difficult climatic and soil conditions of the Altiplano.

Opposite page. Lake Titicaca, at an altitude of 3,800 metres, is one of the highest-lying large lakes in the world. This vast body of water acts as a gigantic heat source, rendering the harsh climate of the Altiplano distinctly more mild than it would otherwise be. In the foreground are neatly arranged bundles of reeds laid out on the lake shore to dry, from which boats, even huts are made by local people, some of whom live on floating islands constructed from the same reeds.

Left. Traditional farming on the Isla Amantini in Lake Titicaca.

The discovery of the raised field systems prompted experimentation. Guided by the findings of the archaeologists, local Quechua farmers reconstructed a ten-hectare area of raised fields. Canals were dug the original distances apart using traditional tools, and the excavated earth was piled up to form raised fields, just as had been done 3,000 years before. The fields were planted with local potato varieties, and native protein-rich crops such as quinoa and cañihua. Without the use of any additional fertilisers, the potato crop from the fields was three times higher than average for the Titicaca region, despite the use elsewhere of both artificial fertilisers and high-yield strains of seed.

The impressive productiveness of the raised fields is probably due to a number of factors. For one thing, nitrogen-fixing algae (which convert atmospheric nitrogen to nitrogen compounds that are then used by plants) settle in the canals, and serve as a green manure when collected and spread on the fields. Probably more significant, though, is the improvement in microclimate brought about by the mere presence

of canals – in 1982 heavy night frosts destroyed the crops in adjacent fields, but those in the raised fields were scarcely affected. Temperature readings showed that on frosty nights air and soil temperatures were several degrees higher on the raised fields than on conventional arable land. So the canal water on the Altiplano seems to be storing the sun's energy, causing a layer of warm air to form which covers and protects the raised fields at night.

Observing how much better harvests were from the raised fields – whether the crops had been grown in extremely wet weather conditions or during prolonged periods of drought – farmers began building more raised fields of their own accord. Soon the original test area had been increased ten-fold. This success contrasts sharply with all the agricultural projects that had failed in the Titicaca region over the years. Artificial fertilisers, new agricultural machinery and imported high-yield seeds had all at some time been introduced, but with little success, and inappropriate high-tech irrigation systems fell into disrepair. None of these imported techniques

was remotely appropriate to the particular, harsh conditions of the Altiplano.

Raised fields are only one of many traditional farming methods developed across the world to suit local water, soil and climatic conditions. Custom-made techniques of this kind are far superior to modern agricultural technology, particularly where extreme conditions prevail, as in semi-arid areas, in hilly regions or at high altitudes. There are a few, scattered examples of local farmers, scientists and non-governmental aid organisations attempting to revive ancient agrarian ecosystems – in Sri Lanka and in the Negev Desert, among other places. But every day, traditional fields are being cleared out in the name of progress – even near Lake Titicaca. High time, then, that the wide range of sophisticated knowledge garnered from the observations and experience of generations is accorded the respect it deserves and put to use in continuing or reviving methods of farming which will otherwise be lost for ever, and which remain the most appropriate ways of providing food for people living in extreme climatic conditions.

SYDNEY
The Greening of the Games

For all the inroads made by environmental policies in recent years, one area of development in particular has been severely neglected: urban planning. In future, initiatives currently being pursued in Sydney may well serve as an important precedent. Here, Greenpeace Australia, with strong grass-roots support, has since 1991 been helping to establish entirely new criteria for planning decisions.

The problems faced by Sydney are typical of a relatively young and fast-growing metropolis: urban sprawl, permanent smog, insufficient means of disposal for huge quantities of domestic waste, and increasingly poor drinking water. In its urban campaigns, Greenpeace Australia is offering a vision of towns and cities that confronts and deals with these harsh realities.

By the year 2011, the city's population is expected to have grown by almost one million, bringing the total to 4.5 million, but if the Greenpeace outline for planning is adopted, this will not result in further urban sprawl (the city will be confined within its current boundaries), nor will extraction of water from the surrounding countryside increase. Air pollution would be drastically reduced, and the city's rivers and marshlands returned to their natural state. Domestic energy consumption would be cut by at least 50 per cent. All of these objectives would be achieved without any drop in living standards.

Adopting a holistic approach, a small team of consultants retained by Greenpeace Australia has drawn up an integrated 'Strategy for a Sustainable Sydney', which constitutes a significant move away from most current, uncoordinated urban planning. Environmental experts have taken a close look at all aspects of the city's infrastructure, and worked out detailed plans for improving public transport, controlling refuse disposal, maintaining sustainable water supplies, improving air quality, and restoring and supporting biodiversity in the city's nature reserves. Redevelopment of inner-city sites with a view to intensifying the settlement density has been put forward for selected districts, in an attempt to house more people in existing residential areas while avoiding overcrowding.

As well as producing an overall development concept for the city, Greenpeace Australia entered the architectural competition for the construction of the Olympic Village that will house athletes in the year 2000. Greenpeace won the competition, and Sydney was awarded the right to host the first games of the 21st century, defeating Beijing by only one vote, a victory widely attributed to its 'green' proposal.

Olympic Village 2000 sets out to show how an ecologically sound infrastructure can be designed and installed in an urban context, especially as far as water is concerned. The aim of so-called total water cycle management is to provide fresh water supplies as far as possible by recycling water, instead of pumping it into the Village from where it goes straight into the sewers after a single use. Waste water from showers and kitchens is to undergo primary biological purification in settling and detention ponds, from where it trickles

Sydney's Olympic Village, to be built 14 kilometres from the city centre, will house 15,000 athletes and officials in a development comprising town-houses and apartments, shops, entertainment areas, recreation facilities and community services. The Village will be set amid parkland reaching down to the water's edge on Parramatta River.

By adopting environmentally sound strategies, the plan offers a glimpse into sustainable life in the 21st century. It combines in one project the use of solar energy, an innovative public transport system and the exclusive use of natural, non-toxic building materials. Conservation of Sydney's scarce water supplies also plays a crucial role: the wetland system around Haslam's Creek, to the east of the Village, which is an important haven for wildlife, is the focus of a scheme to recycle storm- and waste water using natural biological processes.

into reed beds and natural areas of wetland in the Village before being filtered and reintroduced into the water supply. Water containing faecal matter will be biologically treated in separate systems. Rainwater also figures prominently in the scheme – the rain that runs off buildings will be allowed to return to the soil or collected for watering gardens; the rainwater falling on other sealed surfaces like streets and squares will no longer simply flow into the sewers but will be stored in ponds and in marshy areas before flowing into reed beds to be introduced into the drinking water cycle.

Few of these radical changes will be noticeable to the Olympic competitors. Water-saving devices fitted to taps and shower-heads will be scarcely perceptible to the user but will reduce consumption by

half. Toilets will be equipped either with a vacuum system or with highly efficient water-saving cisterns – the final decision on this has yet to be made. The water supplied will be at least as pure and safe as conventional city tap water; there may even be an extra tap providing especially good drinking water. Overall, athletes from the developed world will be using less than half the amount of water they would at home, and the combined effects of recycling and saving water could lead to a reduction of up to 90 per cent in fresh water requirements compared to those of an average Australian town. There will be no need to extend existing water mains and supply systems, or to carry out the costly and disruptive construction and maintenance of a central sewer.

Contrary to what conventional city plan-

ners might believe, systems like this one, which are sympathetic to nature, do not handicap or stand in the way of further urban development. In fact, quite the reverse is true. In cities such as Sydney, which are already exploiting available water resources to the full, they provide scope for development that would otherwise have been impossible or prohibitively expensive. If it turns out that fresh water requirements really can be cut by as much as 90 per cent, a major problem faced by expanding conurbations will have been overcome. Pilot projects like the Greenpeace Olympic Village could point the way for the 21st century, by preventing cities from turning into uncontrollable monstrosities and thus bringing them closer to the ideal of efficiently organised structures for living.

LAKE BAIKAL
Revolutionary Technology

Lake Baikal in southern Siberia, the world's oldest and deepest lake, is considered by many to be the most beautiful on the planet. In the words of the Russian author Valentin Rasputin who wrote some of his most impressive prose in a cabin on its shores, 'Man does not have feelings enough to respond to this wonder'.

The lake is unique in many ways. Filling a tectonic rift which has an average width of 48 kilometres, it is 635 kilometres long, and its depth, of up to 1,637 metres, is more like that of an ocean than a lake; Lake Baikal contains no less than one fifth of the world's fresh water. It takes over 400 years for its waters to be replaced by the 336 rivers and streams that flow into it, which means that its water has been renewed only five times since the Christian calendar began.

The waters in the lake are crystal clear, allowing sunlight to penetrate to depths of up to 100 metres. The unusual purity of its water almost proved to be Lake Baikal's downfall. Engineers discovered that the water, being virtually free of minerals, was perfectly suited for processing the Siberian pine forests into paper and high-quality cellulose; in the 1950s, a pulp and paper industry began operating on the lake.

From the start, there was serious opposition to plans for industrial development. Zoologists, botanists and limnologists (lake scientists) were particularly opposed to the two largest industrial complexes: a cellulose factory in Baikalsk (now a furniture factory) and a cardboard mill in Selenginsk, 60 kilometres upstream on the largest of the rivers that flow into the lake, the Selenga. There were repeated warnings about the pollution of Lake Baikal by the waste-water outfalls of the factories – the huge lake was not easy to pollute, they said, but when it did become contaminated, it would be impossible to clean up. The 1960s and 1970s saw an escalation in the battle between Baikal conservationists and the government in Moscow, and all public criticism of the plans was ruthlessly suppressed; in 1975, the Central Committee prohibited the publication of any information whatsoever concerning the lake, including scientific data. In spite of this, or perhaps for this very reason, Lake Baikal, the pearl of Siberia, became a symbol of ecological resistance in the Soviet Union.

The reasons for comprehensive conservation of Lake Baikal are self-evident. The lake is over 25 million years old, and thus the Earth's oldest body of fresh water – lakes normally silt up with sediment after several hundred thousand years at most. It fills the deepest continental rift on earth – nine kilometres deep and, as there are at least three tectonic plates that meet here and scrape past one another, tearing apart the bedrock, the lake is still becoming wider and deeper more quickly than natural sedimentation can fill it up. Over this colossal period of time, a truly unique freshwater world has developed. To biologists, Lake Baikal is like a museum of evolution, for nowhere else on earth has a freshwater system been able to develop undisturbed for such a long period. With more than 1,500 endemic species of animals and plants, the lake provides a window on the history of life, retaining a biological memory of the time when the Himalayas were thrust up and humanity was just one of a million possibilities of evolution. Only a minute part of this puzzle has yet been pieced together, even though scientists have been examining the complex relationships between biology, geology and the history of the earth for decades.

Zoologists, limnologists, geographers and botanists were able to present their case for the lake's preservation so convincingly that even the authorities gradually began to grasp its importance. In 1987, the Soviet government declared absolute protection for a zone approximately 50 kilometres wide all around the lake. Tight restrictions have since obliged industry to operate without discharging any waste water. Scientific data demonstrated indisputably that merely reducing the volume of waste water pumped into the lake would not protect it in the long term.

For the cardboard mill in Selenginsk this meant that the 170,000 tonnes of unbleached pulp it produced annually would have to be manufactured without the discharge of waste water. The company's engineers shook their heads; there was no such thing as a waste-water-free cardboard manufacturing process. No cardboard mill anywhere in the world fully recycled its waste water. A closer look was taken at all the available knowledge of pulp and paper technology in the hope of discovering some alternative, and after only two years a viable method seemed to be within reach.

Experimental research in small-scale pilot plants proved that it is feasible to use biological and chemical methods to clean up production water for reuse. The solid residues resulting from the treatment processes – precipitates and sludges – can be used to fertilise farmland and tree plantations. Only materials and substances that do not produce harmful chemical residues are used in the manufacturing process.

Industry across the world has begun to pay attention to the example provided by Selenginsk. In the Canadian province of Saskatchewan, on the shores of Meadow Lake, Millar Western Pulp Ltd produces over 240,000 tonnes of chlorine-free bleached pulp annually without discharging a single drop of waste water into the lake. Now there are even companies in the textile and metal sectors – both notorious for pollution via outfalls – that are operating without waste water. Both the environmental dividend and the huge drop in costs (deriving from plummeting water use and the avoidance of waste water discharge levies) have led to rapidly increasing demand for these innovative processes, and there are already specialist engineering consultancies able to advise and provide the relevant technology.

It seems that the Lake Baikal conservationists may achieve a triumph far greater than they could ever have believed possible during the long years of campaigning that were often undertaken at considerable personal risk. Should their protest prove to be the start of a worldwide victory march for waste-water-free industrial production, Lake Baikal may yet become the symbol of a modern revolution, of the final departure from the irresponsible practice of abusing rivers, lakes and oceans as a matter of course through the disposal of waste which need never have been produced in the first place.

Above. From December to April, Lake Baikal is covered with a thick layer of ice that can be up to a metre deep. In the north, this ice layer may persist well into June. The lake owes its extraordinary clarity to the presence of billions of shrimps (Epischura baicalensis), *which in summer make up 97 per cent of the plankton in the lake and filter both algae and bacteria out of the water.*

Right. Water purification vats at the Selenginsk cardboard factory (clearly showing what wastewater discharge to the Selenga River and thence to the lake) would have contained.

CAMBODIA
A Chance for the Mekong

Once the Mekong River pours into the South China Sea through its eight powerful estuarine rivers, its waters have travelled 4,500 kilometres and passed through six countries. The river has dropped some 5,000 metres in altitude from the Tibetan Highlands where it rises, through China, Burma, Laos and Thailand, before becoming calmer as it reaches the wide plains of Cambodia and Vietnam and, finally, the ocean.

Few other regions have been subjected to such massive political upheavals over the past 40 years as the countries along the lower course of the Mekong. In the 1960s, the Vietnam War caused quite literal con-flagration in the region; it will be a long time before either the countryside or the people recover completely. Today, in the aftermath of the Cold War, large parts of Cambodia have been rendered inaccessible by landmines. The Mekong itself, however, in spite of the effects of various ill-conceived schemes including deforestation (causing serious siltation), still survives in virtually its natural state. It supports a vast abundance of fish, and annual monsoon floods carry moisture and fertile soil to millions of hectares of paddy fields.

Of course, for such a powerful river, hydraulic engineering plans to 'improve' it do exist. As far back as the 1950s, Western planners identified enormous potential for hydroelectric power in the river's lower course. A monumental master plan was drawn up, involving a series of huge reservoirs behind gigantic dams – this in itself was thought a sufficient development concept to be applied right across Indochina. Engineers waxed lyrical at the thought of the inexhaustible reservoirs of energy, the safe navigation of the river, effective flood control and the extra harvests that would spring from artificial irrigation.

Political developments forced them to abandon their plans, but the Mekong Committee (set up in 1957 on the initiative of the United Nations by Thailand, Laos, Vietnam and Cambodia to plan, fund and execute the total conversion of the Mekong) survived. A few years ago, the Committee's advisors (mainly from Western nations) began dusting off the files on development in Indochina. Minor modifications were made to the original plans – such as relocating the Pa Mong Dam a few kilometres downstream, but the main intention is still for the river to be denied any free-flowing section over about 2,000 kilometres. This is to be achieved by the construction of eight monumental dams. Even downstream of these, the river will, of course, be forced to adhere to artificial rather than natural rhythms.

A great many changes have taken place in Indochina since the early plans for the Mekong were drawn up in the 1950s, not least as far as economic interests are concerned. Thailand, with its rapidly growing economy, is extremely interested in the expansion of hydroelectric power on the Mekong, especially as it already has to import hydroelectricity from Laos. The other three countries are regarded by the Mekong Committee as 'hopelessly backward' and, according to the Committee's Swedish Head of Information, 'unable to survive without our help and without foreign investments'. Cambodia in particular, because of its long isolation, finds itself inundated with offers of financial help from donor countries and international development banks: ministers from 33 states and representatives from 13 development banks attended a conference for Cambodia organised by Japan in 1992 and promised $880 million for 'reconstruction and economic development'.

However welcome these overtures may be to the Cambodian government, it is nonetheless somewhat suspicious of such a sudden access of interest. Observing that other countries' experiences of dam projects have often been troubled, Cambodia is understandably circumspect about the supposed benefits it will enjoy as a result of the Committee's plans for the construction of two mega-dams on its territory. Why run up vast foreign debts when other, more critical voices from abroad warn of the considerable ecological and social disadvantages that could ensue? Cambodia, after all, would not be the first country to experience financial ruin after embarking on a project of this kind.

Today, Cambodia is a rich, poor country. Luminous green paddy fields line the banks of the Mekong and its tributaries; at the height of the rainy season, one third of the country is covered with a glittering sheet of water. Ancient farming techniques ensure that no crops are lost even when the fields are four or five metres deep in water, and the rivers are abundant with fish. The Cambodians are well aware that it is the Mekong that allows them to eat.

The country may be poor, but it has a lot to lose: the Great Lake – Tonle Sap – for instance. A river of the same name normally

Opposite. Catching shellfish in the Nam Khan, a tributary of the Mekong in the mountainous north of Laos. Here the water is still clear, but many of the country's rivers are now thick with soil run-off caused by the logging out of ancient forests for timber to export to Thailand.

Above. The Festival of the Giant Catfish, Chiang Khong, Thailand, an annual gathering at which people celebrate one of the wonders of the Mekong and pay respect to the river itself. The fish, which can be up to three metres long, swims 3,000 kilometres to spawn in the headwaters of the Mekong in China. If the Mekong Committe has its way, the few remaining wild catfish will find their routes to breeding grounds blocked by dams.

flows from the Great Lake to the Mekong, but in the rainy season, the sheer volume of water in the river forces its current to reverse. The Great Lake expands as a result, quadrupling the area of land that it covers. Huge numbers of fish feed on the vegetation in the flooded woodland near the shores, which also provides ideal breeding grounds. Legendary for the rich variety of its fish, the Tonle Sap also acts as a nursery for fish in the Mekong.

Hydraulic engineers advising the Mekong Committee would prefer to improve control over the lake by cutting it off from the other water systems with a dam. Plans of this nature are strenuously opposed by the Cambodian government, which has no desire to put the country's plentiful and diverse fish stocks at risk. Perhaps it is because of the Tonle Sap that Cambodia's Director of Fisheries always attends meetings of the Mekong Committee as an observer.

The reluctance of the Cambodians to build new dams is not merely normal scepticism about rushed development, but stems from their experience of the possible consequences of redesigning rivers during the time when the Pol Pot regime was in power in the 1970s. Under Pol Pot, the entire population was forced to join work brigades and build dams and dykes for irrigation agriculture. People still clearly remember how fish disappeared from the manipulated waters, and hunger and starvation followed as a result. Rather than any new dams being built in Cambodia today, it is more likely that old Pol Pot dams will be torn down. The government intends to remove what remains of the old dams, which never worked anyway, to allow the fish populations of the country's rivers to recover.

It remains to be seen whether the Cambodian experience can act as a brake on the Mekong Committee's development machine, and thus save the Mekong from being given the full treatment. The war in Indo-China has earned the Mekong a reprieve. Just how long it will remain undisturbed will also depend on whether world public opinion can be made to realise in time the enormous value of the natural asset on which international construction groups have set their sights.

The dam lobby decided without a moment's hestitation in favour of exploiting the Mekong for hydroelectricity, in itself a resounding vote against the preservation of the river's natural riches. Nobody bothered to consult the people who depend on the river for their livelihoods and sustenance. They are well aware that any such transformations will do them no good at all. Nam Mun, the largest tributary of the Mekong in Thailand, has recently been extensively dammed and flooded, in spite of fierce local resistance.

BOTSWANA
A Triumph for Commonsense

Botswana may be larger than France, but it is a lot less densely populated. It has an extremely arid climate and only 1.3 million inhabitants. In the north-west of the country lies the Okavango Delta, an ecosystem of enormous importance. It covers 16,000 square kilometres, making it even bigger than the Rhine delta, and is the largest inland delta in the world – a mighty oasis existing in the middle of a semi-desert. The Okavango River rises in the tropical mountains of Angola and passes into Botswana after dallying briefly in the Namibian Caprivi Strip. For around 90 kilometres, in Botswana, the river has a clearly defined course, before it reaches the large, flat lowlands where it branches out into countless tiny channels. 95 per cent of its water is absorbed by the delta; some seeps down into the groundwater, some is taken up by the vegetation and some evaporates. Around half of the delta is permanent swampland; the rest floods only in the rainy season.

On average, only five per cent of the Okavango's water leaves the delta to feed into a number of smaller rivers; this, in the opinion of Botswana's Department of Water Affairs, is an irresponsible waste of water. Decades were spent drawing up plans to prevent the Okavango's water from evaporating and to place it at the service of the population. These finally crystallised in a project for the canalisation and drainage of the southern part of the Delta over a distance of 42 kilometres. The extra water thus extracted was to be stored in three new reservoirs dedicated to the 'development' of the regions of Ngamiland and Boteti: the additional water was to be used for irrigation projects on large-scale farms growing cash crops, for the diamond mines in Orapa, to increase the volume of water available to poor smallholders in the delta area and to improve domestic supplies for the regional centre, Maun.

From the start, the project met with fierce resistance from the local population.

Farmers living near the small rivers downriver of the delta were quite convinced that the construction of a canal would 'kill their rivers' and dry out their fields and the grazing pastures that are so dependent on water from the rivers. International opposition to the project centres on the importance of the area for wildlife and plants: 160 species of fish have been counted in the Delta to date, and its 63 species of dragonfly give an indication of the diversity of its insect life. Above all, it is an ideal habitat for waterfowl, hippopotamuses and crocodiles. Elephants, giraffes, gazelles and zebras move into the delta when all other water sources dry up in the dry season.

When construction commenced in November 1990, the Botswana government found itself facing both intense local opposition and a storm of international outrage. The Okavango Delta is a mecca for lovers of African big game and attracts thousands of foreign tourists every year. Perhaps the government suddenly realised that it was placing its still fragile but already valuable tourist industry at risk. Whatever the reason, it decided to halt the building work. The next step it took was highly innovative: it commissioned the International Union for the Conservation of Nature and Natural Resources (IUCN) to bring together a team of scientists, including hydrologists, economists, biologists and sociologists, to do a cost-benefit analysis for the project and, if necessary, to suggest better alternatives.

The thirteen scientists in the international team were faced with a task of great responsibility. Not only did they have to assess the canal and dam project for its likely effects on the local people and the natural environment, they were also charged with proposing a better concept for achieving the goals set out by the government: an increase in food production in the region, improvements in water supply for the urban population and greater availability of water for the profitable diamond mine at Orapa.

It quickly became apparent that there were problems with the plans made by the Australian engineering consultancy responsible for the Okavango project. Its engineers had discovered early on that the region's soil was unsuitable for commercial irrigation. Although that removed the main

justification for the project, the company continued as though all was well. Alternative models for satisfying urban and industrial demand for water were either never examined or rejected out of hand. It is easy to conclude that the engineering company was interested only in the construction of the canal and dams and had no intention of taking account of the wider objectives of the Botswana government.

The very people whose standard of living was supposed to be improved, the smallholders, would have lost extensive areas of pastures and fields near the river to the reservoirs. Smallholders make up around 50 per cent of the population in Ngamiland, and it is one of Botswana's declared intentions to support their rural existence in order to save them from the misery of urban migration. The IUCN team therefore made improving the lot of small farmers one of its main priorities. It soon became clear that simply providing water was by no means a sure-fire solution, particularly in this arid climate. Having access to more water for animals, for example, is of little use if it is achieved by flooding their pastures.

At the end of the study, the team came to the conclusion that individual single-issue initatives would not help to solve the complex overall problems faced by farmers caught between traditional and modern lifestyles. So it came up with a whole raft of proposals amounting to a comprehensive strategy for gradually improving the living conditions of rural populations in Ngamiland and Boteti. The main task would be to establish careful links between traditional farming (which has evolved to cope well in the semi-desert) and the modern urban economy. Far from being dismissed as a dying sector of society, village life and skills would be valued for the part they can play within the national economy. Small industry, based on processing local products such as leather and papyrus, could be set up. The team recommended reinstating traditional weekly markets as a stabilising factor, enabling smallholders once again to sell their products in larger towns and thus slowly to be introduced into the formal economy. The scientists even demanded that changes be made to the curriculum at primary schools, because the current one 'biases students against rural development activities'.

The other supposed beneficiaries of the canal and dam project were also subjected to close scrutiny. The regional capital of Maun, which has for years suffered from chronic water shortages, can start to tackle its problems even without the project: the team proposed alternate use of river water during the rainy season and groundwater during the dry season, thus safeguarding long-term water supplies in a way the dam could never have done. The large quantities of water required by the diamond mine at Orapa could also be provided from the groundwater without the need for any new reservoirs. The team emphasised that pumping off non-replenishable groundwater was not an ideal scenario, but if the diamond mine was a given, then at least it was less harmful than the secondary effects of the original project.

The 543-page report by the IUCN team persuaded the Botswana government to abandon the planned project instantly. Reaction in Botswana was almost entirely positive, especially in the region that would have been most directly affected. Only the Department of Water Affairs, under whose aegis the project had been for ten years, was dissatisfied – small wonder, when what had started as a purely hydraulic engineering project had turned into a whole package of alternative measures, most of which barely involved the water ministry.

Once again, the attempt to spark off economic activity with a single large-scale project has been shown up for the illusion it is. In commissioning an interdisciplinary and independent study of the Okavango project and heeding subsequent advice, the government of Botswana has set an example that others would do well to follow.

The consequences of intervention in a region's water regime with canals, dams or irrigation systems extend far beyond the water sector, especially in arid regions. It can remove livelihoods, cause irreparable damage to ecosystems and influence the climate. Water management is not an isolated discipline – any steps to manipulate the natural water regime must be taken in the full knowledge of all likely effects, and be subject to the approval of those likely to be affected. These are questions too important to be left to technocrats – they belong in the realm of political debate.

Right. A traditional mokoro *or dug-out canoe – perfect for negotiating the shallow, winding waterways of the Okavango Delta.*

Opposite page. From the air the sheer richness of this watery landscape is clear. Millions of migrating birds arrive every year in this vast marshy area at the mouth of the Okavango River to rest and breed.

A Fresh Perspective

No matter where you live in the world, there are water problems not far away. The difficulties and destruction often seem so overwhelming that it is easy to turn away in resignation, wearily accepting that this is all the inevitable effect of the seemingly inexorable expansion of the world's human population.

Happily, this is emphatically not the case. The majority of the world's current water problems do not result from a critical shortage of water on the planet or from unavoidable natural phenomena, but are mainly the consequence of at best, inappropriate and at worst, utterly irrational water management. Most current strategy and technology are based on assumptions and practice that date from the 19th century and have never seriously been challenged. For these misguided ideas to be unquestioningly reapplied and extended throughout the industrialised world is bad enough, but they have frequently been foisted on developing countries, so undermining the possibility of installing more enlightened systems.

Cultivating a more sensitive approach to water use requires an openness to every bit of related information and know-how, whether it emerges from traditional systems of water protection and conservation or from ecologically sound modern technology. Any responsible strategy has to be grounded in an awareness of how embedded human life actually is in nature, a recognition of how well it will treat us if we repay the compliment.

There is little point in expecting governments and scientists somehow to change water policies and to come up with solutions to the problems. These can only grow out of a transformation in our own attitudes far more profound than merely deciding to take fewer baths or showers. We need, as a number of environmental writers have pointed out, a new water ethic.

When we use water, we are taking it out of an endlessly self-perpetuating and enriching system. Rediscovering the importance of playing a sympathetic part in this life-giving cycle is the key to building a sounder relationship with water and indeed with the whole natural environment.

Human beings have to realise that they are only some of the consumers and beneficiaries of water on the planet, and that after any use, it inevitably returns to nature. The refreshing splash of water that helps you wake up in the morning might once have been snowflakes settling gently on a mountainside or moisture taken up by the tiny root hairs of a plant. When you enjoy a warming cup of tea or coffee, you might pause to think for a moment of the slow progress of a water drop as it passes through mosses and earth becoming ever purer as it goes. And when you next wash the dishes, spare a thought for how nature is going to cope with cleaning up after you.

We are not and cannot be separate from water in nature. In the words of John Trudell, one of the founders of the American Indian movement: 'Water tells us we are one'.

Ghayl Umar Oasis, Yemen.

SOURCES

Chapter 1 Water and the Planet

History of Nile exploration Georg Brunold, *Nilfieber*, Eichborn Verlag, Frankfurt am Main, 1993; **earth history** Frank Press and Raymond Siever, *Earth*, W.H. Freeman, New York, 1986 (fourth edition); **lake oscillations and seiches** Dieter M. Imboden, 'Mixing and Transport in Lakes: Mechanisms and Ecological Relevance' in Max M. Tilzer and Colette Serruya, *Large Lakes*, Springer Verlag, Berlin and Heidelberg, 1990; **Lake Wakatipu legend** Maika Mason, letter to author, 30 July 1994.

Chapter 2 Drinking Water

Physical symptom of dehydration Michael Stührenberg, *Geospezial Sahara*, Hamburg, 1992; **water loss by perspiration** Gilbert F. White, David J. Bradley and Anne U. White, *Drawers of Water*, University of Chicago Press, Chicago and London, 1972; **qanats** Gerd Michel, 'Kanate in der Volksrepublik China' in *Schriftenreihe der Frontinusgesellschaft*, Heft 11, Bergisch Gladbach, 1988; **Hebrew and Roman water law** Dante Caponera, *Principles of Water Law and Administration*, A.A. Balkema, Rotterdam and Brookfield, 1992; **nypheum** Renate Tölle-Kastenbein, *Antike Wasserkultur*, Munich, 1990; **aqueduct of Tushpa** Wilhelm Wölfel, *Wasserbau in den Alten Reichen*, VEB Verlag für Bauwesen, Berlin, 1990; **pollution of River Tevere in Ancient Rome** Norman Smith, *Man and Water – A History of Hydro-Technology*, Peter Davies, London, 1975; **gravel and sand filters** Martin Wegelin, *Surface Water Treatment by Roughing Filters* in IRCWD [International Reference Centre for Waste Disposal] Report No.10, Dübendorf, Switzerland, 1992; **water pollution by agriculture** *Green Fields, Grey Future*, Greenpeace, Amsterdam, 1992; **maps showing leaching of nitrates and pesticides** National Insitute of Public Health and Environmental Protection (RIVM) and Institute for Inland Water Management and Waste Water Treatment (RIZA) *Sustainable Use of Groundwater; problems and threats in the European Communities*, RIVM/RIZA report 600025001, Bilthoven, The Netherlands, November 1991; **world drinking water statistics and cost of water supplies** J. Christmas and Carel de Rooy, 'The Decade and Beyond' in *Waterlines* 9 (3), 1991; **over-exploitation of British rivers** *Draining Our Rivers Dry*, Friends of the Earth factsheet, London, 1992; **over-exploitation of Spanish groundwater** Angel Muñoz, 'El Agua en España' in *Ecologia y Sociedad*, Suplemento Especial, Madrid, May 1993; **statistics for drinking water treatment** Joni Seager (ed.), *The State of the Earth*, Unwin Hyman Ltd, London, 1990; **privatisation of Scottish waterworks** 'Scotland Rejects Private Water' in *World Water and Environmental Engineer* London, January/February 1993.; **privatisation of waterworks in Belgium and Portugal** *Hydroplus. Magazine Internationale de l'Eau*, No.20, February 1992; **turnover of water industry** *Hydroplus. Magazine Internationale de l'Eau*, No.30, January/February 1993; **expected turnover of water industry** Commission of the European Communities, *The State of the Environment in the European Community* COM (92) 23, Vol. III, Brussels, 1992; **exploitation of deep groundwater** Thomas Kluge, 'Wassersparen als Element einer vorsorgenden Gewässerschutzstrategie' in Thomas Kluge (ed.), *Wassersparen*, Verlag für interkulturelle Kommunikation, Frankfurt am Main, 1992; **international water prices table** *Hydroplus. Magazine International de l'Eau*, No.20, February 1992; **water prices in Germany** Richard Stadtfeld and Gisela Hansen, 'Entwicklung der öffentlichen Trinkwasserversorgung in der Bundesrepublik Deutschland' in *GWF Wasser-Abwasser* 134 (4), 1993; **regional sustainability** Thomas Kluge, 'Regionale Nachhaltigkeit' in *Politische Ökologie*, Sonderheft 5, 1994; **European Water Works Association's initiative to lower drinking water standards** Michael Bond, 'EC Faces Climbdown Over Water' in *The European*, 17 September 1993.

Chapter 3 What Price Cleanliness?

Religious water use Barbara Blum-Heisenberg, *Die Symbolik des Wassers: Baustein der Natur – Vielfalt der Bedeutung*, Kösel Verlag, Munich, 1988; **mikwes** Georg Heuberger (ed.), *Geschichte und Architektur jüdischer Ritualbäder in Deutschland*, Jüdisches Museum, Frankfurt am Main, 1992; **Hindu rituals** Beatrix Pfleiderer, 'Vom guten Wasser' in Hartmut Böhme (ed.), *Kulturgeschichte des Wassers*, Suhrkamp, Frankfurt am Main, 1988; **medieval rural bathing** Wolfgang Kaschuba, ' "Deutsche Sauberkeit" – Zivilisierung der Körper und der Köpfe' in Georges Vigarello, *Wasser Seife und Parfüm*, Reihe Campus, Frankfurt am Main and New York, 1992; **Heinrich Schliemann reference and Japanese bathing customs** Eva Ströber, 'Badefreuden und rituelle Reinigung' in *Quellen. Das Wasser in der Kunst Ostasiens*, Museum für Kunst und Gewerbe, Hamburg, 1992; **Herodotus reference** Wilhelm Wölfel, *Wasserbau in den Alten Reichen*, VEB Verlag für Bauwesen, Berlin, 1990; **ancient water closets** Martin Illi, *Von der Schîssgruob zur modernen Stadtentwässerung*, Verlag Neue Zürcher Zeitung, Zurich, 1987; **history of sewers** Thomas Kluge and Engelbert Schramm, *Wassernöte*, Kölner Volksblatt Verlag, Aachen, 1988; **EU-market for sewage treatment plants** Keith Hayward, 'Money Supply' in *World Water and Environmental Engineer*, January/February 1993; **sewerage directive** Council Directive concerning urban waste water treatment' in *Official Journal of the European Communities* (91/271/EEC), Brussels, 21 May 1991; **Detergent statistics** *Daten zur Umwelt 1990/91*, Umweltbundesamt, Erich Schmidt Verlag, Berlin, 1992; **sociology of washing** Alain Corbin, *Le Miasme et la Jonquille. L'odorat et l'imaginaire social XVIIIe-XIXe siècles*, Editions Aubier Montaigne, Paris, 1982.

Chapter 4 Healing Waters

The Good Well of Jelenia Góra and source of River Seine Fritz Geschwendt, *Der vor- und frühgeschichtliche Mensch und die Heilquellen*, August Lax, Verlagsbuchhandlung, Hildesheim, 1972; **age of Swiss medicinal springs** Hansjörg Schmassmann, 'Geologie und Beschaffenheit der schweizerischen Mineralwässer' in *Thermen der Schweiz*, Offizin Zürich Verlagsgesellschaft, Zurich, 1990; **physiological effects of bathing** Lilian Jaeggi-Landolf, 'Bädermedizin heute' in *Thermen der Schweiz*, Offizin Zürich Verlagsgesellschaft, Zurich, 1990; **Ngawha Springs mythology and history** Paora Maxwell, *The Maori Use of Geothermal Energy. Report for the Waitangi Tribunal*, Wellington, New Zealand, 1991.

Chapter 5 Freshwater Harvest

Bangladesh fisheries statistics Max Finlayson and Michael Moser (ed.), *Wetlands*, Facts on File, Oxford and New York, 1991; **world fisheries statistics** *Review of the State of the World Fishery Resources*, FAO [Food and Agriculture Organisation], Rome, 1990; **environmental effects of salmon farms** Hal Kane, 'Fischzucht auf dem Acker' in *World Watch* Vol.2, No.5 (German edition), October/November, 1993; **Calcutta fish farms** Martin Strauss and Ursula J. Blumenthal, *Human Waste Use in Agriculture and Aquaculture*, IRCWD Report No. 9, Dübendorf, Switzerland, 1990.

Chapter 6 Water in a Straitjacket

Decreasing biodiversity due to drainage Dieter Korneck and Herbert Sukopp, 'Rote Liste der in der Bundesrepublik ausgestorbenen, verschollenen und gefährdeten Farn- und Blütenpflanzen' in *Schriftenreihe der Bundesforschungsanstalt für Naturschutz und Landschaftsökologie*, Heft 19, Bonn-Bad Godesberg, Germany, 1988; **quote on medieval mining** P. Krenkel (ed.), 'Paulus Niavis oder das Gericht der Götter über den Bergbau' in *Freiberger Forschungshefte, Kultur und Technik*, D3, Berlin (DDR), 1953; **Flood Action Plan, Bangladesh** Bimal Kanti Paul and Harun Rasid, 'Flood Damage to Rice Crops in Bangladesh' in *The Geographical Review*, 83, 1993.

Chapter 7 Watering the Land

Modern irrigation in Egypt I.Z. Kinawy, 'The Efficiency of Water Use in Irrigation in Egypt' in E. Barton Worthington (ed.), *Arid Land Irrigation in Developing Countries*, Pergamon Press, Oxford, 1977; **ancient Mesopotamian crops** Wilhelm Wölfel, *Wasserbau in den Alten Reichen*, VEB Verlag für Bauwesen, Berlin, 1990; **hydraulic despotism** Karl A. Wittfogel, *Oriental Despotism. A Comparitive Study of Total Power*, New Haven (Conn.) and London, 1964; **crop yields in Ancient Mesopotamia** Shin Theke Kang, 'Irrigation in Ancient Mesopotamia' in *Water Resources Bulletin (AWRA)*, June 1971; **Marib dam** Joachim P. Chwaszcza, *Jemen*, Edition Erde im BW

Verlag, Nürnberg, 1993; **Nabatean and Islamic irrigation and British irrigation in India** Norman Smith, *Man and Water – A History of Hydro-Technology*, Peter Davies, London, 1975; **raised fields of Lake Titicaca** Clark L. Erickson, 'Raised Fields in the Lake Titicaca Basin', *Expedition*, Vol. 30, University of Pennsylvania, 1988; **British irrigation in India and diversion of Amu-darya River** Fred Pearce, *The Dammed*, The Bodley Head, London, 1992; **bories** letter to author, Hans Weber, 9 July 1994; **table of water consumption in agriculture** The World Resources Institute, UNEP and UNDP (ed.) *World Resources 1992/93*, Oxford University Press, New York and Oxford, 1992; **salinisation and irrigation** Swayne F. Scott, 'Water and Sustainable Agricultural Development' in *Ecologically Sound Resources Management in Irrigation*, DVWK-Bulletin 19, Verlag Paul Parey, Hamburg and Berlin, 1993; **soil salinisation in USA** Sandra Postel, *Last Oasis*, W.W. Norton, New York and London, 1992; **over-exploitation of groundwater in Gujarat, India** Unday Shankar, 'Groundwater: A Disappearing Act' in *Down to Earth*, New-Delhi, India, 15 July 1993; **over-exploitation of Ogallalla aquifer** Erla Zwingle, 'Wellspring of the High Plains' in *National Geographic*, Vol. 183, No.3, Washington D.C., 1993; **schistosomiasis** Mutamad A. Amin, 'Problems and Effects of Schistosomiasis in Irrigation Schemes in Sudan' in Barton E. Worthington (ed.), *Arid Land Irrigation in Developing Countries: Environmental Problems and Effects*, Pergamon Press, Oxford, 1977; **irrigation in Thailand** Liesbeth Sluiter, *The Mekong Currency*, International Books, Utrecht, 1993.

Chapter 8 An End to the Dam Age?

History of hydropower John Shaw, *Water Power in Scotland 1550-1870*, John Donald Publishers Ltd, Edinburgh, 1984; **ecological effects of dams** Ueli Bundi and Elie Eichenberger, *Wasserentnahme aus Fließgewässern. Gewässerökologische Anforderungen an die Restwasserführung*, Bundesamt für Umwelt, Wald und Landschaft (Switzerland), Berne, 1989; **erosion of Nile delta** Asit K. Biswas, 'Irrigation, Environment, and Aswan High Dam: A Reassessment' in *Ecologically Sound Resources Management in Irrigation*, DVWK-Bulletin 19, Verlag Paul Parey, Hamburg and Berlin, 1993; **Three Gorges project China** Chee Yoke Ling, *Who Will Pay for China's Three Gorges Dam?*, Third World Network Features, Hong Kong, 6 December 1993; **greenhouse effect of a tropical dam** S. Gupta and R.K. Pachauri, *Global Warming and Climate Change: Perspectives from Developing Countries*, Tata Energy Research Institute, New Delhi, India, 1990; **Akosombo dam, Ghana** Fred Pearce, *The Dammed*, The Bodley Head, London, 1992; **Batoka dam project, Zambia** Sylvester Chiposa, 'Row Rages over Batoka Dam' in *African Business*, November 1993; **negawatt potential** Sian McCutcheon, *Electric Rivers. The Story of the James Bay Project*, Black Rose Books, Montreal and New York, 1991; **possible effects of an inexhaustible energy resource** Hans-Peter Dürr, letter to author, 5 March 1993.

Chapter 10 The Demands of Industry

Table of water consumption by industry The World Resources Institute, UNEP and UNDP (ed.), *World Resources 1992/93*, Oxford University Press, New York andOxford, 1992; **water consumption in steel production; water saving in US industry; Japanese water efficiency** Sandra Postel *Last Oasis*, W.W. Norton, New York and London, 1992; **water consumption - of pulp and paper industry; by industrial sectors; for manufacture of an automobile** Thomas Kluge, Engelbert Schramm and Aicha Vack, *Aquarius II: Industrie und Wasser*, Greenpeace-Study, Frankfurt am Main, 1994; **water consumption for broilers** 'Watch Water Costs, Food Processors Told' in *Food Chemical News* 33 (23), 1991; **Donbas pollution** Greenpeace Ukraine, 'Water Pollution in Ukraine and Its Effects' in *Literature Review*, Kiev, 1992; **EU waste production and number of contaminated industrial sites in the Netherlands** *Sustainable Use of Groundwater*, RIZA/RIVM, Bilthoven and Lelystad, 1991; **deep well injection USA** *A Shot in the Dark*, Greenpeace USA, Washington D.C., 1990; **environmental problems of mining** John E. Young, *Mining the Earth*, Worldwatch Institute, Washington DC, 1992; **ancient mining problems** Karl-Wilhelm Weeber, *Smog über Attika*, Artemis Verlag, Zürich and Munich, 1990.

Chapter 11 Overexploitation & Neglect

SOUTHERN AFRICA Lesotho water plans Martin Schneider, 'The Rand Water Board' in *SA (South Africa) Inc.*, Johannesburg, 1993; **Lesotho politics** Fred Pearce, *The Dammed*, The Bodley Head, London, 1992; **Zimbabwe water plans** Bruce Berry and Etienne Nel, 'Operation Pipeline – Bulawayo's Search for Water' in *Geography* 78, July 1993, part 3; **irrigation in the Caprivi Strip** Thayer Scudder *et al.*, *The IUCN Review of the Southern Okavango Integrated Water Development Project*, IUCN, Gland, Switzerland, 1993.

THE CASPIAN SEA fluctuation in water level M.S. Ayatollahi, 'Adverse effects of the Caspian Sea Level Fluctuations on the Coastal Areas', lecture at International Atomic Energy Agency, IAEA Vienna, 20 December 1993, and Christoph Neidhart, 'Türkmensiche Wüsten in *Die Weltwoche*, Zurich, 20 May 1993; **rising Caspian Sea** Vera Rich, 'Floods Threaten Cities Around Caspian Sea' in *Science*, 15 June 1991.

THAILAND Molasses disaster Liesbeth Sluiter, *The Mekong Currency*, International Books, Utrecht, 1993; **state of Thai environment** *Thailand. Coping with the Strains of Success*, UNIDO [United Nations Industrial Development Organisation], Oxford, 1992; **spiritual change advocated in South East Asia** Uwe Schmitt, 'Der atemlose Tiger' in *Frankfurter Allgemeine Zeitung*, Frankfurt am Main, 4 December 1993.

BEIJING Eva Sternfeld, *Water Resources: Problems and Strategies for Sustainable Water Management in the Rural Areas of Beijing Municipality*, lecture at 3rd European Conference on Agricultural and Rural Development in China, 15-18 April 1993, Schloß Rauischholzhausen, Germany.

MEXICO CITY percentage of city dwellers in developing world Jürgen Bähr and Günter Mertins, 'Verstädterung in Lateinamerika', *Geographische Rundschau* 44, 1992; **cost of drinking water in Mexico City** Sybille Flaschka, 'Das Wasser von Mexiko-Stadt' in *Die Tageszeitung*, Berlin, 6 May 1993; **population growth** Hans-Jörg Sander, 'Umweltprobleme im Hochtal von Mexiko' in *Geographische Rundschau* 42, 1990; **sewerage** Martin Strauss and Ursula J. Blumenthal, *Human Waste Use in Agriculture and Aquaculture*, IRCWD [International Reference Centre for Waste Disposal], Report No. 9, Dübendorf, Switzerland, 1990.

QUEBEC history of James Bay project Sean McCutcheon, *Electric Rivers. The Story of the James Bay Project*, Black Rose Books, Montreal and New York, 1991; **electricity discounts for industry** Graeme Hamilton, 'Discount Power Could Cost Hydro $5 billion' in *The Gazette*, Montreal, 28 September 1993; **James Bay ecological damage** John G. Mitchell, 'James Bay: Where Two Worlds Collide' in *National Geographic Special Edition – Water*, Washington D.C., November 1993.

EUROPEAN UNION EU Commission's declaration of intent *Commission of the European Communities: Towards Sustainability*, COM (92) 23, Brussels, 1992; **IPPC Directive** *Commission Proposal for a Council Directive (EEC) on Integrated Prevention and Pollution Control*, COM (93), 423 final, Brussels, 30 September 1993; **ecology directive** *Commission Proposal for a Council Directive (EEC) on the Ecological Quality of Water*, DOC XI/239/92-EN Rev.3, Brussels, 26 August 1993; **lowering of drinking water standards** Michaela Schmidt, 'Revision der Trinkwasser-richtlinie' in *GWF Wasser-Abwasser* 135, 1994.

Chapter 12 Hope for the Future

PERU archaeology of raised fields Clark L. Erickson, 'Raised Fields in the Lake Titicaca Basin' in *Expedition*, Vol. 30, University of Pennsylvania, 1988; **discovery of raised fields** Fred Pearce, *The Dammed*, The Bodley Head, London, 1992.

SYDNEY *Solutions for Clean Healthy Cities*; *Strategy for a Sustainable Sydney*; *Water and the Olympic Village* – all Greenpeace Australia, Sydney, 1993.

LAKE BAIKAL ecology of Lake Baikal Don Belt, 'The World's Great Lake' in *National Geographic*, Washington D.C., June 1992; **waste-water-free cardboard production** N.A. Aldokhin et al., 'Recycling of wastewater and solid waste at the Selenginsk Pulp and Paper Plant' in *UNEP Industry and Environment*, July-December 1990.

CAMBODIA Tonle Sap and Pol Pot dams Liesbeth Sluiter, *The Mekong Currency*, International Books, Utrecht, 1993; **plans for dams on the Mekong** Rolf Bökemeier, 'Aufbruch am Mekong' in *GEO*, No.1, Hamburg, 1994.

BOTSWANA Okavango study Thayer Scudder *et al.*, *The IUCN Review of the Southern Okavango Integrated Water Development Project*, IUCN, Gland, Switzerland, 1993.

INDEX

GREENPEACE ADDRESSES

Greenpeace Argentina
Mansilla 3046
1425 Buenos Aires
Argentina

Greenpeace Australia
41 Holt Street
Surry Hills NSW 2010
Australia

Greenpeace Austria
Auenbruggergasse 2
1030 Vienna
Austria

Greenpeace Belgium
Vooruitgangstraat/Rue du Progrès 317
1210 Brussels
Belgium

Greenpeace Brazil
Rua de Mexico, 21
grupo 1301 A/B
Centro CEP 20031144
Rio de Janeiro-RJ
Brazil

Greenpeace Canada
185 Spadina Ave.
6th Floor
Toronto M5T 2C6
Ontario
Canada

Greenpeace Central America
10 Calle 3-15 zona 1
Guatemala 01001
Guatemala

Greenpeace Chile
Loreto 20
Recoleta
Santiago
Chile

Greenpeace Czechoslovakia
U Prasne brany 3
116 29 Praha 1
Czech Republic

Greenpeace Czechoslovakia Bratislava
c/o MV SZOPK
Godrova 3 B
811 06 Bratislava
Slovakia

Greenpeace Denmark
Bredgade 20
Bagh. 4
1260 Copenhagen K
Denmark

Greenpeace Finland
Kirkkokatu 2 B
P.O. Box 177
00171 Helsinki
Finland

Greenpeace Germany
Vorsetzen 53
20450 Hamburg
Germany

Greenpeace Greece
Zoodohou Pigis 52
GR-10681 Athens
Greece

Greenpeace International
Keizersgracht 176
1016 DW Amsterdam
Netherlands

Greenpeace Ireland
44 Upper Mount Street
Dublin 2
Ireland

Greenpeace Italy
Viale Manlio Gelsomini, 28
00153 Rome
Italien

Greenpeace Japan
4F Yoyogi-Kaikan
1-35-1 Yoyogi
Shibuya-ku
Tokyo 151
Japan

Greenpeace Luxemburg
24 rue Dicks
P.O. Box 229
4003 Esch/Alzette
Luxemburg

Greenpeace Med.
33 Paula Square
PLA04
Paula
Malta

Greenpeace Mexico
Calle La Escondida No. 110
Colonia Coyoacan
C. P. 04000 Mexico, D. F.
Mexico

Greenpeace Netherlands
Keizersgracht 174
1016 DW Amsterdam
Netherlands

Greenpeace New Zealand
22 York Street
Private Bag 92-507
Wellesley Street
Auckland
New Zealand

Greenpeace Norway
St. Olavs gt. 11
P.O. Box 6803
St. Olavs Plass
N-0130 Oslo 1
Norway

Greenpeace Russia
21, Dolgorukovskaya 21
Moscow 103006
Russia

Greenpeace Spain
Rodriguez San Pedro 58
28015 Madrid
Spain

Greenpeace Sweden
Herkulesgatan 3 A
P.O. Box 8913
402 73 Gothenburg
Sweden

Greenpeace Switzerland
Muellerstr. 37
Postfach 276
8026 Zurich
Switzerland

Greenpeace Tunisia
51 AV Abdelaziz Thaalbi
El Manar II
2092 Tunis
Tunisia

Greenpeace UK
Canonbury Villas
London N1 2PN
UK

Greenpeace Ukraine
Apt. 6
5 Pyrogoc Str.
P. O. Box 500
252010 Kiev-10
Ukraine

Greenpeace USA
1436 U Street, NW
Washington
DC 20009
USA